CRITICAL INSIGHTS

Literature of Protest

Editor
Kimberly Drake
Scripps College

SALEM PRESS
A Division of EBSCO Publishing
Ipswich, Massachusetts

GREY HOUSE PUBLISHING

Cover Illustration: Diego Bervejillo

Editor's text © 2013 by Kimberly Drake

Copyright © 2013, by Salem Press, A Division of EBSCO Publishing, Inc.

Critical Insights: Literature of Protest, 2013, published by Grey House Publishing, Inc., Amenia, NY, under exclusive license from EBSCO Publishing, Inc.

∞ The paper used in these volumes conforms to the American National Standard for Permanence of Paper for Printed Library Materials, Z39.48-1992 (R1997).

Library of Congress Cataloging-in-Publication Data

Literature of protest / editor, Kimberly Drake, Scripps College.
    pages cm. -- (Critical Insights)
  Includes bibliographical references and index.
  ISBN 978-1-4298-3826-9 (hardcover)
 1. Protest literature, American--History and criticism. 2. Justice, Administration of, in literature. 3. Social justice in literature. 4. Protest literature, English--History and criticism. 5. Protest literature, Russian--History and criticism. I. Drake, Kimberly, 1965- editor of compilation.
  PS228.P73L58 2013
  810.9'353--dc23

                                                                    2013007386

ebook ISBN: 978-1-4298-3842-9

Contents

About This Volume, Kimberly Drake   vii
On the Literature of Protest: Words as Weapons, Kimberly Drake   1

Critical Contexts

Countering the Rhetoric of Slavery: The Critical Roots and Critical
     Reception of *Uncle Tom's Cabin,* Lydia Willsky   27
Brutish Behavior: Joseph Conrad, Mark Twain, and Anticolonial
     Protests, 1899–1905, Jeremiah Garsha   44
Nella Larsen and Langston Hughes: Modernist Protest in the
     Harlem Renaissance, Kimberly Drake   66
The Meaning of Rape in Richard Wright's *Native Son,* Kimberly Drake   87

Critical Readings

Radical and Nationalist Resistance in David Walker's and Frederick
     Douglass's Antislavery Narratives, Babacar M'Baye   113
The New Woman Chafes against Her Bonds, Adeline Carrie Koscher   144
The Solidarity of Song: Proletarians, Poetry, and the Public
     Sphere of the Lawrence Textile Strike of 1912,
     Tara Forbes and Mikhail Bjorge   167
Dystopia as Protest: Zamyatin's *We* and Orwell's *Nineteen
     Eighty-Four,* Rachel Stauffer   191
Paranoia and Pacifism in E. E. Cummings's *The Enormous Room,*
     Seth Johnson   211
Holiness and Heresy: Viramontes, *la Virgen,* and the
     Mother-Daughter Bond, Christi Cook   233

Resources

Additional Works on the Literature of Protest   257
Bibliography   263
About the Editor   269
Contributors   271
Index   273

About This Volume

Kimberly Drake

This volume was created for the express purpose of filling gaps in the critical coverage of works of protest and liberation. It brings together a set of critical perspectives on a fairly diverse set of texts, although most fall into the category of fiction, and most were written by American authors. While the texts covered here, or the historical events that led to their creation, or both, are fairly well known and have been studied before, they are not usually examined as part of a tradition of protest literature. In the few existing critical examinations of protest literature, the texts covered usually do not venture outside of focused geographical, cultural, historical, or generic boundaries the way that this one does. What draws these texts together is their related set of approaches for conveying socially progressive ideas to readers in an emotionally compelling, consciousness-altering way.

A discussion of the tradition of protest literature can be found in the introduction to the volume, "Words as Weapons: The Literature of Protest and Liberation." As a way to dispute the widespread notion that protest literature is "bad writing," this chapter discusses the way aesthetics functions in protest literature, and the various, often experimental approaches protest writers use to penetrate readerly defense mechanisms. These approaches were dictated by the target audience or by the circumstances of a particular social movement to which the author was connected in various ways. Added to these constraints were the problems inherent in trying to represent a group of people (whether or not the author belonged to this group) fairly and accurately, without doing any more damage to their image in the social mainstream. Ultimately, aesthetics were crucial to these authors, who could not afford to create work whose political messages might be misinterpreted, or whose effects would be mild and transitory.

The next four chapters each provide a specific "critical context" for the text or texts that are being discussed. These chapters illuminate the text by using a particular critical angle to approach it. The first of these chapters is "Countering the Rhetoric of Slavery: The Critical Roots and Critical Reception of *Uncle Tom's Cabin*," by Lydia Willsky. Willsky examines what was perhaps the most popular and most effective protest novel of all time, outsold during the nineteenth century only by the Bible. Since *Uncle Tom's Cabin* first appeared in print, its critical reception has run the gamut from high critical praise to explicit condemnation on the basis of the author's gender, her choice of genre, her politics, her religious views, the accuracy of her portrayal, and her characters. Indeed, Stowe's multifaceted treatment of its subject matter, American slavery, seems almost designed to elicit controversy and wildly different views. This is certainly a common strategy in protest literature, one used by many of the works studied in this volume; Willsky shows here how particular aspects of the novel elicited passionate reactions and political discussions, ultimately helping it achieve its goals.

The next chapter is a comparative treatment of texts by two well-known novelists, Mark Twain and Joseph Conrad, both of whom wrote about colonialism. In "Brutish Behavior: Joseph Conrad, Mark Twain, and Anticolonial Protests, 1899–1905," Jeremiah Garsha examines the way Twain builds on Conrad's *Heart of Darkness* in his texts "To the Person Sitting in Darkness" and *King Leopold's Soliloquy* to create a brief convergence of European and American protest against the supposed "civilizing mission" of imperialism. In portraying the atrocities committed in the Belgian Congo under the authority of King Leopold II, these texts take on the point of view of the colonial henchman (in Conrad's case) and Leopold himself (in Twain's text). They do not lament the colonial power's treatment of the Congolese so much as depict colonial violence as a metaphor for colonial corruption.

The chapter that follows discusses how two authors found their calling in the New Negro arts movement. In "Nella Larsen and Langston Hughes: Modernist Protest in the Harlem Renaissance," Kimberly Drake examines a few representative poems from among Hughes's widespread oeuvre as well as Larsen's *Quicksand*. She comments on the way these authors' texts and their own literary personae were shaped and used by a cultural and artistic movement that was confronting racial and literary hegemony in a variety of ways. Hughes was best known for his leftist and jazz-inspired poems that relied on the vernacular of the working classes, while Larsen wrote psychological novels concerned with the middle class. Situated on seemingly opposite ends of a Harlem Renaissance literary and political spectrum, Hughes and Larsen nevertheless shared an interest in the critique of class lines, bourgeois imitation, and experimentalism in form and content.

The period following the end of the Harlem Renaissance produced some extremely powerful fiction, but only recently has the literature of this period been recognized for its achievements. Richard Wright has been called the father of the protest novel, and *Native Son* is an essential text in the protest literature tradition. In "The Meaning of Rape in Richard Wright's *Native Son*," Kimberly Drake investigates the most controversial acts of that novel: the protagonist's self-empowerment through rape and murder. She does so using a combination of two critical "lenses" or approaches: a psychoanalytic approach and a feminist approach. By combining these lenses, she seeks to address two issues readers have repeatedly brought up: the protagonist's misogyny and his interactions with and views of white characters. In the process, she emphasizes the complexity and artistry of this novel, aspects that have been often overlooked in favor of a simplistic assessment of Wright's creative process.

The next six chapters provide extended examinations of particular works of protest, drawing on their historical, political, and/or cultural contexts. In Babacar M'Baye's chapter, "Radical and Nationalist Resistance in David Walker's and Frederick Douglass's Antislavery Narratives," we journey back to Wright's political predecessors, David Walker and Frederick Douglass. As M'Baye argues, Walker's *Appeal* was the forerunner of a black radical and black nationalist tradition that insisted on the indomitable desire for liberty in all African Americans and that called for violent uprisings of all slaves around the world. This tradition would eventually inspire writers such as Richard Wright, Angela Davis, Amiri Baraka, Maya Angelou, Nikki Giovanni, and Malcolm X, but initially, it inspired Frederick Douglass. Most of Douglass's critics have not seen him as part of the black radical tradition but as an integrationist. Yet, in contrast to Harriet Beecher Stowe, who supported the American Colonization Society's plans to force free African Americans to immigrate to Africa, Douglass insisted, "Individuals emigrate—nations never." This emphasis on the black nation within America is evidence that Douglass's rhetoric as well as aspects of his *Narrative* had a decidedly black nationalist bent.

Adeline Carrie Koscher directs our attention to the turn of the century, when the New Woman was making her first appearances in literature, in her chapter "The New Woman Chafes against Her Bonds." Examining the New Woman as portrayed primarily in novels by Charlotte Perkins Gilman and Kate Chopin, Koscher notes that while laws regarding marriage and other social institutions had begun to change, women needed to imagine these institutions in entirely new, even utopian ways—ways perhaps only possible in fiction. It was through fictional New Women and their protests against accepted gender roles, Koscher argues, that Gilman and Chopin could encourage their readers to rethink their safe social harbors and strike out for the open water.

Reimagining life's possibilities is a protest strategy also featured in the next chapter, "The Solidarity of Song: Proletarians, Poetry, and the Public Sphere of the Lawrence Textile Strike of 1912," by Tara Forbes and Mikhail Bjorge. Forbes and Bjorge view the songs created during this strike as intellectual work that allowed strikers a critique of the capitalist power structure and a reconception of the world of labor. Songs on all aspects of the strike, from the bosses and scabbing to the solidarity of the strikers, enabled the diverse group of workers—a significant number of them women—to remain engaged and united in their successful protest.

In "Dystopia as Protest: Zamyatin's *We* and Orwell's *Nineteen Eighty-Four*," Rachel Stauffer turns to dystopia as a motivator for social change. Said to have been influenced by H. G. Wells, Yevgeny Zamyatin's *We* is a significant influence on George Orwell's *Nineteen Eighty-Four*. Both *We* and *Nineteen Eighty-Four* end with the collapse of human resistance to the indoctrination programs of totalitarian regimes, which is meant to be profoundly unsettling to readers, Stauffer argues. Additionally, *We* seemed to accurately predict the Soviet-era repression of individuality and individual liberty, as well as the collapse of the Soviet Union, and the text was censored in the 1920s. Stauffer suggests that when it was finally published in the 1980s, *We* became a text of protest *and* liberation as it contributed to the revolution and the glasnost era.

In "Paranoia and Pacifism in E. E. Cummings's *The Enormous Room*," Seth Johnson turns to World War I to examine a different kind of despotic restriction of individuality and liberty: Cummings's portrayal of the paranoid repressions that European and American governments inflicted on their own citizens during wartime. In his autobiographical novel, a text of the secular peace movement, Cummings contrasts an ironic and detached tone with touching portraits of his fellow prisoners, a diverse group of people whose presence in the "enormous room" only serves to highlight the bizarre and convoluted manipulations of free speech, civil rights, and social justice perpetrated by so-called democratic nations at war.

Finally, in the last chapter of the volume, Christi Cook examines the particular forms protest takes in young-adult Chicano/a literature. Entitled "Holiness and Heresy: Viramontes, *la Virgen*, and the Mother-Daughter Bond," her chapter analyzes the connections between Rudolfo Anaya's *Bless Me, Ultima* and Helena María Viramontes's *Under the Feet of Jesus*. Frequently banned even in recent years, Anaya's novel challenged Catholic religious hegemony by depicting its integration with earth-based spirituality; it also challenges patriarchal ideology by portraying strong female characters. Viramontes similarly allows her characters to practice a range of religious beliefs, while also directly commenting on the conditions for migrant workers in the United States and on the patriarchal and economic structures that tend to keep women fixed in poverty. Both authors reconfigure Mexican cultural elements in ways that are more useful to their Chicano/a protagonists, thus forming new tools in their protest against the social injustice for Chicanos and Chicanas in the United States.

The protest texts covered in this volume are clearly connected to particular social movements and directed at specific audiences, but they share the same general goals: to show readers the inner workings of social injustice and to help them resist such injustice. The chapters in this volume go further, we hope, in providing readers with useful approaches to and interpretations of these texts. In choosing these chapters, we inevitably left out many other ways of approaching many different works of protest literature, and a list of the texts that could have been covered is appended at the end of this volume. We hope that the list serves to inspire further work in this area.

On the Literature of Protest: Words as Weapons_____

Kimberly Drake

I have every so often been termed a propaganda or protest writer. . . . That designation has probably grown out of the fact that I write about what I know best, and being a Negro in this country is tied up with difficulties that cause one to protest naturally. I am writing about human beings and situations that I know and experience, and therefore it is only incidentally protest—protest in that it grows out of a live situation. (Langston Hughes, 1952)

I think we writers . . . can be dangerously revolutionary. We believe wholeheartedly in the power of the imagination to create the possible, and no one, no one can control that fact. We have breathed new life into social engagement. We are knocking at the door demanding change. (Helena María Viramontes, 2000)

What would happen if one woman told the truth about her life? / the world would split open. (Muriel Rukeyser, 1968)

In his article "How a Revolutionary Counter-Mood Is Made," Jonathan Flatley examines the most basic question that can be asked about protest literature: how can a narrative, lyric, or dramatic description of oppression ignite resistance to that oppression? Adding Martin Heidegger's analysis of "mood" in *Being and Time* to Vladimir Lenin's discussion of party newspapers in "What is to Be Done?," Flatley discusses the way protest writing can "facilitate[e] a mood-shifting affective attunement" among a group of oppressed workers (504). By reading a narrative description of "the mistreatment of other persons," workers come to "share an affective state," or a common emotional experience, and "indeed to become aware of themselves as a collective"; this process "invoke[s] a counter-mood," one that is the precursor to

---

organizing and resistance (504). For Lenin, the most "powerful agitational effects are achieved by straightforward reporting" about particular acts of oppression, not by a text that produces "pity or sympathy," according to Flatley (504). Reading such a "report," Lenin argues, readers will not only "understand, but will *feel* (Lenin's emphasis) that they are being oppressed by the same 'dark forces' oppressing the persons they read about" (Flatley 509). Once they realize this, they will not only experience an "irresistible desire to act," but also "a knowledge of *how* to act, what to do" (Flatley 509; emphasis in orig.). As Flatley notes, it is the combination of knowledge and emotion that inspire readers to form or join a social movement.

While this project is a unique and compelling contribution to the study of protest literature, Flatley's focus is on a 1968 instance of labor organizing at a Dodge plant inspired by a party newspaper. He thus leaves two of Lenin's notions a bit murky: that "straightforward reporting" works to create "powerful agitational effects" and that readers derive the "knowledge of how to act, what to do" spontaneously after reading this kind of writing. The first notion suggests that a transparent, authentic form of writing produces the correct response, or the one suggested in the second notion. Flatley describes the "correct response" as a "militant, collectively self-aware mood" (504) and a clear course of action. Pity and sympathy are to be avoided, and given what other literary critics have said about these emotions, I suggest that this is because they are thought to fritter away revolutionary energy in self-indulgent catharsis. Might "straightforward reporting" still produce "pity and sympathy," though? How exactly does "straightforward reporting" work? Flatley describes a successful piece of "reporting" as one that relies in part on "defamiliarization or 'making strange,'" one that takes readers out of "automatic modes of perception in which something is recognized instead of seen, since those things perceived by habit, the things we already think we know, are scarcely perceived at all" (516). In other words, we are accustomed to the unjust treatment of others, and as a result, accounts of this treatment fail to arouse the right "countermood" that will break through the hegemonic mood keeping us following normative patterns of behavior. The right description of oppression can catapult us into another emotional state or "mood," and since that description has affected many readers similarly, all we need is a revolutionary social movement to channel our countermood into militant action. Lenin's "straightforward reporting" in this light seems more like fiction, if not poetry, both of which can effectively defamiliarize and can produce sudden shifts in perception.

This volume has come into being because in fact protest literature does not usually work in the straightforward manner Lenin envisioned; the chapters in this volume examine the ways particular novels, stories, poems, songs, and works of creative nonfiction attempt to create social change.[1] A number of modes of literature[2] apart from "straightforward reporting" can inspire and have inspired social change, and the process of creating that inspiration is in fact both complex and historically contingent. While Lenin's ideal reader would seem to be a male member of the working class, most writers cannot count on such a stable group identity for their readers, nor could they presume that the writing would have the same impact upon all or most readers within that group. Further, Flatley cites the work of Eve Kosovsky Sedgwick, among others, in acknowledging that "affect and cognition are always in deep and complex interface with each other," so efforts to influence both emotion and understanding are "mediated, variable, and situated" (505), rather than automatic and direct, as Lenin would have us believe. What stands out to one reader will be overlooked by another, and what affects a working-class man one day might not affect him on another, depending on events in his life, other influences on him, and yes, his mood.

These challenges might seem insurmountable in our postmodern understanding; nevertheless, throughout the literature of protest and liberation (which continues to be written despite postmodernism), we see writers attempt to engage not only the reader's empathy, outrage, disgust, or horror, but also the reader's cognitive understanding of the workings and effects of oppressive social practices. Tactics that attempt to engage readers show up in a variety of ways in a given text, but certainly, identification with the text's protagonist[3] is an important tactic. For Lenin, the reader's "feeling" of identification with the protagonist seems limited to a kind of spontaneous recognition of similarity that is both cognitive and emotional and that gives rise immediately to a political self-awareness. Perhaps in the case of factory workers who have chosen to read a newspaper produced by one or more of their colleagues, such a recognition of similarity might lead quickly to the formation of a union movement. In cases where a readership includes not only members of the oppressed group, but also members of the oppressing group and people who are not members of either group, identification with the protagonist would necessarily lead readers to different kinds of social action. Most writers of protest know that their readers are from various parts of society and that they may not be looking for political enlightenment; they also know that readers may hold opinions and have experiences and emotions that interfere with the correct workings of the identification process. In other words, connecting readers to what Flatley calls the "countermood" of the political protest driving the text is difficult because of conscious and unconscious resistance on the part of the reader or audience.

During the writing process, writers can never be sure exactly whether (or how) their readers will resist experiencing the "mood" of their texts. Nor are there exact ways to measure the impact of a text, to tell when it has moved readers to the point of changing their minds about an issue or even committing themselves to social action. Although current technology may give us those capabilities, writers of previous decades used one tool to understand the way readers experienced their texts: the book review. Established and respected review journalists typically have a background in particular areas of arts criticism and perhaps some expertise in particular cultural modes of expression; they often are and have been professors, librarians, and/or practicing artists, creative writers, or musicians as well as journalists.

However, reviewers are also writing for a publication with a particular readership.[4] Ideally, a reviewer compares the text to others in its genre, culture, tradition, and historical moment, attempting to be fair in the analysis of the book, but the reviewer must also reflect the values of the reviewer's publication in the review. A journalist reviewer, then, delivers an expert opinion to readers about whether they should read or experience the text under review; the reviewer also suggests to the author how the text is being understood. Reviews of a text thus signify a culturally mediated set of responses or resistances to a writer's text. Writers use reviews, of their own work and the work of similar writers, to understand readers' responses and defenses, which then lead them to abandon, embrace, create, or combine literary or artistic tactics that might penetrate these defenses.

These tactics run the gamut in the tradition of protest literature,[5] but few protest writers rely solely on "straightforward reporting." They certainly do portray incidents of oppression and typically do so realistically, often showing graphic violence in detail (although not all depictions of violence, such as rape, were felt to be appropriate in earlier times). In some cases, the "reporting" of injustice had a secondary purpose, as did early African American abolitionist pamphlets. While the primary goal was certainly to convince whites to eradicate slavery, another goal was simply to allow "a broader national community of black leaders and white citizens" to "see African-American arguments" and allow "subsequent generations of black as well as white readers" to "refer back to African-American documents," thus establishing "a public literary identity [that] transformed African-American protest" (Newman, Racl, and Lapsansky 4). There were often even more goals in literary portrayals of violent oppression, such as in Frederick Douglass's 1845 *Narrative*. Douglass's depictions are relatively free from appeals to emotion, but they are loaded with religious or moral imagery in varying degrees of subtlety; besides showing that slavery should be abolished and that African Americans should be equal citizens, this text is designed to show white readers how their political views on slavery may be morally corrupt. The more intricate the text, the more goals it might be trying to achieve, so some protest writers rely on more emotional depictions and heightened language, sometimes bordering on the manifesto, to ensure that readers interpret the text as the author has desired. Authors such as Harriet Beecher Stowe and Tillie Olsen use fiction but rely on authorial intervention and the direct address to readers at key points to ensure that readers are on the right track. Olsen's narrator seems at one point to be reacting in disappointment to the poor reactions of a fictional reader.

Olsen's authorial intervention suggests her concern that readers will not react correctly to her text, a concern that has produced a number of literary tactics. Fearing that a reader will not identify with a socially marginal protagonist, in other words, some authors include several characters with which the reader can identify. The author might include portrayals of the moral corruption of the oppressors to supplement the protagonist's struggle to overcome oppression or might create "positive stereotypes" of socially marginalized characters in order to change narrow-minded readers' negative views of such types of people. Similarly, using familiar or "classic" forms such as the sonnet or well-known song tunes and giving them new content that conflicts with the original or expected content can startle readers through "defamiliarization." Creating protagonists who are both victims and perpetrators of violence, as does Richard Wright in most of his fiction, can shock and even traumatize readers, giving them a new perspective on their society; conversely, presenting admirable protagonists who are destroyed physically, emotionally, or even ideologically by their oppressive social systems can create anguish in empathetic readers. While they are not the norm for protest writing and art, the portrayals of utopian solutions to contemporary social problems can give readers a model toward which to direct their social actions. Similarly, humor in songs, stories, or essays is a rare but effective way to get readers or audiences to lower their defenses, connect emotionally to the wording that made them laugh, and accept the text's social messages. All of these tactics, from those that attack the reader to those that invite the reader to participate in group expression (such as singing on a picket line), are intended to raise the reader's consciousness and create a "revolutionary counter-mood" that will lead to social action.

These tactics succeed or fail at different times and in different ways, not only because of the author's skill set, but because readers learn how to defend themselves against the emotional and rhetorical force of such texts. One common defense has been the claim that the oppression depicted is fictional, that the author is telling lies; various chapters in this volume describe how protest writers work to create a sense of "truth" in their texts. I want to focus, however, on what might be considered the most successful defense mechanism against protest literature, one that has become attached to the concept of "protest literature" itself: the idea that it is not really literature or that it is bad writing. The word "protest" conjures up images of marches, strikes, sit-ins, political propaganda, and indoctrination—all of which have been portrayed by various critics as antithetical to the subtle art that goes into writing literature. Readers have absorbed the idea that if a work of protest literature has been written with political, not aesthetic, goals in mind, then reading the text will be like trudging grimly through a series of political pamphlets rather than being carried away by a "symphony" of images designed to "lift up the spirit, to release it from the dreariness of reality" (Smedley 7). This "symphony" of images is the way Agnes Smedley's authorial persona describes what *Daughter of Earth* is *not* going to do for readers. The subject matter will be grim, she notes, and the writing will keep readers mired in dreary reality. Many reviewers interpret these choices as indicating that the text is a failure, because the prose should be moving and transcendent no matter the topic.

Authors of best-selling protest novels of the nineteenth and twentieth centuries were often denigrated for inferior artistry, as if they were unable to produce figurative language or transcendent prose. Certainly some of them were less talented than others were, but for some writers, the "straightforward reporting" mode was a choice. Mike Gold, the proletarian writer and editor of the radical literary magazine *The Liberator*, explicitly called for working-class writers to avoid being "verbal acrobats," another form of "bourgeois idleness" (207). The literature, he said, must "deal with the real conflicts of men and women who work for a living" and must be "useful," in that "every poem, every novel and drama, must have a social theme, or it is merely confectionary" (Gold 206, 207). Many highly talented writers made a conscious choice to write using raw, unadorned language and/or a fragmented writing style. "Feel" the "supreme melodrama" of life, Gold admonished, and "everything becomes poetry—the new poetry of materials, of the so-called 'common man'" (208). This "new poetry" would be, as Gold hoped, itself a form of action, transforming readers who would then "sweep this mess [capitalism and class stratification] out of the world forever" (207). Protest literature, then, is not unconcerned with aesthetics. It is concerned rather with the creation of a style that reflects its subject matter, a style that sets it apart from the style and goals of "bourgeois" or even mainstream art and literature.

The difference between protest literature and nonprotest literature is not in its quality, but in its use of tactics of form and contest in the service of its goal, which is ultimately to create social change. Like all literature, the literature of protest and liberation is designed to touch readers in some way. However, the difference between touching a reader and pushing her toward a political goal is significant. As Jane Tompkins notes, early twentieth-century literary critics believed that "literature is by definition a form of discourse that has no designs on the world. It does not attempt to change things but merely to represent them, and it does so in a specifically literary language whose claim to value lies in its uniqueness" (125). This idea has probably become less dominant in more recent times, as seen in the following example: a former college student of mine, now on a Fulbright scholar teaching high school English literature, recently stated in her blog that she fears for the future of her students' country because they show no interest in reading literature. Students who do not read literature, my student fears, never develop the capacity to live in someone else's world, which enables empathy and compassion and presumably enables better relationships with "others." I agree with this assessment and with its political implications. Protest writers tend to use empathy to achieve specific political goals. These goals could be any or all of the following: to raise readers' consciousness about a particular social issue or to educate them on a deep level about an oppressive situation; to challenge preconceived notions about a particular class of people; to provide readers with an ideological mirror of themselves and their society, one that is perhaps unflattering; to provide readers with tools—in terms of critical perspectives and theories, alternative ways of being, knowing, or thinking, role models and/or a community, and even survival strategies—to use for social analysis and political action. Protest literature would not by necessity achieve all of these goals, but most of it achieves more than one. A literature of "liberation" can be defined as a literature that does not stop at protest, but goes further to imagine a way that an oppressed group might liberate itself. Most slave narratives and a great deal of proletarian literature, for example, depict the protagonist successfully achieving freedom or class consciousness, as the case may be, by relying on the critical tools or the actual aid of a relevant social movement such as abolitionism or the labor movement. On the other hand, poetry, fiction, and plays about lynching or military violence tend to involve grucsome death and the complete lack of social justice—an unhappy (and realistic) ending designed to push readers toward social action.

I would argue that the presence of political goals in literature, no matter how "poetic" the text in question might be, has tended to cloud the critic's vision. Literary critics' standards for literary value were far more rigid and narrow in decades past than they are today, and critics were far less willing to presume equal value in approaching an unfamiliar genre or authorial demographic (something that began to change in the 1970s). As Jane Tompkins has noted, it was expected up through the mid-twentieth century that the so-called masterworks of literature, or books included in what we call the "literary canon," would be characterized by "stylistic intricacy, psychological subtlety, epistemological complexity" (126). Canonical books would also be imaginative rather than autobiographical, "universal" and "timeless" in their appeal, layered with imagery suggesting submerged patterns of meaning, and focused (in most cases) on issues that were important to white men. While many scholars of protest literature or literatures of socially marginal groups have challenged the exclusionary application of these criteria, they continue to accept most of the criteria themselves. Indeed, I would have trouble arguing that a text could lack stylistic intricacy, psychological complexity, and epistemological subtlety and still be compelling to a wide readership. However, it is the subjective understanding of these qualities, and the ways that "universal" and "timeless" have been historically contingent and politically loaded, that is contested by these scholars.

In her essay "The Novel as Social Criticism," Ann Petry describes these hegemonic values as follows: literature should be written "for art's sake," and it is "prostituted, bastardized" when it is "used to serve some moral or political end" (33). The implication here is that art for "art's sake" is free of politics, that it transcends social claims and attachments. Such a notion is consistent with the notion of "white" or other kinds of "privilege," an idea describing the way that hegemonic ideologies favoring a particular group of people disguise themselves to appear invisible and normative, thus giving those recognized by dominant society the sense that their society is egalitarian and their values universal. A great deal of protest literature has been excluded based on the standard of "universality." However, as noted by Richard Long and Eugenia Collier, "the demand for universality in the writings of the Afro-American cloaks a disapproval which the critic cannot articulate," and by accepting the idea that African American literature is not universal, "even the most liberal critic turns out to be a racist" (5). As it turns out, this particular criterion is self-perpetuating: reviewers and college professors select the works that that they consider "great" in their own time and that they believe will be considered "classic" in subsequent decades—a selection that determines to a great extent which texts will stay in print because they will be included in high school or college curricula and/or reprinted in published anthologies.[6]

A text like Harriet Beecher Stowe's *Uncle Tom's Cabin*, one that brought a clear social message to millions of readers all over the world, was not considered part of the literary canon and probably is still not, although I would suggest progress in that area has been made.[7] That the book emotionally moves readers even today, that it is accessible to a wide variety of readers, and that it delivers a nuanced critique of the particular social institution it treats (all features of an effective protest novel for its era): these are the very aspects that earn it the labels "popular" and "protest," meaning "nonliterary" and more than likely, "bad." In a 2006 review of *The Annotated Uncle Tom's Cabin*, edited by Henry Louis Gates Jr., Edward Rothstein notes that Gates is attempting to "resurrect" the novel as "a central document in American race relations," challenging the prevailing dismissal of Stowe's novel for its conservative racial politics. His term "resurrect" indicates his own view that the novel had been "dead" until Gates took it up in a new context. Rothstein goes on to state, "Characters may reflect the era's varied views of slavery, *but* many of them possess distinctive voices as well. This is how Stowe writes a protest novel *that is also moving*" (emphasis added). Rothstein implies a set of protest novel qualities— that the characters must represent certain political views and thus are not fully realized as characters or that they typically are not "moving" because they are taken up with political concerns—and then contrasts them with Stowe's achievements—to create characters with "distinctive voices" and to move readers. In other words, he implies that her text has managed somehow to overcome the inherent problems of its genre. This is not to say that protest literature has not been considered valuable by scholars, but its value has often been said to lie in its status as history or cultural artifact or as sociological examination of particular social groups.

The work of Langston Hughes has also been viewed by various critics as noncanonical, or canonical only in the context of the Harlem Renaissance. Hughes has been long considered the Harlem Renaissance poet laureate, yet his work has been frequently criticized for being too accessible, too simplistic. In the epigraph used at this chapter's beginning, Hughes apparently feels constrained to deny that his work is consciously protesting racial discrimination (among other issues that it did, in fact, protest). His work, he says, comes from his experience. But even a claim that one's work is a product of one's experience is problematic in terms of its value; one's literary talent is expected to be limited if it is too closely tied to one's personal experiences. More importantly, authors who write about their "real" experiences, it is thought, believe that they can transparently represent their "reality," the same "reality" that readers experience. As Jane Gallop notes, the "belief in simple referentiality," or the idea that one can accurately represent reality, "is not only unpoetic but ultimately politically conservative" (qtd. in Lauret 3). Any representation of "reality" is in fact an ideological conception of a conventional reality—one that then presents itself as normative. Taken at his word, Hughes could seem to express a "simplistic, instrumental view of the role of culture in social change" (Lauret 7), and as noted above, many reviewers believed his poetry to be simplistic, even childish. However, more recent criticism of Hughes's work notes his innovative formal approach, which fuses blues and jazz forms with poetic forms in a kind of experimentalism that turns out to be deceptively simple yet thoroughly modernist. In this formal innovation, one that lends itself well to the subjects of his poems, Hughes avoided the problem that has plagued many marginalized writers: the creation of a "body of literature capable of capturing the political and cultural realities of their experiences while using literary forms created by and for white, upper class men," as Lorraine Bethel explains (qtd. in Lauret 4).

Most protest writers, I would argue, have wrestled with this dilemma. To the extent that they used new forms, they might deviate from prevailing standards for literary value. Relying on traditional forms might garner them praise from the literary critical establishment, but the praise would be condescending and the ability to create a "countermood" in readers would be diminished. To quote Audre Lorde, "the master's tools will never dismantle the master's house. They may allow us temporarily to beat him at his own game, but they will never enable us to bring about genuine change" (112). Lorde was talking specifically about academic feminism rather than about literary forms, but her idea is echoed by literary critic Maria Lauret, who argues that the arts and literatures of "non-dominant groups" has to "define itself against the practices and ideology of the dominant group," which inevitably involves issues of form (5). In *Resistance Literature*, Barbara Harlow examines the "significant corpus of literary writing, both narrative and poetic," that serves as a weapon in the "struggle for national liberation and independence" on the "part of colonized peoples" (xvi). This literature, she notes, not only "demands recognition of its independent status and existence as a literary production," but it also "presents a serious challenge to the codes and canons of both the theory and the practice of literature and its criticism as these have been developed in the West" (Harlow xvi). It does so self-consciously and deliberately, Harlow argues, "call[ing] attention to itself, and to literature in general, as a political and politicized activity" (28–29). In this sense, negative value judgments of resistance literature by Western-trained literary critics are at best irrelevant, and the writer's acceptance of Western conventions or literary values could be a sign that the writer has fallen victim to cultural imperialism or "the 'strategies of containment' that [Fredric] Jameson examined in his work *The Political Unconscious*" (Harlow 17, 20). Innovative forms and challenges to convention thus seem vital to the political goals of protest literature.

Langston Hughes's discussion of the minority artist's relationship to conventions in his essay "The Negro Artist and the Racial Mountain" is useful in describing the workings (and lack thereof) of cultural imperialism. He critiques the "urge within the race toward whiteness," which results in the "desire to pour racial individuality," including literature, "into the mold of American standardization" (Hughes para. 1). Hughes describes this drive as emanating from middle-class African Americans; on the other hand, the "low-down folks, the so-called common element" are "not ashamed of him [the black artist]—if they know he exists at all" (Hughes para. 4). This ironic twist at the end of this section presents the real dilemma here: the "low-down folks" may have resisted the pernicious influence of bourgeois "standardization," but do they actually read the protest poetry that depicts their struggles, that was written in a form intended to appeal to them? Ultimately, issues of form are tied to the text's readership. If formal innovations are intended to convey a revolutionary countermood among the oppressed group, they must not succumb to forms aligned and associated with the oppressors, but they must also avoid alienating those readers. If the innovations are intended to penetrate the readerly defenses of mainstream readers or readers from the "oppressor" demographic, they must still avoid ignoring or alienating readers from the oppressed group, but they must also depart from convention to the extent that they create new ways of seeing for readers who tend to see conventionally.

I would suggest that the most effective protest writing has typically taken on reader-friendly experiments in form and in context—reader-friendly in terms of accessibility, not of emotional comfort. These experiments were admittedly subtle in the past century, because of the great physical risk oppressed writers took (on behalf of themselves and their communities) in "speaking truth to power" as well as because their readership or audience required a great deal more grounding in convention than our contemporary equivalents. Writing about the protest poetry of the Harlem Renaissance and the black arts movement of the 1960s, Margaret Reid states that early black writers had to be "deceptive in their works, for if there were the remotest hint of protest in their writing, their slim chances of publication became nil.

So for matters of survival, those writers who wanted to protest about the status quo had to couch their protest in language which had two meanings—one for Blacks and one for Whites" (5). This coded language of protest can be found in most US literary protests during the nineteenth century as well as in songs and literature around the world. James Scott elaborates on this need to hide "critique of power," which each produce what he calls a "hidden transcript" (xii). Not only does each "subordinate group" create a hidden transcript (or many such), but "the powerful, for their part, also develop a hidden transcript representing the practices and claims of their rule that cannot be openly avowed" (Scott xii.) Most protest writers before Richard Wright (late 1930s through the 1940s) avoided the most dangerous parts of each of these "hidden transcripts" while deploying less risky parts to disrupt what Scott calls the "public transcript," or the narrative of power relations that conforms to the status quo (14). One prominent exception to the rule is antilynching activist Ida B. Wells, whose *Southern Horrors* is so blatant in its critique of the "hidden" white transcript and so straightforward in its style that its publication resulted in death threats and the destruction of her office.

Indeed, one of the primary goals of any piece of protest literature is to make the reader feel uncomfortable, outraged, or shocked. Experiments with form as well as the inclusion of shocking content were done to this end. As Petry notes in discussing novels protesting racism, "If emotion is aroused merely by the use of certain words" or concepts such as intermarriage or mixed marriage, and if "the emotion is violent, apoplectic, then it seems fairly logical that novels which deal with race relations should reflect some of this violence" (38). Petry acknowledges that such shocking violence in the book will reduce the book in the eyes of mainstream literary critics, but as she states, "the average reader seems to like" these novels, perhaps because "we all feel guilty because of the shortcomings of society and our sense of guilt is partially assuaged when we are accused, in the printed pages of a novel, of having done those things that we ought not to have done and of having left undone those things we ought to have done" (35). Petry thus links the denigration of protest novels to their level of success in making readers experience "emotional pain and guilt," as Jerry W. Ward Jr. argues (176). Similarly, Amiri Baraka felt that "violence (rhetorical at least) was a key component of black arts, an element necessary to break though crusted layers of internalized oppression in blacks" (Reed 47), yet also "instill pride" in blacks by celebrating culture and developing a "black aesthetic" (47). The violence in Baraka's plays, in other words, was experienced by the audience as a "penetrating" of the "layers" of resistance, but the results of the penetration would differ depending on the particular audience member.

I argue that readers' emotions are more frequently the targets of protest writers than readers' conventional understandings of social relations. The goal of literature of protest is to invite the reader into a fully realized world and into the consciousness of a compellingly portrayed protagonist and then to depict that protagonist in a society where to "conform to the local taboos and mores" is to "live, miserably," but to "refuse to conform" is to die (Petry 37). In a work of protest, then, a reader vicariously experiences being misrecognized and silenced, as in Myung Mi Kim's poem "Into Such Assembly," about the loss inherent in linguistic assimilation: "One gives over to a language and then / What is given, given over?" (lines 34–35). A reader identifies with a protagonist who is physically and emotionally damaged, and perhaps even destroyed, simply by being, as June Jordan states in "Poem about My Rights," "the wrong / sex the wrong age the wrong skin" (lines 8–9). These vicarious experiences are uncomfortable, particularly if we like the protagonist. But readers can also be made uncomfortable when they find themselves positioned as the oppressor, as Jordan does to her readers at the end of her poem: "from now on my resistance / my simple and daily and nightly self-determination / may very well cost you your life" (lines 105–6). Enabling reader identification with an oppressed protagonist as well as with the oppressor are tactics of protest literature that produce emotional effects in the reader; these effects ask the reader to understand her unique form of connection to the oppression of the protagonist, and they thus seek "to endow the individual subject with some new heightened sense of its place in the global system," as Fredric Jameson put it (qtd. in Harlow 13).

The ability to shock a mainstream reader diminished with each decade of the twentieth century to the point that Richard Wright's 1940 portrayal of interracial sex and violence, while shocking, did not result in physical violence to himself or his publisher (as did Ida B. Wells' discussion of these issues four decades earlier), but instead became a Book of the Month Club best seller. This does not mean *Native Son* was not shocking, but it did not appear to have provoked violent attacks on the author. On the contrary, as Alain Locke noted in 1947, with many crisis novels on the best sellers' lists, "the theme of interracial tension and intolerance may become a beaten path to today's big audience" (4). Crisis novels are valued by Locke for their ability to create "revolutionary changes of public thought and social behavior" (4), but he is also clearly calling on writers to exploit the popularity of these novels. One could argue that the ability to reach a "big audience" (Locke 4), meaning a mainstream one, can only broaden the social impact of the protest text, but as we know from other revolutionary forms such as punk rock, the machinery of mainstream literary and artistic production tends to dampen the revolutionary elements of the work. Mainstream success is probably a sign, in other words, that one's revolutionary text has accommodated itself to the status quo. As Chester Himes noted in discussing the troubling publication history of his novel *Yesterday Will Make You Cry*, "white American readers of novels . . . are not interested in black writers unless they bleed from white torture" (*Quality* 72–73). Rather than being offended by portrayals of graphic violence and social injustice, mainstream readers seemed to enjoy such portrayals.

In the five decades since the advent of postmodernism, not only is it ever more difficult to create a literary "countermood" for the cynical globalized readers of today, but newer ways of thinking about representations and truth have called into question some of the basic tactics of protest literature. Some of these problems have already been alluded to, and some will be further discussed in the chapters to follow. One significant example is the mainstream understanding of the psychology of trauma, specifically post-traumatic stress disorder (PTSD), gleaned from television personalities such as Oprah Winfrey and Dr. Phil. We now understand that psychologically speaking, moments of trauma are unspeakable, almost unknowable, and often entirely or partly repressed. As scholars Cathy Caruth, Jeffrey Alexander, and Sheldon George have noted, the traumatic "event is not assimilated or experienced fully at the time, but only belatedly, in its repeated possession of the one who experiences it" (Caruth, *Trauma* 4). Further, Franz Fanon's work on psychoanalysis and the trauma of colonialism in *Black Skin, White Masks* (1967) and Edward Said's work on colonialism and representations of Asia and the Middle East in *Orientalism* (1978) have complicated contemporary understandings of racial oppression by adding theories of the ways knowledge and power are constructed and maintained at all levels of society. What has been destabilized by these and related theoretical paradigms are two sets of binary oppositions that protest writers have relied on for decades: the idea that the experience of oppression was either true (and accurately recalled) or a deliberate lie for the sake of politics and the idea that one was either an oppressor or a survivor of oppression. With the collapse of such binaries, the protest writer's ability to move readers to social action becomes more difficult.

A related issue concerns what has been called the "crisis of representation." It connects the idea of realism and mimetic portrayals to the problem of being able to adequately speak for and represent a group of people, even if the author is a member of that group. The problem is most visible, however, when "persons from dominant groups" attempt to "speak for others," they are inevitably "treated as authenticating presences that confer legitimacy and credibility on the demands of subjugated speakers" (Roof and Wiegman 99). Even when the "person from the dominant group" is attempting to destroy social hierarchies, his or her presence maintains those hierarchies. This is because when any person attempts to speak for another, that person is "representing the other's needs, goals, situation, and in fact, who they are," based on his or her "own situated interpretation" and not the interpretation of the person being represented (Roof and Wiegman 100). Finally, even when a person speaks for herself, she is "representing" herself in a particular way contingent on the time and place; she ("momentarily) create[s] . . . a public, discursive self" that "will in most cases have an effect on the self experienced as interiority" (Roof and Wiegman 100–101.) Jesse Cohn has written about this problem as it appears in works of protest art: "even those motivated by a wish to lend a voice to those who have been silenced, involves a further silencing" (12). Similarly, Sneja Gunew and Gayatri Chakravorty Spivak discuss these failures of representation as leading to tokenism (in which one individual gets chosen routinely to speak for the group) and homogenization of the self (because "there are many subject positions which one must inhabit," 413), but these are elided when one attempts to speak for him or her "self." Ultimately, these scholars agree, "this question of representation, self-representation, representing others, is a problem" (Gunew and Spivak 416–17), and the related notion of "authenticity" in representation is a kind of fantasy constructed by the oppressor.

Are we thus unable to represent others or even ourselves? Is protest literature doomed to failure, no longer able to create clear and believable representations of oppression? Writers and artists are still creating such representations, despite their failings. In *The Violence of Representation*, Nancy Armstrong and Leonard Tennenhouse recommend a dialectical understanding of the problems of representation. They state that every misrepresentation actually incites agency in the misrepresented individual by compelling that person to create a counter-representation; in other words, a "self on the other side of words" will burst free of representational categories and contribute a momentary understanding (Armstrong and Tennenhouse 7). I agree with this approach, which certainly reflects the circumstances leading to the production of protest writing in a number of the chapters included in this volume. As Gunew and Spivak note, "as long as one remains aware that it [representation] is a very problematic field, there is some hope" (417). Without losing track of this, however, I would suggest that we continue to trust in "the power of the imagination to create the possible," as author Helena María Viramontes has stated (153). In the 2011 Arab Spring protests and in the US Occupy movements, we all have witnessed various ways that "straightforward reporting" and imaginative uses of social media can create "revolutionary countermoods" out of isolated incidents of social action. Protest writers are continuing to create formal innovations that will engage today's readers. Writers and readers from various social strata will continue to misrepresent each other and respond to those misrepresentations in dialectical (or to use a more up-to-date term, "networked") fashion, hoping to create if not progress, then social "movement" or "action."

Notes

1. As Margaret Reid states, "protest" means "to state positively, to affirm solemnly," while "affirm" means "to declare fairly" (1). She notes, "The difference between protest and affirmation is weakened if one considers that if a people have to affirm their existence . . . then they are protesting to the persons who wish to deny them their existence" (1).
2. The majority of the chapters in this volume study fiction; fiction or creative nonfiction narratives, such as slave narratives, focus on psychological portraits and are extremely effective consciousness-raising tools. In this introduction, I have focused mostly on fiction and creative nonfiction narratives because they are my research subjects.
3. By "protagonist," I mean the primary character or hero of the text, if it is a narrative or dramatic text, and the speaker, the narrator, the "I" or "we" of a poem or song, or a particular personage described in that poem or song with whom we are directed to sympathize.
4. I am differentiating "journalistic reviews" from "critical reviews" here. The latter are interpretations of texts produced almost entirely by academics (professors and graduate students), and they are primarily geared toward other academics as well as undergraduate and some high school students. They are usually published in relatively obscure publications long after the original text has been

published, and for these reasons, they would seem to have a greatly diminished effect, if any, on writers and artists.

5. Most of the texts I cover in this introduction, and the majority of the texts covered in this volume's chapters, are works of American literature. This is in part due to the predominance of American texts in the field of protest literature. As T. V. Reed notes, "the United States was created through a social movement, the American Revolution, and social movements have helped make and remake our nation since" (xiii). They have done so by giving "substance" and "wider applicability" to "the important but vague and still unfulfilled promises of 'freedom' and 'democracy' announced in the revolution's best known manifesto, the Declaration of Independence" (Reed xiv). Also, it is important to note that while protest can occur across the political spectrum, the protests examined here reflect the ideologies of what Reed terms "progressive" social movements (xiv), which tend to broaden, not restrict social equality and social justice.

6. See Paul Lauter's *Canons and Contexts* for a groundbreaking discussion of the politics of canon formation.

7. I gauge the acceptance of *Uncle Tom's Cabin* into the canon of American literature by the fact that more and more of my high school students have read all or part of the book when they arrive in my college classrooms. However, in the mid-eighties, when Jane Tompkins wrote her crucial essay "Sentimental Power: *Uncle Tom's Cabin* and the Politics of Literary History," the novel was not considered canonical.

Works Cited

Alexander, Jeffrey. "Towards a Theory of Cultural Trauma." Ed. Alexander et al. *Cultural Trauma and Collective Identity*. Berkeley: U of California P, 2004. Print.

Armstrong, Nancy, and Leonard Tennenhouse. "Representing Violence, or 'How the West Was Won.'" *The Violence of Representation: Literature and the History of Violence*. Ed. Armstrong and Tennenhouse. London: Routledge, 1989. 1–26. Print.

Baldwin, James. "Everybody's Protest Novel." *Notes of a Native Son*. Boston: Beacon, 1984. Print.

Caruth, Cathy. Introduction. *Trauma: Explorations in Memory*. Ed. Caruth. Baltimore: Johns Hopkins, 1995. 3–12. Print.

___. *Unclaimed Experience: Trauma, Narrative, and History*. Baltimore: Johns Hopkins UP, 1996. Print.

Cohn, Jesse. *Anarchism and the Crisis of Representation: Hermeneutics, Aesthetics, Politics*. Selinsgrove, PA: Susquehanna UP, 2006. Print.

Douglass, Frederick. *The Narrative of the Life of Frederick Douglass, an American Slave*. Ed. William L. Andrews. New York: Norton, 1997. Print.

Flatley, Jonathan. "How a Revolutionary Counter-Mood Is Made." *New Literary History* 43.3 (2012): 503–25. Print.

George, Sheldon. "Trauma and the Conservation of African-American Racial Identity." *Journal for the Psychoanalysis of Culture and Society* 6.1 (2001): 58–72. Print.

Gold, Michael. "Proletarian Realism." *Mike Gold: A Literary Anthology*. Ed. Michael Folsom. New York: International, 1972. 203–8. Print.

Graham, Maryemma. "The Practice of a Social Art." *Langston Hughes: Critical Perspectives Past and Present*. Ed. Henry Louis Gates Jr. and Anthony Appiah. New York: Amistad, 1993. 213–36. Print.

Gunew, Sneja, and Gayatri Chakravorty Spivak. "Questions of Multiculturalism." *Women's Writing in Exile*. Ed. Mary Lynn Broe and Angela Ingram. Chapel Hill: U of North Carolina P, 1989. 412–20. Print.

Harlow, Barbara. *Resistance Literature*. New York: Methuen, 1987. Print.

Himes, Chester. *The Quality of Hurt: The Early Years. The Autobiography of Chester Himes*. New York: Thunder's Mouth, 1971. Print.

Hughes, Langston. "The Negro Artist and the Racial Mountain." *Nation* 23 June 1926: 692–94. *Nation Archive*. Web. 7 Jan. 2013.

Jordan, June. "Poem about My Rights." *Contemporary Period (1945 to the Present)*. Vol. E of *The Heath Anthology of American Literature*. Ed. Paul Lauter. New York: Wadsworth, 2005. Print.

Kim, Myung Mi. "Into Such Assembly." *The Forbidden Stitch: An Asian American Woman's Anthology*. Ed. Shirley Geok-Lin Lim, Mayumi Tsutakawa, and Margarita Donnelly. Corvallis, OR: Calyx, 1989. 152. Print.

Lauret, Maria. *Liberating Literature: Feminist Fiction in America*. New York: Routledge, 1994. Print.

Lauter, Paul. *Canons and Contexts*. New York: Oxford UP, 1991. Print.

Locke, Alain. "A Critical Retrospect of the Literature of the Negro for 1947." *Phylon* 9.1 (1948): 3–12. Print.

Long, Richard A., and Eugenia W. Collier, eds. *Afro-American Writing: An Anthology of Prose and Poetry*. University Park: Pennsylvania State UP, 1985. Print.

Lorde, Audre. "The Master's Tools Will Never Dismantle the Master's House." *Sister Outsider: Essays and Speeches*. Freedom, CA: Crossing, 1984. 110–13. Print.

Morrison, Toni. "Conversation with Alice Childress and Toni Morrison." *Black Creation Annual* 1974–75 (1974): 90–92. Print.

Newman, Richard S., Patrick Rael, and Phillip Lapsansky. Introduction. *Pamphlets of Protest: An Anthology of Early African-American Protest Literature, 1790–1860*. Ed. Newman, Rael, and Lapsansky. New York: Routledge, 2001. 1–31. Print.

Petry, Ann. "The Novel as Social Criticism." *The Writer's Book*. Ed. Helen Hull. New York: Harper, 1950. 31–39. Print.

Reed, T. V. *The Art of Protest: Culture and Activism from the Civil Rights Movement to the Streets of Seattle*. Minneapolis: U of Minnesota P, 2005. Print.

Reid, Margaret Ann. *Black Protest Poetry: Polemics from the Harlem Renaissance and the Sixties*. New York: Lang, 2001. Print.

Roof, Judith, and Robyn Wiegman, eds. *Who Can Speak? Authority and Critical Identity*. Urbana: U of Illinois P, 1995. Print.

Rothstein, Edward. "Digging through the Literary Anthropology of Stowe's Uncle Tom." *New York Times*. New York Times, 23 Oct. 2006. Web. 3 Jan. 2013.

Rukeyser, Muriel. "Käthe Kollwitz." *The Speed of Darkness*. New York: Random, 1968. 99. Print.

Scott, James C. *Domination and the Arts of Resistance: Hidden Transcripts*. New Haven: Yale UP, 1992.

Smedley, Agnes. *Daughter of Earth*. New York: Feminist, 1987. Print.

Tompkins, Jane. "Sentimental Power: *Uncle Tom's Cabin* and the Politics of Literary History." *Sensational Designs: The Cultural Work of American Fiction, 1790–1860*. New York: Oxford UP, 1985. 122–46. Print.

Viramontes, Helena María. "Praying For Knowledge: An Interview with Helena Maria Viramontes." Interview by Bridget Kevane. *Latina Self-Portraits: Interviews with Contemporary Women Writers*. Ed. Bridget Kevane and Juanita Heredia. Albuquerque: U of New Mexico P, 2000. 141–54. Print.

Ward, Jerry W., Jr. "Everybody's Protest Novel: The Era of Richard Wright." *The Cambridge Companion to the African American Novel*. Ed. Maryemma Graham. Cambridge: Cambridge UP, 2004. 173–88. Print.

CRITICAL
CONTEXTS

Countering the Rhetoric of Slavery: The Critical Roots and Critical Reception of *Uncle Tom's Cabin*_____

Lydia Willsky

"Is this the little woman who made this great war?" American legend has it that Abraham Lincoln spoke those words, or some version of them, upon meeting Harriet Beecher Stowe (qtd. in Fields 181). Though the factuality of this exchange is difficult to prove, the sentiment that inspired it is not. One twentieth-century reviewer, Jane Tompkins, notes unequivocally that "*Uncle Tom's Cabin* was, in almost any terms one can think of, the most important book of the century" (124). By sheer numbers alone (it was the first American novel to sell over one million copies), it was clear to both European and American readers that this "little woman" and her book had done something rather incredible. Very few novels have had the social, political, and cultural impact that Stowe's *Uncle Tom's Cabin* had on American culture, and the novel continues to stir debate among literary critics and scholars of history and religion.

During the tense decade prior to the outbreak of the American Civil War in 1861, *Uncle Tom's Cabin* often stood at the center of debate. It is impossible to extricate Stowe's book from the broader discourse occurring during the years leading up to the Civil War, because so many of the ideas on which she writes—slavery, Christian duty (and hypocrisy), abolition, redemption—were seminal to the discussions between the North and the South, the proslavery and the antislavery debaters. *Uncle Tom's Cabin* did not introduce these subjects or arguments into the antebellum dialogue. Rather, Stowe's novel shed new light on these topics and introduced them to a far broader audience. *Uncle Tom's Cabin* brought the fight to the populace, to the housewives, the timid husbands, and the ambivalent supporters of abolition. Effectively, Stowe asked her readers to pick a side: proslavery or abolition, which, in Stowe's mind represented either the side of the devil or the side of God.

For its critique of southern slaveholders and the seeming indifference of northerners, *Uncle Tom's Cabin* was controversial. For Stowe's portrayal of African Americans and her support for colonization, Stowe's novel has proven *timelessly* controversial. The critical response to Stowe's novel differed from person to person and has changed over time, according to the needs of its readers and critics. This chapter examines the critical responses from the time of the novel's publication into the twenty-first century. It is a testament to the impact of Stowe's novel that it has sustained the interest of so many readers and that it has inspired both praise and critique from so many different demographic groups. In addition, this chapter addresses not just *who* has critiqued the novel, but *what* they have critiqued. Various critics have passionately honored or attacked the gender of the author, the novel's apparent agenda of abolition or colonization, and Stowe's choice of telling the story of slavery in a novel. *Uncle Tom's Cabin* made people think and feel something—ranging from anger and defensiveness to inspiration and motivation to enact substantive change—toward slavery that other books and pamphlets of its kind and of that time simply did not. Further, the novel has been dually enraging and inspiring readers for more than 170 years, another measure of its profound impact. For this reason, the story of the critical response to *Uncle Tom's Cabin* is as important as the story of the novel itself.

Harriet Beecher Stowe and the Creation of *Uncle Tom's Cabin*

Before discussing the critical reception of *Uncle Tom's Cabin*, one must look first at the book itself and its author. Harriet Beecher Stowe was born in 1811 into a family of renowned writers, reformers, and preachers. For this reason, both religion—specifically, her father's moderate Calvinism and her own evangelicalism—and reform played a major factor in Stowe's upbringing, influences that would continue into her later life and as she began to write *Uncle Tom's Cabin*.

What ultimately inspired Stowe to put pen to paper was her own experiences with runaway slaves and slave catchers during the years she spent in Cincinnati, Ohio, after marrying her husband, Calvin Stowe (Ammons 6–7). In 1850, Congress passed the Fugitive Slave Act, which mandated that any person who encountered a runaway slave must return that slave to his or her master or risk severe punishments under the law. Up to this point, the blight of slavery had remained far away in the South. However, the Fugitive Slave Act, as one writer put it, suddenly made "active participation in the institution of slavery a Northern as well as a Southern reality" (Ammons 7). The act had a polarizing effect on the North, especially. Genteel antislavery, or the position that favored a gradual emancipation of slavery while eschewing any hasty attempts to abolish the institution, was no longer a viable option. The question was put to the North: if you see a runaway slave, will you reveal your complicity in the slave system by returning the slave, or will you defy the federal government and refuse to remand this slave to certain punishment, even death? In Ohio, Stowe witnessed firsthand the ruthlessness of slave catchers, who would capture slaves and sell them down south for a fee. The region was also rife with antislavery activity, perhaps as a reaction to Ohio's particularly harsh and racist laws.[1]

Prior to 1850, Stowe had been "opposed to slavery," even if she was not "active on the issue" (Ammons 7). Stowe, referring to herself in the third person in the "Concluding Remarks" of the novel, explained:

> Since the legislative act of 1850, when she heard, with perfect surprise and consternation, Christian and humane people actually recommending the remanding escaped fugitives into slavery, as a duty binding on good citizens—when she heard, on all hands, from kind, compassionate, and estimable people, in the free states of the North, deliberations and discussions as to what Christian duty could be on this head—she could only think, These men and Christians cannot know what slavery is; if they did, such a question could never be open for discussion. (622)

The Critical Roots and Critical Reception of *Uncle Tom's Cabin*

29

Stowe determined to "exhibit" the institution "in a *living dramatic reality*" (622; italics in orig.). Helping to strengthen Stowe's resolve, her sister-in-law wrote her a letter, asking Stowe to write something about the horror of the Fugitive Slave Act and slavery in general, as Ann Douglas notes in her introduction to *Uncle Tom's Cabin* (8). At that time, Stowe had dabbled in writing but had not produced anything of any great note. Then in 1851, while receiving communion at church, Stowe reported that she had received a vision of "a saintly black man being mercilessly flogged and praying for his torturers as he died," as Douglas recounts in her introduction (8). From this vision, the character of Uncle Tom arose. These events, precipitated by the passing of the Fugitive Slave Act, converged to prompt Stowe to begin her project that would make her, then a relative unknown, into a national figure and spokesperson for the antislavery cause.

Before it became a book, *Uncle Tom's Cabin* appeared as a series in antislavery activist Gamaliel Bailey's newspaper, *The National Era*. The set of installments, of which Stowe originally envisioned there would only be three or four, expanded until it grew into an epic tale of suffering and redemption spanning across years and, eventually, across continents (Kirkham 67). The plot involves two parallel stories, one ultimately tragic but triumphant and the other perilous but happily resolved by the end. The first, titular story involves Uncle Tom, a pious, loyal slave of the Shelby family, who awakens one morning to find himself sold to a slave trader, Mr. Haley. The story follows Tom's journey down the Mississippi and then into the various homes of his new masters—from the kind, albeit indifferent, Augustine St. Clair and his angelic daughter Eva to the cruel Simon Legree. The St. Clairs, though they begin to make provisions for Tom's freedom, both tragically die, leading to his purchase by Legree, the man ultimately responsible for Tom's death as a martyr to the slave system. The second, parallel story of Stowe's novel followed Eliza and George Harris as they both attempted to escape the clutches of slave catchers. Eliza, prompted by the news that her master Mr. Shelby had sold her young son, Harry, flees with the boy. She manages to evade slave catchers and rejoins her husband, George. Prior to this, George had determined to escape his own cruel master, flee to Canada, and eventually send for Eliza once he was settled. Eliza's own decision to flee expedites her journey considerably. Once they are reunited, they are able to reach Canada safely and joyously set out to begin a new life together, as free people.

The two plots intertwine only briefly at the beginning and again at the end, creating the effect of a bifurcated story. This appeared to perturb critics of the novel (Gossett 101). Strange literary device though it was, each story and each of Stowe's main characters—particularly Tom and Eliza—represent a particular element of the author's critique of the slave system. In the story involving Uncle Tom, Tom's impending death, the climax of the novel, evokes two separate responses from its characters. Tom, broken in body but not in his faith, is overwhelmed with joy at the prospect of his death and the certain glory he will experience in heaven. Legree, on the other hand, grows increasingly disturbed and fearful, knowing, but unwilling to admit, that his soul is damned for his crimes against Tom. Through the story of Tom, Stowe reveals her adamancy that the slave system is damaging to both slave and master. The subject of the hard and depleting life of an African American living under slavery was hackneyed at that time and not new in this regard, as abolitionists had been hammering on this point for some time (Hochman 26). However, the concept that the slave system did irreparable damage to the souls of slave masters became a trademark of Stowe's antislavery message. "Have you not," Stowe asked the people of the South,

> in your own secret souls, in your own private conversings, felt that there are woes and evils in this accursed system far beyond what are here shadowed or can be shadowed? Can it be otherwise? Is *man* ever a creature to be trusted with wholly irresponsible power? And does not the slave system, by denying the slave all legal right of testimony, make every individual owner an irresponsible despot? (622)

The slave system, by its nature, turned good-natured people into tyrants and bad-natured people into brutal oppressors.

With the story of Eliza and in multiple other instances in the novel, Stowe depicted one of the most tragic aspects of the slave trade: the breakup of families, particularly the parting of mothers from their children. Slave mothers had no rights to their offspring under the slave system; masters and slave traders could forcibly part mothers from children. The only options were to flee, as in the case of Eliza; to submit, as was the case of most unfortunate slave women; or, most tragically, to take one's life (as in the story of Lucy in *Uncle Tom's Cabin*). In the conclusion, Stowe appeals directly to "northern mothers" to speak out against this atrocious practice (624). By appealing to their motherhood and motherly instincts, Stowe effectively closes the distance between black and white women, making the actions of escaping slaves "who are driven to defy law and convention" out of "despair and defiance," seem like "acceptable responses to injustice and pain" (Hochman 40).

In her series of installments, Stowe had done what the abolitionist press had failed to do: engage and move people by her description of the terrible institution of slavery. By humanizing the slave experience through Tom's humble piety and Eliza's motherly desperation and courage, Stowe effectively broke the barrier between the intellectually sound arguments of abolitionists and the general populace, for whom such rhetoric had had little effect. Abolitionist presses spoke to the head, whereas Stowe, in her "sentimental" novel, spoke to the heart. Stowe did this, as Barbara Hochman writes, by establishing an "emotional identification" between the (predominantly) white readers and the black characters (26). Furthermore, Stowe took aim not only at the South, but also at the apparent apathy of the North. Stowe asked her northern readers, "Do you say that the people of the free state have nothing to do with it, and can do nothing? Would to God this were true! But it is not true. The people of the free states have defended, encouraged, and participated; and are more guilty for it, before God, than the South, in that they have not the apology of education or custom" (624). Who are the greater sinners, Stowe asked, the slaveholders or the observers who see evil persist and do nothing? With her holistic critique of the slave system, of both the North and the South, alongside her controversial expedient for dealing with slaves post-emancipation (colonization), Stowe opened herself up to an array of response and critique. Readers and critics differed in their efforts to either augment or redirect, even dull, its effects, though none could doubt the power of the book.

Readers Respond: Critical Responses to *Uncle Tom's Cabin*

Abraham Lincoln was the potentially the most renowned, but certainly not the first, individual to express a strong opinion about *Uncle Tom's Cabin*. The array of critical responses in the nineteenth century through the present tend to converge on four particular themes: Stowe's depiction of the slave system; Stowe's literary abilities and her use of the novel as the chosen vehicle of her message; the "right" of Stowe, as a woman, to engage in political discourse; and her own genteel racism. Stowe's reviewers crossed demographic and geographic lines: men, women, freed slaves, and overseas admirers all lent their voices to respond to Stowe's novel.

The crux of the book—its portrayal of slavery as a corrupt institution—drew the greatest praise as well as the greatest ire. Reviews of the novel by antislavery activists and abolitionists were generally full of praise for Stowe, viewing *Uncle Tom's Cabin* as a new rallying point for the abolitionist cause. "*Mrs. Beecher Stowe* has deserved well of her country," wrote antislavery activist William J. Wilson, "in thus bringing *Uncle Tom's Cabin*, and all its associations, from the sunny *South*, into these *Northern regions*, and placing it upon the *Northern track*, and sending it thence round the land" (466).[2] The abolitionist and journalist William Lloyd Garrison, though critical of certain aspects of *Uncle Tom's Cabin*,[3] praised Stowe for her ability to evoke

---

pathos in her readers and for her depiction of Uncle Tom, whose "character is sketched with great power and rare religious perception. It triumphantly exemplified the nature, tendency, and results of CHRISTIAN NON-RESISTANCE" (50).

Perhaps Stowe's greatest fan, Frederick Douglass, a former slave and leader in the abolitionist movement, felt he found in Stowe the spokesperson for his cause of bettering the life of slaves and of freed blacks. Douglass published a review of *Uncle Tom's Cabin* in his newspaper *Frederick Douglass' Paper*, which was most likely written by Douglass's managing editor, Julia Griffiths (Levine 525). The author of the review noted that "the friends of freedom owe the Authoress a large debt of gratitude for this essential service rendered by her to the cause they love" ("Literary Notices" 2). What is clear from the review, as literary historian Robert Levine notes, is that its author believed that the work (then still a serial) served an important "social function" in support of the antislavery cause (526). Stowe had actually written to Douglass in 1851 requesting information "from one who has been an actual laborer" on a cotton plantation so that she might depict the life the slave accurately (Douglass 15). They continued their correspondence for years thereafter, though their letters became increasingly marked by Douglass's urgency to enlist Stowe in his many projects to "elevate the black man" (not least of which was his idea for a new university) and Stowe's increasing coolness and eventual silence on the subject altogether (Levine 538–40).[4]

To say praise and criticism were divided evenly between North and South is an oversimplification. There were many reviews that offered both praise *and* criticism. There were also northerners sympathetic to the southern cause and southerners who were moved by Stowe's novel. Such instances, however, were the exception, rather than the rule. Strangely, in the introduction to the 1879 edition of *Uncle Tom's Cabin*, Stowe revealed that she believed southerners would be *more* receptive to her novel than northerners, because she "had painted slave-holders as amiable, generous, and just. She had shown examples among them of the noblest and most beautiful traits of character; had admitted fully their temptations, their perplexities, and their difficulties" (xviii).

In spite of her belief to the contrary, many southerners were outraged at her portrayals of the slave system, slaveholders, and the experience of slaves. The author of one particularly scathing review challenged what he believed were the three "points upon which the authoress rests her abuse of the Southern States"—namely, "the cruel treatment of the slaves, their lack of religious instruction, and a wanton disregard of the sacred ties of consanguinity in selling members of the same family apart from each other" (Holmes 475). Point by point, he refuted Stowe's account, arguing that reports of cruelty toward slaves were "absolutely and unqualifiedly false"; that the charge of negligence in slaves' religious instruction was highly hypocritical coming from northerners who were "deplorably in want of 'religious instruction' themselves"; and that the "sundering of families," while dreadful, was not so callous as Stowe portrayed it in her novel (475; 476–77). From the reviewer's perspective, Stowe's greatest sin was her breach of the ninth commandment "THOU SHALT NOT BEAR FALSE WITNESS AGAINST THY NEIGHBOUR" (477). This reaction to Stowe as a slanderer, and to *Uncle Tom's Cabin* as a libelous book, was a common critical response from readers and reviewers in the South (Gossett 202–3). Stowe responded to such remarks through her publication of her *Key to "Uncle Tom's Cabin"* that included the various sources, including firsthand accounts of the slave system and advertisements for escaped slaves, intended to prove the basic truthfulness of her story. Thus, the aim and effect of this book was to silence all critics claiming that she had fabricated her depiction of slavery.

Critiques of Stowe even assumed their own literary form, a genre that cultural historian Thomas Gossett calls "anti–Uncle Tom literature." Authors of such books came from both the North and the South. For example, William J. Grayson, a southerner, composed the well-known anti–Uncle Tom book *The Hireling and the Slave*, whereas Robert Criswell, author of the boldly titled *"Uncle Tom's Cabin"*

Contrasted with Buckingham Hall, the Planter's Home; or, A Fair View of Both Sides of the Slavery Question, was a northerner.[5] The one difference between such northern and southern critics is, as Gossett argues, "the northerners are a little less vehement than the southern ones" (Gossett 213). Northern authors hoped to tame the passion for abolition brought on by *Uncle Tom's Cabin*, whereas southern writers often could not contain their rage at Stowe. The aim of these books was, ostensibly, to defend the institution of slavery using the same means as Stowe, hoping that by doing so they could elicit the same popular response as *Uncle Tom's Cabin*. In these books, most slave owners are kind and patriarchal, most slaves are bumbling, hapless fools who love their masters, and most characters who are initially skeptical of the slave system become convinced of its fairness and its necessity by the end of the book (Reynold 154–55). Such books are as plain in their agenda as *Uncle Tom's Cabin*, while lacking the depth of character and plot development that made Stowe's novel so powerful and so popular.

In fact, the popularity of *Uncle Tom's Cabin* was one of the most perplexing aspects of the book for both nineteenth-century and modern critics. Nicholas Brimblecomb, author of a scathing book of letters to Stowe published in 1853, wrote bitterly that "inasmuch as your book, entitled 'Uncle Tom's Cabin,' has seemed to attain, by some means, considerable notoriety—a notoriety by the way, of which I judge it to be utterly undeserving—it has occurred to me to address you a few communications" (7). That *Uncle Tom's Cabin* found a welcome place on the bookshelves of many readers made it more insidious than abolitionist pamphlets, which had not achieved the same degree of "notoriety."

Fear or anger over the book's popularity by slaveholders was one thing. For antislavery writers and literary critics, their confusion over the book's popularity had to do with two facts: its literary form and the gender of its author. Particularly galling to antebellum critics of *Uncle Tom's Cabin* was the fact that Stowe's chosen medium was a literary form theretofore read only by "sentimental" women, a fact of which Stowe was well aware (Hochman 28). Sentimental fiction, the genre of most novels at that time, was geared toward women and was known for its emotionality, religiosity, and its female protagonists.[6] The fact that sentimental fiction novels on the whole ranked among the best sellers seemed to prove that popularity was not a measure of great literature. For the most part, this was true, as most sentimental fiction novels tended to fizzle in relevance and notoriety. Not so for *Uncle Tom's Cabin*.

Writing about the novel in 1969, literary scholar John William Ward wrote, "For the literary critic, the problem is simply how a book so seemingly artless, so lacking in apparent literary talent, was not only an immediate success but has endured" (75). As Jane Tompkins puts it, critics have denied Stowe's novel's "power to work in, and change, the world" (130). Tompkins adds that Stowe's ability to speak to "many of the culture's central concerns in a narrative that is immediately accessible to the general population" is the reason why "she is able to move so many people so deeply" (135). The fact that Stowe's novel fell outside the standards of enduring literary classics made it difficult for modern creators of the standard literary canon of American literature to accept Stowe as a peer of such masters as Ralph Waldo Emerson, Mark Twain, and James Fenimore Cooper. Twentieth-century critics eschewed the "emotionality," "religiosity," and "domesticity" of nineteenth-century female authors in favor of stoicism, individuality, and liberty, as Tompkins notes (123). Yet, its undeniable *and* enduring popularity made the book impossible to ignore. Stowe's novel broke the barrier between belles lettres and sentimental fiction, by taking on a serious issue and making it both accessible *and* popular. One admirer of the book acknowledges this fact and admits that he cannot in fact offer any critique in his review of *Uncle Tom's Cabin*, only "homage" (Sand 459). In his review of the novel, George Sand argues that the overemphasis on Stowe's lack of literary skill is secondary to the social and political impact of the book. The "defects" of Stowe's writing, he argues, "exist only in relation to the conventional rules of art. . . . If its [the book's] judges, possessed with the love of what they call 'artistic work,' find unskillful treatment in the book, look well at them to see if their eyes are dry when they are reading this or that chapter" (460).

Certain people credited Stowe's gender for her ability to tug at the heartstrings and affect the religious sensibilities of her readers, particularly women. "With the instinct of her sex," writes one anonymous reviewer for the London *Times*, "the clever authoress takes the shortest road to her purpose, and strikes at the convictions of her readers by assailing their hearts" (478). In line with this view, literary historian Jean Fagan Yellin argues that Stowe's intention in writing *Uncle Tom's Cabin* was to "politicize a female audience" (100). Women were certainly one of the primary demographic groups reading *Uncle Tom's Cabin*. Writing forty years after the novel's initial publication, reviewer Helen Gray Cone stated that in *Uncle Tom's Cabin*, "the artist's instinct and the purpose of the reformer were fused, as far as they are capable of fusion, in a story that still holds its reader" (489). Cone adds that, with the book, Stowe had forever eradicated the view that women writers were somehow weak or inferior (490). Yet, women comprised some of Stowe's most vehement critics. Much of the anti–Uncle Tom literature produced in the nineteenth century came from the pens of women authors (Jordan-Lake xvii–xix). These women were shocked that Stowe had so easily convinced a female audience that they assumed should have been more discerning.

Yet, the most shocking element for some was not Stowe's ability to reach women, but Stowe's audacity to write *at all*. "[We] beg to make a distinction between *lady* writers and *female* writers," wrote reviewer George Holmes,

> We could not find it in our hearts to visit the dullness or ignorance of a well-meaning lady with the rigorous discipline which it is necessary to inflict upon male dunces and blockheads. But where a writer of the softer sex manifests, in her productions, a shameless disregard of truth and of those amenities which so peculiarly belong to her sphere of life, we hold that she has forfeited the claim to be considered a lady. (468)

The fact that Stowe had departed from the truth (and therefore the bounds of her virtuous gender) exempted him from withholding criticism out of respect for her sex.

Ultimately, such criticism did little to undermine Stowe's message. In truth, the greatest threats to Stowe's arguments were not her gender or her opinions on slavery, but her depiction of black people and her method for dealing with them. African American author and social critic James Baldwin critiqued *Uncle Tom's Cabin* in his 1949 review "Everybody's Protest Novel," a piece that arguably led to the modern critical backlash against Stowe.[7] Stowe, in Baldwin's view, had committed the cardinal sin of further Othering the black characters. Stowe appeared to give special favor to the mulatto characters such as Eliza, George, and Harry, who Stowe had created "as white as she can make them," according to Baldwin (497). The thoroughly black characters, like Tom, succeed (or are redeemed) only by "purifying" their blackness through "good works" and becoming white through forbearance, piety, and, ultimately, death (498). According to Baldwin, Stowe distanced white people, herself among them, from black slaves, which contradicted her goal of making white readers identify with the black characters of the book.

Lending fuel to the idea that Stowe wished to distance herself from blacks was her pro-colonization stance. At the end of the novel, George Harris expresses his plans to return to Africa to create a new life for himself and his family. The novel leaves the reader with the impression that Stowe, through her characters, thinks the best solution for African Americans post-abolition is, simply, to leave. Stowe eventually apologized for this stance, though at the time of the book's publication, many saw the potentially devastating impact such a statement could have on the abolitionist cause (Gossett 294). Reverend Henry Clarke Wright, Lydia Maria Child, and Martin Delany, all prominent figures in the abolition movement, nearly rejected *Uncle Tom's Cabin* wholeheartedly because of Stowe's pro-colonization stance (Gossett 170–74). Still, some, while apprehensive about Stowe's support of colonization, found great merit in *Uncle Tom's Cabin* for the antislavery movement. Both William Lloyd Garrison and Frederick Douglass were disappointed by Stowe's seeming retreat from the boldness of her book's message, while still maintaining that the book's positives outweighed the negatives. Like them, the nineteenth-century lecturer and activist William G. Allen "had one regret, with regard to the book, and that is that the chapter favoring colonization was ever written" (464). However, Allen, like Garrison and Douglass, did not "apprehend so much harm from it," especially since many of "the bad features of that chapter are modified by the admission . . . of the right of the colored people to meet and mingle in this country—to rise by their individual worth, and without the distinction of caste and color" (464).

That Stowe's novel acknowledged the potential elevation of African Americans—an outcome so desired by Frederick Douglass and many others—was an incredible feat for that time and for an unknown, woman author. Stowe knew that the dialogue on slavery needed to change; it needed to involve the masses in a way that abolitionist discourse had not. Stowe's admirers and detractors alike were all aware of the power held by the novel and its diminutive author. For what seemed like the first time, a work of fiction *moved* people in a way that lofty rhetoric had during the Revolutionary War. Sentiment and pathos won the hearts of some and enraged others, past and present. Since its publication, Stowe's protest novel has caught the attention of people worldwide. More than likely, *Uncle Tom's Cabin* will continue to provoke, move, enrage, and engage people now and in years to come.

Notes

1. Long before Stowe arrived in Cincinnati, the state of Ohio put into action laws requiring free blacks to post bonds promising good behavior. These laws eventually became increasingly lax, and in 1829, the region had acquired a sizeable black population. The increasing black presence caused a great deal of anxiety among the white majority, leading to a strict enforcement of the bond laws of 1804 and 1807. Mobs began to form, attempting to expedite the departure of not just those black persons without bonds, but also those with bonds. Thus, the city

as a whole, when Stowe arrived, was incredibly hostile to any sort of black presence in its midst (Gossett 32).

2. William J. Wilson wrote under the alias Ethiop.

3. Garrison was critical of Stowe for overburdening the slaves with the duty of nonresistance. Garrison wrote, "We are curious to know whether Mrs. Stowe is a believer in the duty of non-resistance for the white man, under all possible outrage and peril, as well as for the black man" (50).

4. For certain critics, Douglass's insistence that Stowe would serve as a spokesperson for his cause seemed naive. Critics such as Martin Delany criticized Douglass for seemingly ignoring Stowe's pro-colonization stance. Douglass downplayed this aspect of Stowe's book, choosing instead to emphasize the good work that the book did for the antislavery cause, rather than the disheartening message of colonization. However, Douglass did address the subject of colonization in a letter printed in his paper in December 1853: "The truth is, dear madam, we are *here*, and we are likely to remain. . . . We have grown up with this republic, and I see nothing in her character, or even in the character of the American people as yet, which compels the belief that we must leave the United States" (2).

5. Other books include Thomas Bang Thorpe's *The Master's House: A Tale of Southern Life* (1854), William Gilmore Simms's *Woodcraft; or, Hawks about the Dovecote; A Story of the South at the Close of the Revolution* (1854), and Sarah J. Hale's *Liberia; or, Mr. Peyton's Experiments* (1853).

6. For more on sentimental fiction, see Jane Tompkins's *Sensational Designs* (1985), Ann Douglas's *The Feminization of American Culture* (1977), and Lori Merish's *Sentimental Materialism* (2000).

7. For more on the modern critical reception, see Thomas Gossett's essay "The Critical Reception of Uncle Tom's Cabin: 1941 to the Present" (388–408).

Works Cited

Allen, William G. "About *Uncle Tom's Cabin*." Rev. of *Uncle Tom's Cabin*, by Harriet Beecher Stowe. *Frederick Douglass' Paper* 20 May 1852: n. pag. Rpt. in Stowe, *Authoritative Text* 463–65. Print.

Ammons, Elizabeth. Introduction. *Harriet Beecher Stowe's* Uncle Tom's Cabin: *A Casebook*. Ed. Ammons. Oxford: Oxford UP, 2007. 3–14. Print.

Baldwin, James. "Everybody's Protest Novel." *Notes of a Native Son*. Boston: Beacon, 1955. Rpt. in Stowe, *Authoritative Text* 495–501. Print.

Brimblecomb, Nicholas. Uncle Tom's Cabin *in Ruins! Triumphant Defence of Slavery in A Series of Letters to Harriet Beecher Stowe*. Boston: Waite, 1853. Print.

Cone, Helen Gray. "Harriet Beecher Stowe and American Women Writers." *Women's Work in America*. Ed. Annie Nathan Meyer. New York: Holt, 1891. Rpt. in Stowe, *Authoritative Text* 489–90. Print.

Douglas, Ann. *The Feminization of American Culture*. New York: Knopf, 1977. Print.

___. "Introduction: The Art of Controversy." *Uncle Tom's Cabin or, Life among the*

Lowly. By Harriet Beecher Stowe. Ed. Ann Douglas. New York: Penguin, 1986. Print.

Douglass, Frederick. "Letter to Harriet Beecher Stowe." *Frederick Douglass' Paper* 2 Dec. 1853: 2. Print.

Fields, Annie. *Authors and Friends*. Cambridge: Riverside, 1897. Print.

Garrison, William Lloyd. Rev. of *Uncle Tom's Cabin*, by Harriet Beecher Stowe. *Liberator* 26 Mar. 1852: 50. Print.

Gossett, Thomas F. Uncle Tom's Cabin *and American Culture*. Dallas: Southern Methodist UP, 1985. Print.

Hochman, Barbara. Uncle Tom's Cabin *and the Reading Revolution: Race, Literacy, Childhood, and Fiction, 1851–1911*. Amherst: U of Massachusetts P, 2011. Print.

Holmes, George F. Rev. of *Uncle Tom's Cabin*. *Southern Literary Messenger* 18 (1852): 631. Rpt. in Stowe, *Authoritative Text* 467–77. Print.

Jordan-Lake, Joy. *Whitewashing* Uncle Tom's Cabin*: Nineteenth-Century Women Novelists Respond to Stowe*. Nashville: Vanderbilt UP, 2005. Print.

Kirkham, E. Bruce. *The Building of* Uncle Tom's Cabin. Knoxville: U of Tennessee P, 1977. Print.

Levine, Robert S. "*Uncle Tom's Cabin* in *Frederick Douglass' Paper*: An Analysis of Reception." *American Literature* 64 (1992): 77–93. Rpt. in Stowe, *Authoritative Text* 523–42. Print.

Lewis, R. W. B. *The American Adam: Innocence, Tragedy and Tradition in the Nineteenth Century*. Chicago: U of Chicago P, 1955. Print.

"Literary Notices." *Frederick Douglass' Paper* 8 Apr. 1852: 2. Print.

Merish, Lori. *Sentimental Materialism: Gender, Commodity Culture, and Nineteenth-Century American Literature*. Durham: Duke UP, 2000. Print.

Reynolds, David. *Mightier than the Sword:* Uncle Tom's Cabin *and the Battle for America*. New York: Norton, 2011. Print.

Sand, George. Rev. of *Uncle Tom's Cabin*, by Harriet Beecher Stowe. *La Presse* 17 Dec. 1852: n. pag. Rpt. in Stowe, *Authoritative Text* 459–63. Print.

Stowe, Harriet Beecher. Introduction. *Uncle Tom's Cabin; or, Life among the Lowly*. Boston: Houghton, 1879. ix–xlii. Print.

___. *The Key to* Uncle Tom's Cabin*; Presenting the Original Facts and Documents upon which the Story Is Founded, Together with Corroborative Statements Verifying the Truth of the Work*. Boston: Jewett, 1854. Print.

___. "Letter to Frederic Douglass." *Harriet Beecher Stowe 's* Uncle Tom's Cabin*: A Casebook*. Ed. Elizabeth Ammons. Oxford: Oxford UP, 2007. 15–17. Print.

___. Uncle Tom's Cabin*: Authoritative Text, Backgrounds and Contexts, Criticism*. Ed. Elizabeth Ammons. New York: Norton, 1994. Print.

___. *Uncle Tom's Cabin; or, Life among the Lowly*. Ed. Ann Douglas. New York: Penguin, 1986. Print.

Tompkins, Jane. "Sentimental Power: *Uncle Tom's Cabin* and the Politics of Literary History." *Sensational Designs: The Cultural Work of American Fiction 1790–1860*. Oxford: Oxford UP, 1985. 122–46. Print.

"Uncle Tom in England." Rev. of *Uncle Tom's Cabin*, by Harriet Beecher Stowe. *Times* [London] 3 Sept. 1852: 1–8. Rpt. in Stowe, *Authoritative Text* 478–83. Print.

Ward, John William. *Red, White, and Blue: Men, Books, and Ideas in American Culture*. New York: Oxford UP, 1961. Print.

Williams, Grant G. "Reminiscences of the Life of Harriet Beecher Stowe and Her Family." *Colored American Magazine* Dec. 1902: 81–160. Print.

Wilson, William J. [Ethiop]. Rev. of *Uncle Tom's Cabin*, by Harriet Beecher Stowe. *Frederick Douglass' Paper* 17 June 1852: n. pag. Rpt. in Stowe, *Authoritative Text* 466–67. Print.

Yellin, Jean Fagan. "Doing it Herself: *Uncle Tom's Cabin* and Woman's Role in the Slavery Crisis." *New Essays on* Uncle Tom's Cabin. Ed. Eric Sundquist. New York: Cambridge UP, 1986. 85–105. Print.

Brutish Behavior: Joseph Conrad, Mark Twain, and Anticolonial Protests, 1899–1905_____

Jeremiah Garsha

> My task which I am trying to achieve is, by the power of the written word, to make you hear, to make you feel—it is, before all, to make you see. That—and no more, and it is everything. If I succeed, you shall find . . . that glimpse of truth for which you have forgotten to ask. (Joseph Conrad, Preface, *The Nigger of the "Narcissus"*)

Joseph Conrad's statement, quoted above, was a prophetic one. Penned while the author was drafting his masterpiece *Heart of Darkness* in the last months of 1898, the quote reveals Conrad's quest to use his work as a protest to reveal the truth of the European colonialism. Born out of his personal experience as a steamer captain traversing the Congo River basin in 1890, the forgotten truth Conrad wanted the reader to uncover was his firsthand account of the very nature of the colonial project and the unimagined horror of European-inflicted violence. The publication of *Heart of Darkness*, first as a serial in 1899 and then as a bound novella in 1902, punctuated a rare and overlooked public backlash to African colonialism and the ideology of imperialism.[1] In the years that followed, other authors and artists picked up Conrad's call to make audiences hear, see, and feel the brutal truth of colonialism by exposing them to the unspeakable, and unspoken, acts of violence.

Mark Twain championed Conrad's motifs in two subsequent works, "To the Person Sitting in Darkness" and *King Leopold's Soliloquy*. Published in 1901 and 1905, respectively, these works can be read as reflections of *Heart of Darkness*. In the latter, Twain uses the real Belgian king as a stand-in for Conrad's fictional Mr. Kurtz. Twain also incorporates many of Conrad's motifs within his own characteristically satirical prose, supplementing his fiction with actual photographs and official colonial reports. Twain's and Conrad's publications are united by their depictions of colonial violence as a metaphor for colonial corruption. The brutish behavior illustrated by Conrad and Twain shows that the imperial backlash was not necessarily a call for humanitarianism toward colonized people but rather a protest centered on the concept that colonialism was flawed because it turned "good" Westerners into excessive brutes.[2]

Heart of Darkness opens with an internal monologue about the nature of colonialism. Writing in a third-person narrative style, Joseph Conrad attempts to distance himself from his personal experience in triplicate. The character of Charlie Marlow is the main narrator of the story, and his tale in *Heart of Darkness* closely resembles Conrad's own experience sailing through the Belgian Congo in 1890.[3] Yet Conrad is also the unnamed narrator of the story, a middle-class former sailor who shares Marlow's account directly with the reader. In this way, Conrad appears in two forms. As Marlow, he exists in the story as a witness, a sailor who has been transformed by his experience within the Belgian Congo and has seen firsthand the brutality of imperialism as it played out in the colonial periphery. As the unnamed narrator, Conrad presents himself, perhaps, as he wished he was: a successful British businessman who remains idealistically unaware of the darker truths of the world and, at the beginning of the novella, ignorant of the colonial project's true nature.

Conrad juxtaposes each of the narrators' seemingly opposed versions of colonialism within the opening pages of *Heart of Darkness*. Seated aboard the *Nellie*, a cruising yawl anchored in the Thames, the unnamed narrator first muses about the British colonizing mission: "Hunters for gold or pursuers of fame, they all had gone out on that stream, bearing the sword, and often the torch, messengers of the might within the land, bearers of a spark from the sacred fire" (5). The narrator sees the British imperial agents acting as a modern-day Prometheus, bringing the sacred fires of civilization into the darkness of the world. He views the Thames as the umbilical cord connecting the British Empire to the British metropole[4] and wonders, "What greatness had not floated on the ebb of that river into the mystery of an unknown earth! . . . The dreams of men, the seed of commonwealths, the germs of empires" (5; ellipsis in orig.).[5] The protagonist Marlow, on the other hand, offers up a much more cynical, and perhaps more accurate, viewpoint. Before he even tells the men of his voyages abroad, he states that imperial agents are "no colonists" (7). While this is a seemingly innocuous remark, Marlow is making the point that these men are not venturing out to build settlements where the sparks of civilization can burn. Rather, Marlow tells us, "They were conquerors, and for that you want only brute force . . . your strength is just an accident arising from the weakness of others. . . . It was just robbery with violence, aggravated murder on a great scale, and men going at it blind—as is very proper for those who tackle a darkness" (7). Unlike the naive narrator, who looks upon the Thames as a passageway to spread the sacred fire and join the corners of the world into the British Empire, Marlow interjects that "the conquest of the earth" simply means "taking it away from those who have a different complexion or slightly flatter noses than ourselves" (7–8). Conrad sets up *Heart of Darkness* as a dialogue between the ideology and idealization of the "civilizing mission" and the stark reality of colonial corruption.

Conrad had a unique perspective on the concept of British imperialism and the European colonial project. Born Józef Teodor Konrad Korzeniowski in the Polish portion of the Russian Empire in 1857, he did not become a British national until 1886, the same year he changed his name to Joseph Conrad (Stape 8). Escaping a life of political turmoil and personal hardships, like both narrators in *Heart of Darkness*, Conrad "followed the sea" (*Heart* 4). At seventeen he traveled to Marseilles, where he joined the French Merchant Service and sailed extensively for two decades across the world. Traveling throughout the Far East, the Americas, and Africa, Conrad journeyed through British, French, German, and Belgian colonial outposts (Stape 51). When the unnamed narrator draws a distinction between himself and Marlow, he states that Marlow "was a seaman, but he was a wanderer, too"

(Conrad, *Heart* 5). Marlow tells us that he was attracted to the places on the map that were not filled in, the "blank space of delightful mystery" (9). Conrad was an international wanderer who, like Marlow, found comfort in a solitary life as a sailor. He was a native Polish speaker, fluent in French, who learned English as his third language. For the sailors in *Heart of Darkness*, "home is always with them—the ship; and so is their country—the sea" (5), and the same could be said of Conrad himself. Certainly no one would question Conrad's grasp of English or his British patriotism, but his personal history as a Polish national, who thought in French and wrote in English, gave him an outside perspective into his adopted British culture. *Heart of Darkness*, at its core, is the story of the contradictions between "civilized" and "brutish" behavior. As Marlow and, to a certain extent, Conrad traveled down the Congo River toward the Inner Station, they were both representatives of European civilization, but also detached witnesses of European barbarity.

Marlow is commissioned by "the Company," a stand-in for the real Association Internationale Africaine (International African Association), itself a fake nongovernmental organization privately run by the Belgian king Leopold II (Hochschild 45). Marlow receives his appointment because the last captain, a Dane named Fresleven, was killed in an episode of African violence. Later Marlow finds out that the captain was involved in a "quarrel [that] arose from a misunderstanding about some hens. Yes, two black hens. Fresleven . . . thought himself wronged somehow in the bargain, so he went ashore and started hammering the chief of the village with a stick" (Conrad, *Heart* 10). Before Marlow has even recounted his personal voyage, he has already digressed into an episode of violence. Marlow shares with his audience the contradiction between civilized behavior and brutish force when he states, "Oh, it didn't surprise me in the least to hear this [about the beating], and at the same time to be told that Fresleven was the gentlest, quietest creature that ever walked on two legs" (10). For Conrad, Fresleven was corrupted by a few years engaged in "the noble cause" of colonial activities, and while he was a "civilized" European, in the colonial setting, "he probably felt the need at last of asserting his self-respect in some way. Therefore he whacked the old nigger mercilessly, while a big crowd of his [the chief's] people watched him, thunderstruck, till some man . . . made a tentative jab with a spear," killing Fresleven. When Marlow recovers Fresleven's body, he notes that "the supernatural being had not been touched after he fell" and that "a calamity had come to it [the village], sure enough. The people had vanished. Mad terror had scattered them . . . and they had never returned" (10). The black hens that caused the original argument with Fresleven can be read as metaphorical representations of the native villagers. Marlow is unsure what happened to the hens but says, "I should think the cause of progress got them" (11). The cause of progress is clearly the imperial project, which blazed a path of death and destruction on the backs for the indigenous locals while financially enriching Europeans.

Conrad's and Marlow's trips through the Congo occurred at the high point of European imperial fervor, when imperialist activity was resurging after a steady decline in the earlier part of the nineteenth century (Rich 263). The scramble for Africa was launched following the Berlin Conference of 1884–85, where the European Great Powers converged and divided up Africa (Wesseling 111). Britain and France increased their already sizable African colonies, while Germany, an emerging power, took a few strategic colonies, notably in southwest and southeast Africa. King Leopold II was given complete and private control of the euphemistically named Congo Free State, which encompassed most of central Africa. When Marlow is awaiting his departure instructions at the Company office, he notices "a large shining map, marked with all the colours of a rainbow," each depicting the colonial control of various European powers. Britain is depicted in red, which, Marlow remarks, is "good to see at any time, because one knows that some real work is done in there" (Conrad, *Heart* 11). Here, we see that Conrad, through Marlow, struggled, in a small way, to show his critique of colonialism while still maintaining his, and the readers', allegiance to Britain and the colonizing mission. In an 1899 letter to Aniela Zagórska, his cousin's granddaughter, Conrad wrote, "Liberty . . . can only be found under the English flag all over the world" (qtd. in Simmons 200). Marlow, while narrating his tale with hindsight, is still filled with excitement as he heads off, thinking of himself as "one of the Workers, with a capital—you know. Something like an emissary of light, something like a lower sort of apostle" (Conrad, *Heart* 14). Marlow departs on his journey, like the unnamed narrator, taken up with an idealized vision of the colonial mission as spreading the sacred spark of British civilization. Upon his arrival, however, reality quickly sets in.

As *Heart of Darkness* progresses, the Thames, which the unnamed narrator originally calls a "luminous space" (3) between the sea and the sky, morphs into Marlow's corrupted description of the Congo River basin. The Thames has transformed into "streams of death in life, whose banks were rotting into mud, whose waters, thickened into slime, invaded the contorted mangroves, that seemed to writhe at us in the extremity of an impotent despair" (16–17). The duality of the rivers, the pristine Thames and the murky Congo, is a literary transition between the supposed civilizing waters of Europe and its invasion of African shores. Conrad's description suggests a one-way flow that leads to corruption and death. Like the water, Marlow's travels through the *Heart of Darkness* reveal the true extent of the brutality that the civilizing mission had inflicted on the indigenous populations. With each atrocity Marlow witnesses, his narration grows more and more cynical, and episodes of violence punctuate his every stop.

Marlow's first encounter with African natives in the Congo is deliberately set in contradiction with European imperial agents. During his stopover at the first Company station, Marlow hears the sounds of colonialism before he sees the natives: "A horn tooted to the right, and I saw the black people run. . . . A slight clinking behind me made me turn my head. Six black men advanced in a file" (18). The sounds of European colonialism are the noises of forced labor, whistles, and chains. Marlow finds the natives conscripted as slaves, building a railroad to further Belgian trade: "I could see every rib, the joints of their limbs were like knots in a rope; each had an iron collar on his neck, and all were connected together with a chain whose bights swung between them, rhythmically clicking" (18). A few pages later, Marlow encounters a cluster of dying natives in a jungle clearing. "They were not enemies," Conrad writes, "they were not criminals, they were nothing earthly now—nothing but black shadows of disease and starvation, lying confusedly in the greenish gloom" (20). This description is juxtaposed with the first colonial agent Marlow encounters, standing in view of the jungle clearing. The man is impeccably dressed in "a high starched collar, white cuffs, a light alpaca jacket, snowy trousers, a clean necktie, and varnished boots" (21). The white man, robed in white clothing, outwardly embodies the European civilized ideal. Marlow tells us that he respects the man himself because he respects the man's "collars, his vast cuffs, his brushed hair" (21). The man is able to keep his starched "achievements of character" while surrounded by dying slaves because he taught domestic servitude, with professed difficulty, to "one of the native women about the station" (21). The colonial agent maintains his outward appearance of whiteness and purity through his unequal, forced relationship with his domestic servant, just as Europe was engaged in a forced and exploitative relationship with the African colonies. The colonial agent, like Europe, hides his true intentions of exploitation and personal riches under the façade of the "civilization duty."

It is this imperial agent who first tells Marlow of Mr. Kurtz, the Company agent running a trading station deep in the jungle that brings in more ivory than all the others combined. After this exchange, the well-dressed white agent reveals his inner corruption. While writing in his ivory inventory sheets and staring at enslaved natives, the man tells Marlow, "When one has got to make correct entries, one comes to hate those savages—hate them to the death" (22). The agent sees only numbers and profits in the colony, and the natives are merely the expendable means needed to extract ivory riches. The ominous phrase "hate . . . to the death" signifies the abandonment of civilized behavior, underscoring that within the colonial setting, violence and atrocities are an encouraged way of making profit "the correct entry."

The motif of color paints ivory in this scene as both whiteness and the economic product desired by European markets and extracted from the colonies by brutal methods. Marlow is unable to leave the colonial outpost without gazing back to "still tree-tops of the grove of death" (22–23). Color is Conrad's central trope, and Marlow's departing view of the European outpost underscores that beneath the gaze of the "snowy" white-dressed colonial agent are the "black" shadows of death and starvation and that colonialism has brought Africa only a "greenish" gloom of destruction (20).

Conrad's depiction of the Belgian Congo is historically accurate. The Congo Free State was clearly one of the most violent, brutal, and oppressive colonies of the era. Britain had officially abolished the slave trade in 1833, and one of the agreements at the Berlin Conference was that the Congo Free State was to be administered in accordance with British abolition. Leopold II portrayed himself as an antislavery crusader, running the Congo Free State on altruistic and humanitarian grounds (Hochschild 46, 131). In reality, slave labor in the Belgian-run colony was the modus operandi. Laborers were routinely beaten with the *chicotte* (a flesh-ripping hippo-hide whip), purposefully starved, and often worked to death. Colonial troops, often themselves African natives conscripted under the colonial divide-and-rule tactic, raided villages in order to capture female hostages. These women were then sold back to the district chiefs in exchange for harvested raw materials (160–61). Most distressing of all, for every cartridge of ammunition used by the colonial troops, they were required to provide the severed right hand from a corpse in order to show that the bullet had been used to kill someone (165). This policy led to forced mutilation of thousands of men, women, and children.

Marlow encounters the remnants of atrocities and slavery as he journeys deeper toward Kurtz and the Inner Station. "Now and then," he tells us, he passes "a carrier dead in harness . . . with an empty water-gourd and his long staff lying by his side." He passes many abandoned and destroyed villages, and he literally stumbles upon "the body a middle-aged negro, with a bullet-hole in the forehead" (Conrad, *Heart* 23). When he finally encounters Mr. Kurtz, however, Marlow sees the true extent to which civilized morals had been abandoned. Kurtz's home is decorated by shrunken heads, impaled on stakes and facing inward, in worship of Kurtz.

In *Heart of Darkness*, the character of Kurtz is an embodiment of the infectious, violent nature the colonial system fostered in the imperial agents. Many historians and biographers of Joseph Conrad have tried to pinpoint the historical inspiration for the fictional character of Kurtz. Conrad tells us that Kurtz's "mother was half-English, his father half-French" (50), and Marlow knows that "Kurtz . . . means short in German" (74). It has been argued that this is Conrad's allusion to Georges Antoine Klein, as *klein* means "small" in German (Baines 117; Hochschild 144). Klein worked as a French agent for an ivory-gathering enterprise in the Congo and died aboard the ship Conrad himself was piloting in 1890, similarly to Kurtz. Historian Adam Hochschild makes a compelling case that Kurtz's real-life counterpart was Captain Léon Rom, who was a station chief at Stanley Falls in the Congo and, according to contemporary accounts, used severed heads "as a decoration round a flower-bed in front of his house" (qtd. in Hochschild 145). The fact that Kurtz was modeled from a real-life counterpart historically grounds *Heart of Darkness* and shows that Conrad's depictions of violence are far from fictitious.

Irrespective of the actual inspiration for Kurtz, the character can be read as the personification of the imperial impulse to inflict unspeakable acts of violence outside of the public gaze. Marlow says, "All Europe contributed to the making of Kurtz," and in this way Kurtz is the ultimate source of European colonial corruption, as the "powers of darkness claimed him for their own" and "he had taken a high seat amongst the devils of the land" (Conrad, *Heart* 50). Kurtz thus represents all of Europe, wildly out of control in the colonial setting, concerning himself with economic profit via violent means.

Kurtz runs the Inner Station like a colonial empire in miniature. Early on, an imperial agent tells Marlow, "Anything—anything can be done in this country. That's what I say; nobody here, you understand, *here*, can endanger your position" (34; emphasis in orig.). Kurtz's actions give a literal interpretation to this quote. Using brutality and thievery, Kurtz raids villages, plundering more ivory than all the other colonial agents, and positions himself as a god to his colonized natives. Kurtz tells Marlow that the International Society for the Suppression of Savage Customs has tasked him with drafting a report to guide future colonial agents. The pamphlet opens with Kurtz's statement that "whites, from the point of development we had arrived at, 'must necessarily appear to them [savages] in the nature of supernatural beings—we approach them with the might as of a deity'" (51; interpolation in orig.). Here we see that Kurtz practices what he preaches, and at first Marlow is nearly converted. According to the pamphlet, Kurtz's support of the colonial project is guided by humanitarianism: "By the simple exercise of our will we can exert a power for good practically unbounded." Marlow tells us, "From that point he soared and took me with him. The peroration was magnificent. . . . It gave me the notion of an exotic Immensity ruled by an august Benevolence. It made me tingle with enthusiasm." But Kurtz's micro-empire does not run under his supposed civilizing mission. Marlow is awakened from his intoxication with Kurtz's charm when he encounters the final words of the pamphlet, written later as a postscript. At the foot of the last page, Kurtz has written, "Exterminate all the brutes!" (51).[6]

The postscript underscores Kurtz's abandonment of the civilizing-mission pretense. Added to his pamphlet on benevolent theocracy, Kurtz's call for extermination embodies Conrad's own understanding of the European hypocritical notion of civilization and progress in the colonial setting. The civilizing mission in Kurtz's mind is a corrupted, abandoned notion, destroyed by his years in the colonial setting and his active engagement with his own violent impulses. Earlier in the story, Marlow encounters an old oil painting done by Kurtz a year before he disappeared into the heart of darkness. The painting is of "a woman, draped and blindfolded, carrying a lighted torch." This is the corrupted version of the unnamed narrator's idealistic vision of colonialism as spreading the Promethean spark. Marlow notes, "The effect of the torch-light on the face was sinister" (26). The carrying of the civilizing ember has only corrupted and blinded the torchbearer, twisting the idealistic imperialist into a brutish thug. While colonial agents may venture out of Europe under the guise of torchbearers of civilization, Conrad, through Kurtz, shows how quickly the benevolence of colonization transforms into brute force. This central trope, popularized by *Heart of Darkness*, resonated deeply with American audiences across the Atlantic, who were just beginning their own colonial campaigns. The exploration of Conrad's colonial violence particularly soared when a self-confessed reformed imperialist, Mark Twain, took up the protest.

Born in 1835 in the slave-owning state of Missouri, Twain witnessed the subjection of people firsthand. Nevertheless, in 1866, while working as a newspaper reporter for the *Sacramento Daily Union*, Twain's first publications were a series of articles calling for annexation of the Hawaiian Islands. He argued that the United States could "loosen that French and English grip" on Hawaii and "fill these islands full of Americans and regain her lost foothold" (*Letters* 12). Beyond commercial and geostrategic political grounds, Twain championed Hawaiian annexation based on democratic ideology, arguing that, as a former colony, it was the United States' duty to liberate the Hawaiian people from their monarchy. Using phrases accusing the Hawaiian king of stripping away the inalienable rights of native Hawaiians by ruling with "absolute authority" and creating a "hideous pyramid of brutality, and superstition, and slavery" ("Our Fellow Savages"), Twain appealed to American audiences who would have identified themselves as former subjects of England, liberated by the Revolutionary War (Zmijewski 61; Caron 379–80).

Mark Twain's turn from imperialist to anti-imperial crusader crystallized in 1898, with the conclusion of the Spanish-American War. As a result of the 1898 Treaty of Paris, the United States annexed former Spanish colonial holdings, including Guam, Puerto Rico, and the Philippines. While the United States greatly increased its global colonial sphere, it was slowly dragged into conflict with local Filipino revolutionaries, who had been allies during the war with Spain but now sought independence from American rule.

At the outbreak of the Spanish-American War, Twain was a confessed "red-hot imperialist" who viewed the conflict as "the worthiest one that was ever fought" (qtd. in Capozzola 62). In an October 15, 1900, interview published in the *New York Herald*, Mark Twain described his imperial patriotism by saying, "I wanted the American eagle to go screaming into the Pacific. . . . Why not spread its wings over the Philippines . . . here are a people who have suffered for three centuries. We can make them as free as ourselves" ("Excerpts"). Like his argument for Hawaiian annexation, Twain once again used the image of American liberation from colonial rule to justify the United States' obligation to expand overseas.

Twain was not the only major literary figure of his day to see American colonialism in a positive light. Heralding the duties of imperialism, British-born writer Rudyard Kipling published his poem "The White Man's Burden" in *McClure's Magazine* with the subtitle "The United States and the Philippine Islands." Kipling's poem, published the very same month as *Heart of Darkness*, urges the United States to follow the British and French example and take overseas colonial holdings. In it, Kipling argues that the United States has a duty to:

> Take up the white man's burden—
> Send forth the best ye breed—
> Go bind your sons to exile
> To serve your captives' need (lines 1–4)

Strangely, Twain was, initially, convinced that the United States, as urged by Kipling, had the ironic democratic duty of freeing the oppressed Filipinos by occupying the Philippines.

It is interesting that Twain was able to justify colonialism as an American ideal, as he had witnessed firsthand the realities of colonialism. On a literary speaking tour in 1895–96, Twain saw the subjection of indigenous people across the British Empire. His visits to India, Australia, New Zealand, and South Africa during this tour formed the basis of his 1897 book *Following the Equator*; while there, he directly witnessed the contradictions between the "civilizing mission" touted by imperialists and the more accurate reality of colonial exploitation (Zwick 236). Moreover, Twain had grown infuriated by the brutal mistreatment of African Americans in the southern United States, particularly the widespread practice of lynching in his home state of Missouri.[7]

These experiences culminated when Twain read reports of American conduct against the Filipino revolutionaries. In order to combat the insurgent groups, American soldiers tortured captured soldiers and suspected revolutionaries, waged retaliatory attacks against unarmed women and children, and implemented concentration camps, a tactic invented by Spanish soldiers in the Philippines and Cuba ten years before. American abuses were so widespread, in fact, that in 1899 the United States Senate formed the Committee on the Philippines to investigate atrocities committed by American soldiers. This resulted in the court-martial and conviction of newly appointed Brigadier General Smith, who had earlier bragged to media reporters that the Filipinos were "worse than fighting Indians" and that he would adopt the same genocidal tactics he honed in the American West (Miller 212–14, 95). These publicized instances of brutish behavior marked the turning point for Mark Twain, who had once argued for the American eagle to "spread its wings over the Philippines" but now realized that "we have gone there to conquer, not to redeem." Twain, the once "red-hot imperialist," had become, in his words, "an anti-imperialist. I am opposed to having the eagle put its talons on any other land" ("Excerpts").

In 1901 Twain joined the newly created American Anti-Imperial League, which was dedicated to opposing a United States–led campaign of colonialism. Similar to Conrad's protest against the colonial project in *Heart of Darkness*, the Anti-Imperial League's protest did not oppose American colonialism on humanitarian grounds, but rather on the grounds that it corrupted the uniquely American ideals of self-government and freedom from tyranny, which had liberated American from British imperialism in 1776 (Schurz 77n1). Like the Anti-Imperial League, Twain felt that the United States' occupation of the Philippines showed that the nation had betrayed the fundamental values of liberal democracy (Zwick 244).

Beyond the ongoing atrocities occurring in the Philippines, the first few years of the twentieth century were marked by global episodes of colonial violence. While *Heart of Darkness* documented the crimes of the Belgian Congo, the German Empire waged campaigns of violent suppression against Chinese dissidents in what was known as the Boxer Rebellion (1899–1901); the Wahehe uprising in German East Africa, today Tanzania (1891–93); and the genocide of the Herero and Nama people in German South West Africa, today Namibia (1904–8). Even more alarming for readers at the time was the war between Great Britain and the Boers (Dutch-descended Afrikaaners) in South Africa, known as the Boer Wars (1880–81 and 1899–1902).[8] For the first time, colonialism had resulted in a white-on-white slaughter that galvanized anti-imperial support in Western nations. Most damning were reports of the staggering death rates surrounding the British tactic of using concentration camps, like the United States in the Philippines, to stop the Boer insurgency. These atrocities, which received daily media coverage, galvanized Twain and his supporters to herald the anticolonial cause.

Twain's first major protest essay, "To the Person Sitting in Darkness," debuted the same year he formally became vice president of the Anti-Imperial League. Published in February 1901, the essay is filled with subtle and direct allusions to the supposed "civilizing mission" (Robinson 46). The title alone is meant to counter the notion that

European imperialism brought enlightenment and civilization to the colonial periphery. Twain uses it as a reference to the biblical passage Matthew 4:16, "The people who sat in darkness have seen a great light" (qtd. in Emerson 257). "To the Person Sitting in Darkness" may also be a reference to *Heart of Darkness*, in both title and theme. Twain carries forward the trope of colonialism as corruption, with the added Gilded Age notion that it was funded by capitalism.[9] He writes, "Extending the Blessing of Civilization to our Brother who sits in Darkness has been a good trade and paid well . . . and there is money in it yet" ("To the Person" 165). Twain sees that colonialism is primarily funded by economic motives and is quick to point out that "our Civilization" is "the Actual Thing that the Customer Sitting in Darkness buys with his blood and tears and land and liberty . . . but it is only for Export" (166). In his classic satirical prose, Twain argues that civilization is something that the colonized cannot afford. In this way, Twain's essay shows that civilization enriches the coffers of empire while morally bankrupting the metropole. While he was opposed to the mistreatment of the Boers and the Chinese, the heart of his essay is the corruption of the United States due to its imperial treatment of Filipinos.

Twain uses the reported colonial atrocities to show that the United States was playing "The European [Colonial] game" and "playing it badly" ("To the Person" 169). He compares the United States to England in South Africa, perhaps referring to the brutal use of concentration camps in both South Africa and the Philippines. He argues that the American flag under colonialism would be corrupted and transformed into "our usual flag, with the white stripes painted black and the stars replaced by the skull and cross-bones" (176). While recounting the American occupation of the Philippines, Twain writes, "There must be two Americas: one that sets the captive free, and one that takes a once-captive's new freedom away from him . . . then kills him to get his land" (170). For Twain, and the American Anti-Imperialist League he represented, the first America was the nation that freed itself from British rule in 1776 and had an obligation to liberate the oppressed in the name of democracy. The second America, which occupied the Philippines, served only to corrupt and morally bankrupt American liberalism. Twain writes that the United States has "crushed a deceived and confiding people," "stabbed an ally in the back," "robbed a trusting friend of his land and his liberty," and "debauched America's honor and blackened her face before the world" (174). The latter quote uses a racially charged and gendered image, depicting Lady Liberty's white countenance replaced with blackface, signifying that the United States' entry into the colonial game has literally left America morally in the darkness, staining liberal democracy's reputation and corrupting "white ideals" into "black savagery."

While "To the Person Sitting in Darkness" is a work of Twain's typical satirical prose, he uniquely interweaves real quotes, diary entries, and reports of colonial violence directly into the essay. Twain's use of the motif of light as a stand-in for colonial enlightenment also echoes back to Conrad's dual narrators in *Heart of Darkness*, who see the sacred spark illuminating only violence and corrupting the torchbearer. "To the Person Sitting in Darkness" documents the corruption of Christian and capitalist pursuits throughout the European colonial empires, with Twain's essay echoing Conrad's notion that the great horror of colonialism is its corrupting influence on the colonizers.

Twain's 1901 essay picks up on many of the anticolonial tropes popularized by Conrad, yet he omits any direct reference to the Belgian Congo. Four years later, however, Twain published *King Leopold's Soliloquy*, his most famous anticolonial protest. The novel debuted in 1905, during the high point of European and American anticolonial fervor. *Heart of Darkness* was first published in 1899, the very year Great Britain went to war in South Africa, and was bound into a novella for wider distribution in 1902, the year the war ended. The European media, capitalizing on the popularity of *Heart of Darkness*, which contributed greatly to the growing anticolonial discourse, continued to expose the public to the harsh realities of colonialism, galvanized by detailed reports of concentration-camp systems used by the British in

South Africa. The widespread success of Conrad's work was due to its resonance with audiences already coming to terms with the contradictory "civilizing mission." American readers, guided by Twain and the Anti-Imperial League, were also forced to reflect on their own history as former colonial subjects becoming colonial masters. Coupling this with the coverage of global colonial atrocities, Conrad and Twain questioned the myth of colonization as a civilizing duty, which perfectly aligned with the documented violence occurring in the Belgian Congo.

Heart of Darkness was based on Conrad's personal journey through the Congo in 1890, when the Congo Free State was in its fifth year of existence. By 1905, when Twain published *King Leopold's Soliloquy*, the Congo Free State had become the world's largest exporter of rubber. Mr. Kurtz, in Conrad's work, uses brutal tactics to amass large riches of ivory, which he exports to European markets, enriching the Company and himself. With the invention of the inflatable tire and the proliferation of automobiles, global demand for rubber skyrocketed, making it the single most valuable resource in the colony (Jones 42). The level of violence and brutality inflicted on rubber harvesters surpassed anything described in *Heart of Darkness*. Indigenous Congolese were conscripted as forced laborers, their families held hostage until they collected Belgium's quota of rubber. When the enslaved laborers were unable to meet the quota, entire villages were razed and burned. Children were slaughtered or mutilated, having their hands cut off for every shot fired by the colonial troops (42). In total, Leopold II's bloody reign over the Congo is estimated to have killed more than ten million (Hochschild 233).

Like many of the colonial atrocities committed at the turn of the twentieth century, the horrors of the Congo were publicized, yet largely unknown to the general public. Twain's motivation for writing *King Leopold's Soliloquy* may have been to disseminate these crimes to his large audience of readers. As in "To the Person Sitting in Darkness," Twain interweaves the actual reports directly into his writing. *King*

Leopold's Soliloquy, as the title suggests, is nothing more than King Leopold conversing with himself. Twain therefore has Leopold pick up and read aloud reports that he has directly transcribed into the book, thus forcing the audience to confront the actual crimes in the Congo. Beyond the many graphic descriptions Twain has King Leopold recount to the reader, the book takes the novel approach of reprinting the photographs of mutilated men, women, and children, their hands chopped off at the wrist.

The photographs reprinted in *King Leopold's Soliloquy* are distressing. Twain has Leopold pick up a stack of photographs and lament, "The kodak has been a sore calamity to us. The most powerful enemy that has confronted us, indeed" (73). "Kodak" refers to the Kodak camera, invented in 1888 as the first handheld camera, allowing amateurs to capture photographic images. For Leopold it was "the only witness . . . [he] couldn't bribe." By 1905, the Kodak had shrunk in size to the point that Leopold sees it as "that trivial little kodak, that [even] a child can carry in its pocket" (74). Leopold is troubled by the fact that "every Yankee missionary and every interrupted trader sent home and got one [a Kodak]; and now . . . the pictures get sneaked around everywhere, in spite of all we can do to ferret them out and suppress them" (73). Indeed, there was no shortage of photographic evidence documenting Leopold's crimes. The king consoles himself when he remembers that even though the Congo Free State is "a land of graves . . . and the ghastliest episode in all human history," the world does "*not wish to look*" (74–75; emphasis in orig.). The book ends with Leopold comforting himself with the knowledge that "he is the King with Ten Million Murders on his Soul," which "hurts us, it troubles us . . . and we shrink from hearing the particulars. . .We *shudder and turn away* when we come upon them in print" (55, 75–76; emphasis in orig.). Twain challenges the reader with these final lines. Leopold knows that the reader's instinct when confronted with violence and horror is to turn away, for "THAT IS MY PROTECTION. And you will continue to do it. I know the human race" (76). The entire premise of *King Leopold's Soliloquy* is Mark Twain's attempt to turn the reader's attention to the colonial project and to keep us from looking away.

Twain paints Leopold II as an alternate version of Mr. Kurtz, had he returned from the Congo. Rather than decorating his home with decapitated heads, Leopold enjoys the riches and palace that his colonial empire has brought. Mr. Kurtz, like Leopold, ran his colony like a brutish god, enriching himself at the expensive of the colonized. He dies on his way home to his fiancée, who is named in *Heart of Darkness* as "Kurtz's Intended"; corrupted by his experience and actions in the Congo, Kurtz fails to reach his fiancée and is unable to reclaim his humanity. Leopold, in Twain's work, is the corrupted Kurtz who has returned and stands as a challenge to the reader to hold a criminal accountable for his actions.

The final line of *King Leopold's Soliloquy*, printed beneath a drawing of a handless child, is a quote attributed to Joseph Conrad, saying, "To Them it must appear very awful and mysterious . . ." (76). Twain leaves the reader to ponder this quote, which is left intentionally vague. One can read the ambiguous term "them" as referring back to Africans, as represented by the depiction of the mutilated child. Interpreted this way, the quote emphasizes that to the colonized, the "civilization mission" is a strange and terrible experience that has brought only destruction and pain. The quote, however, can be read a second way, casting the reader as the subject, and can thus be interpreted as "to [you] it must appear very awful and mysterious." Read this way, Twain uses Conrad's voice to damn the reader into action. The quote comes immediately after the reader encounters Leopold assuring himself that the inaction of the West is his protection. By placing the quote directly beneath an image of brutal violence, and only a paragraph after stating that the readers' instinct will be to turn away, the words serve as a challenge to the audience to prove Leopold's self-assurance wrong. Twain tasks the audience with protesting against colonialism by punishing Leopold for his crimes.

The quote from Conrad in *King Leopold's Soliloquy* can also be read like the postscript at the foot of Mr. Kurtz's report, telling the reader to "exterminate all the brutes" (Conrad, *Heart* 51). The image of the mutilated child, like the corrupted torchbearer in Kurtz's painting, is a stand-in for the corrupted reality of the civilizing mission. The final reference back to Conrad also signifies that *King Leopold's Soliloquy* is Twain's direct attempt to carry forward the protest and tropes of *Heart of Darkness*. He argues that in the colonial setting, brutish power inevitably corrupts the imperial agent and then returns home to weaken the metropole morally and ideologically.

The overall message in both Conrad and Twain's anticolonial works is that colonialism has corrupted European and American values. The imperial agents are no longer bearers of the sacred light, spreading civilization, but have become excessive brutes. From this perspective, colonialism is protested not on humanitarian grounds, but rather as a corrupting influence on the imperial nation. Conrad and Twain can be credited with leading the way in their critique of the "civilizing mission." While small works on their own, these publications, released within a six-year span, show that the sparks of an anticolonial protest rode on a wave of public disenchantment following publicized European and American atrocities in the colonial periphery. Using photographs and actual colonial reports, Twain forced his readers to not turn away from the images of brutish behavior and challenged the public to reassess the "civilizing mission" in a specifically American context. The first major cracks in the imperial discourse, however, can be traced back to Joseph Conrad, who, through his own personal experience and the power of his prose, made his audience feel, hear, and see the horrors of brutish colonial corruption.

Notes

1. *Heart of Darkness* was published in a three-part series in *Blackwood's Magazine*, debuting in February 1899 and concluding in April 1899. See "Serialization."
2. "Westerners" here refers to the Anglophone audiences of America and Europe.

3. While it is not in the scope of this chapter, readers can find large overlaps by comparing *Heart of Darkness* with Conrad's "Congo Diary," published in its entirety as "Joseph Conrad's Diary (Hitherto Unpublished) of His Journey up the Valley of the Congo in 1890" (1925).

4. "Metropole," from the Greek word *metropolis* (literally, "mother city"), is a term used to denote the imperial home nation.

5. While "germ" may be a pejorative-sounding term for a microorganism today, Conrad's use is intended to illustrate empire as something that grew or germinated.

6. This is the infamous line that launched author Sven Lindqvist on an investigation of the European colonial project as an antecedent to many twentieth-century genocides. See his very excellent *"Exterminate All the Brutes": One Man's Odyssey into the Heart of Darkness and the Origins of European Genocide* (1992).

7. Responding to a newspaper account of the lynching of Will Godley in Pierce City, Missouri, Twain penned "The United States of Lyncherdom" in the summer of 1901. The essay, detailing the horrific practice and its American prevalence, remained unpublished until thirteen years after his death (Twain, *Europe and Elsewhere* 239–49).

8. Historians now refer to these Boer Wars as the South African War.

9. "The Gilded Age," a term coined by Twain, refers to the period in American history (approximately 1877 to 1893) when a façade of wealth covered deep social and political issues like a golden shell. See Twain and Warner's *The Gilded Age: A Tale of Today* (1873).

Works Cited

Baines, Jocelyn. *Joseph Conrad: A Critical Biography.* London: Weidenfeld, 1993. Print.

Capozzola, Christopher. "Thomas Dixon's War Prayers." *Journal of Transnational American Studies* 1.1 (2009): 61–65. Print.

Caron, James E. *Mark Twain: Unsanctified Newspaper Reporter.* Columbia: U of Missouri P, 2008. Print.

Conrad, Joseph. *Heart of Darkness.* New York: Random, 1999. Print.

___. "Joseph Conrad's Diary (Hitherto Unpublished) of His Journey up the Valley of the Congo in 1890." *Blue Peter* 5 (1925): 318–25. Print.

___. Preface. *The Nigger of the "Narcissus."* 1897. Garden City: Doubleday, 1914. 11–16. Print.

Emerson, Everett H. *Mark Twain: A Literary Life.* Philadelphia: U of Pennsylvania P, 2000. Print.

Hamner, Robert D., ed. *Joseph Conrad: Third World Perspectives.* Washington: Three Continents, 1990. Print.

Hochschild, Adam. *King Leopold's Ghost: A Story of Greed, Terror, and Heroism in Colonial Africa.* Boston: First Mariner, 1998. Print.

Jones, Adam. *Genocide: A Comprehensive Introduction*. New York: Routledge, 2006.
Print.

Kipling, Rudyard. "The White Man's Burden." *The Writings in Prose and Verse of
Rudyard Kipling*. Vol. 21. New York: Scribner's, 1903. 78. Print.

Lindqvist, Sven. *"Exterminate All the Brutes": One Man's Odyssey into the Heart of
Darkness and the Origins of European Genocide*. New York: New, 1992. Print.

Miller, Stuart Creighton. *'Benevolent Assimilation': The American Conquest of the
Philippines, 1899–1903*. New Haven: Yale UP, 1982. Print.

Rich, Norman. *Great Power Diplomacy, 1814–1914*. Boston: McGraw, 1992. Print.

Robinson, Forrest. "Mark Twain, 1835–1910: A Brief Biography." *A Historical Guide
to Mark Twain*. Ed. Shelley Fisher Fishkin. New York: Oxford UP, 2002. 13–54.
Print.

Schurz, Carl. "Platform of the American Anti-Imperialist League." *Speeches, Correspondence, and Political Papers of Carl Schurz*. Vol. 6. Ed. Frederick Bancroft.
New York: Putnam, 1913. 77 n1. Print.

"Serialization: *The Heart of Darkness*." *Conrad First: Joseph Conrad Periodical Archive*. Dept. of English, Uppsala U, 2009. Web. 18 Dec. 2012.

Simmons, Allan H. "Politics." *Joseph Conrad in Context*. Ed. Simmons. Cambridge:
Cambridge UP, 2009. 195–203. Print.

Stape, John. *The Several Lives of Joseph Conrad*. New York: Random, 2009. Print.

Twain, Mark. *Europe and Elsewhere*. New York: Harper, 1923. Print.

___. "Excerpts: From the New York *Herald*, 15 October 1900." *The World of 1898:
The Spanish-American War*. Lib. of Congress, 2011. Web. 18 Dec. 2012.

___. *King Leopold's Soliloquy*. New York: International, 1970. Print.

___. *Mark Twain's Letters from Hawaii*. New York: Appleton, 1966. Print.

___. "Our Fellow Savages of the Sandwich Islands." Brooklyn, New York. 8 Feb.
1873. Lecture. *Mark Twain and His Times*. Stephen Railton and the U of Virginia
Lib., 2012. Web. 18 Dec. 2012.

___. "To the Person Sitting in Darkness." *North American Review* 172.531 (1901):
161–76. Print.

Twain, Mark, and Charles Dudley Warner. *The Gilded Age: A Tale of Today*. 1873.
Stilwell: Digireads, 2007. Print.

Wesseling, H. L. *Divide and Rule: The Partition of Africa, 1880–1914*. Westport:
Praeger, 1996. Print.

Zmijewski, David. "The Man in Both Corners: Mark Twain the Shadowboxing Imperialist." *Hawaiian Journal of History* 40.13 (2006): 55–73. Print.

Zwick, Jim. "Mark Twain and Imperialism." *A Historical Guide to Mark Twain*. Ed.
Shelley Fisher Fishkin. New York: Oxford UP, 2002. 227–56. Print.

Nella Larsen and Langston Hughes: Modernist Protest in the Harlem Renaissance_____

Kimberly Drake

> Between me and the other world there is ever an unasked question: . . . How does it feel to be a problem? (W. E. B. Du Bois, *The Souls of Black Folk*)

The Harlem Renaissance, also known as the New Negro movement, has been called the "happy hour" of African American art and literature, despite the continuation of racial and economic oppression (which in various ways worsened) throughout the period (roughly 1917–29). Because the Harlem Renaissance was a self-conscious literary and cultural movement, intent on using the power of artistic and literary representation to intervene in political and social policies, it has tended to be viewed by critics and historians through the terms with which its major players conceptualized it. In fact, it was far more diverse and less cohesive as a movement than it has typically been portrayed. This chapter examines the literary protests and personae of two of its star writers, Langston Hughes and Nella Larsen. Hughes is best known for his leftist and jazz-inspired poems that rely on the vernacular of the working classes, while Larsen wrote psychological novels focusing on the middle class. Situated on seemingly opposite ends of a Harlem Renaissance literary and political spectrum, Hughes and Larsen nevertheless shared an interest in the critique of class lines and bourgeois imitation, and both practiced experimentalism in form and content. Both were interested in creating literary representations of how "it feel[s] to be a problem."

Because literature can so powerfully influence its readers, members of oppressed groups have successfully used it to represent themselves as worthy of citizenship and equal treatment. African Americans began writing slave narratives, poetry, and other literary works as early as the 1730s, most of which protested slavery and racial oppression and made a case for social equality for blacks. The basic strategy of these literary protests had been to overturn slavery- and Reconstruction-era racial stereotypes by portraying the African American protagonists as intelligent and literate, religious and moral, emotionally complex, and noble—in other words, idealized human beings, according to prevailing norms. These norms happened to be defined by the white middle class, so an African American who manifested them was considered a "credit to the race," helping to "uplift" the race in the eyes of whites, which might result in social acceptance and political rights. Characters who reinforced racial stereotypes were often members of the black working class, and they were meant to appear degraded and/or static and outmoded, something to be left behind.

A critical issue writers felt compelled to address in the Reconstruction era was the dominant ideology of gender and sexuality; slavery-era stereotypes used aspects of this ideology in their dehumanizing portrayals. In this ideology, physical strength and vigor, reason, social responsibility, and devotion to liberty were the province of white men, setting a standard for masculinity that protest writers adopted in their portrayals of black men (or of themselves, as Frederick Douglass does in his *Narrative*). On the other hand, compassion, delicacy, and virtue were the special province of white middle-class women; therefore writers felt a particular responsibility to demonstrate these qualities in their female protagonists. Authors anxious to combat prevailing views of African American women had to focus particular attention on the jezebel stereotype. This slavery-era image of African women as hypersexual and therefore incapable of being raped was created so that white men could rape them with impunity (Lerner 193). Begun in slavery as an attempt to "facilitate the continued [sexual] exploitation" of black women (193), the jezebel stereotype has been a powerful force in and symbol of racial and gender oppression. Traditionally, black women writers responded to this myth about black women's "sexual licentiousness" by creating characters who were virtuous to the point of lacking sexual desire (Lerner 193; McDowell xii–xiii). Before Larsen created Helga Crane, virtually all African American women writers (and some men) depicted their black female protagonists as chaste and respectable. They could not feel "sexual desire" but instead had to feel a "desire to uplift the race" (Carby 240) or to help African Americans achieve a higher standard of morality. This is true of male characters as well, who by the Reconstruction era were being constructed as counterarguments to the rapist stereotype used as the excuse for lynching.[1] In novels and short stories, male and female protagonists would be interested in each other because of their mutual attraction to political uplift, not because of sexual desire. Because participation in the project of "uplift" involves establishing a public presence, the black heroine typically becomes involved in uplift only after her marriage.

The rhetoric of uplift became entangled with scientific racism around the turn of the century in the form of eugenics, something that also affected gender discourses. Scientific racism describes efforts to use science to establish white superiority; eugenics has been described as a "science" used to predict human traits and behaviors and to control human breeding. Through eugenics, people with the "best" genes were to reproduce and "improve the species" (*PBS*).[2] The idea that an elite class of people, which Du Bois called the "talented tenth," probably had the best genes and so should reproduce, was a fairly normative idea for whites and blacks in the early-to-mid twentieth century. As Du Bois stated, "We in America are becoming sharply divided into the mass who have endless children and the class who through long postponement of marriage have few or none"; the "Best of the race" must "guide the Mass away from the contamination and death of the Worst" (qtd. in English 294, 297). Despite his fairly radical views about economics and his immense interdisciplinary body of work promoting social and political justice for African Americans and colonized peoples around the world, here readers see Du Bois uncritically reinforcing existing ideologies about class differences, "uplift," and gender.

In her article "Rethinking Recognition," Nancy Fraser explains such problematic statements when she discusses what can happen when members of a "disesteemed group" organize a response to the "dominant culture's demeaning picture" of their group and the resulting harm to their identities:

> Jettisoning internalized negative self-identities, they must join collectively to produce a self-affirming culture of their own. . . . The result, when successful, is "recognition," an undistorted relation to oneself. . . . [However, t]he overall effect is to impose a single, drastically simplified group-identity, which denies the complexity of people's lives, the multiplicity of their identifications, and the cross-pulls of their various affiliations. Ironically, then, the identity model serves as a vehicle for misrecognition . . . promot[ing] conformity, intolerance, and patriarchalism. (24, 26)

In other words, a group identity created in response to oppression may be structured around a simplistic and inflexible rejection of some aspect of that oppression; this group identity, meant to provide a nurturing and protected space in which to develop individual identity, can be, in fact, a space in which individual identity is stifled. Some aspects of African American literary self-portrayals can be explained using Fraser's ideas: to destroy damaging and deadly racial stereotypes, authors tended as a group to avoid any hint of them in the behavior of their characters. A certain political and psychological uniformity among nineteenth-century African American characters was the result.

Aspects of this protective group identity were challenged in various ways by Harlem Renaissance writers, especially Larsen and Hughes. In Larsen's *Quicksand*, for example, James Vayle, Helga's former fiancé, expresses Du Boisian ideas about reproduction and the responsibility of the educated classes to produce more children:

> James was aghast. He forgot to be embarrassed. "But Helga! Good heavens! Don't you see that if we—I mean people like us—don't have children, the others will still have. That's one of the things that's the matter with us. The race is sterile at the top. Few, very few Negroes of the better

class have children . . . we're the ones who must have children if the race is to get anywhere." (103)

James's response is to Helga's flippant comment that she will not have children; after this exchange, he suggests that he is planning to propose to her again in the near future. Helga is uninterested in James's proposal and his plans to breed "better" children with her, but her sarcastic treatment of the entire episode is a critique of the kind of rigid "group identity" model that had been imposed by leaders like Du Bois as a strategy for improving the race. Larsen's novels and Hughes's poetry often use an "outsider" perspective to engage in such crucial critiques of conventional ways of thinking, critiques that are characteristic of the Harlem Renaissance as a cultural movement.

Larsen and Hughes were at different times considered representative of and rising stars in the Harlem Renaissance movement. Like any cultural movement, the Harlem Renaissance is hard to define, in part because attempts to define and classify often result in homogenizing and the erasure of difference. Scholars tend to agree, though, that a number of events in the very early part of the twentieth century provided the conditions that enabled the movement. Among these were the Great Migration of roughly two million southern blacks to northern cities (and also to California and big southern cities); a large drop in Harlem real estate prices that enabled the purchase and rental of properties by African Americans; an increasingly militant political consciousness following African American soldiers' participation in World War I and the establishment of organizations such as the NAACP and Marcus Garvey's Universal Negro Improvement Association; economic growth; and an increased interest in forms of cultural production that were also of interest to white intellectuals and artists (Hutchinson, *Harlem* 3). While it should be recognized that something special certainly did take place in Harlem, it is also important to note, as Hazel Carby does, that the "intense literary and artistic production" and "intellectual awakening" (163) did not occur only in Harlem or only in the 1920s. Earlier intellectual and literary movements in African American politics and art are made to disappear in this kind of description; also erased are the "intellectuals, leaders, organizations, and journals" devoted to "economic radicalism" at this time (165). The Harlem Renaissance cannot be accurately described as a liberal or accommodationist movement.

Similarly, previous studies of the Harlem Renaissance have implied that population density alone created an African American artistic revolution, but as George Hutchinson reminds readers, the 1920s saw an "explosion of literary output in the US" across racial lines, and the "publishing industry expanded and diversified" because "writers and artists generally were in vogue, especially young ones" (*Harlem* 8). Furthermore, virtually all of the "significant new publishers and magazines" were in New York, "along with a mix of pragmatist philosophers, Boasian anthropologists, socialist theorists, and new journalists," a combination that expanded and diversified the "print culture" and brought "like-minded culture-workers" together for intellectual and social exchange (6). Massive migration to New York City helped to connect this "mix" of people with emerging African American artists and writers, creating cross-racial relationships. One result was new or adapted "institutions that supported the creation of a literary movement" (5). Among these were new publishing houses, intellectual and political organizations, museums, theaters, the jazz industry, and the 135th Street branch of the New York Public Library.

An important characteristic of the Harlem Renaissance, then, was its interracial communal nature: artists and writers in this movement were not struggling in isolation or small enclaves against waves of white racism, but rather were consciously engaging with members of a substantial literary and artistic community, one that included white intellectuals, artists, critics, and art patrons. This interracial community was focused on African American art and literature and helped to promote a kind of cultural solidarity among black artists and writers, who were recognized as cultural experts in this movement. Speaking from the midst of the Harlem Renaissance as its self-proclaimed critic (called by C. W. E. Bigsby the "black Matthew Arnold"), Howard philosophy professor Alain Locke notes that up until the inception of the renaissance, "Negroes have been a race more in name than in fact . . . the chief bond between them has been that of a common condition rather than a common consciousness. . . . In Harlem, Negro life is seizing upon its first chances for group expression and self-determination" (qtd. in Christian, *Black Women* 37). The "common consciousness" was not characterized by homogeneous ideology, but rather by enthusiasm for the immense potential of the New Negro arts movement.

However, this new artistic community coincided with a fragmentation of African Americans along class lines. Hazel Carby notes that "after World War I and the migration," there was "no longer a unitary 'people'"; by the 1920s, black artists sought "artistic autonomy" and separated themselves "from the task of writing for the uplifting of the race as a whole" (166). The split between "folk" and the elite or middle class became visible and permanent in the Harlem Renaissance; the "folk" residing in the South and the North (the urban "underclass") were the subject of its art, but not the creators of it, and in fact were not entirely aware of its existence. As Hughes states in *The Big Sea*, "the ordinary negroes hadn't heard of the Negro Renaissance" (228). The movement provided no real benefit for "non-theatrical, non-intellectual Harlem," Hughes goes on to say, and this group was the "unwilling victim of its own vogue" (229) in that white tourists and gangsters took over their nightclubs (228). In Hughes's view, the Harlem Renaissance ended in the spring of 1929 with the onset of the Great Depression. Financial patronage had been important to the movement, which exposed, in the views of Hughes and others, the movement's "'bourgeois' weakness" (Hutchinson, *Harlem* 13). On the other hand, one should not dismiss the power of strategic appeals to bourgeois aesthetics. Those who denigrate the middle-class character of the Harlem Renaissance "blind themselves to the strategic importance of middle-class contests for cultural power in the United States" (13). If social ideologies of race are dictated by the ruling elites and promulgated and maintained by the middle class, any successful movement for social justice using the arts as its medium will probably be (at least in part) shaped by and targeted to these demographics.

The precise beginning of the Harlem Renaissance has also been debated, though scholars often credit the publication of Claude McKay's "Harlem Dancer" poem in 1917. Highlights of the movement include James Weldon Johnson's *Book of American Negro Poetry* (1922); the Civic Club dinner sponsored by *Opportunity, A Journal of Negro Life* (a National Urban League publication), which was attended by white publishers and black writers and resulted in cross-racial networking and publications (1924); and the literary contest and award dinner of *Opportunity* (1925), which similarly was attended by important literary figures both white and black. Also notable was the *Harlem* special issue of the social work magazine *Survey Graphic* (1925), guest edited by Alain Locke, which was later expanded into *The New Negro: Voices of the Harlem Renaissance* (1925). Despite such self-conscious attempts to codify the literary output of this period, Harlem Renaissance authors characterized the New Negro identity quite differently. One can see in Hughes's poetry and in Larsen's *Quicksand* an expression of the "crisis of representation of the period": the location of an "authentic" yet modern black identity (Locke 51). The New Negro movement ultimately did not establish a clear understanding of New Negro identity; on the contrary, one might note that the search for such an identity came to characterize the New Negro artist and highlights the modernist bent of much of the New Negro cultural production.

Despite the fact that New Negro artists like Larsen and Hughes "were profoundly invested in positioning African American culture squarely within the discursive space of 'the modern'" (Kuenz 509), the Harlem Renaissance has until very recently been seen as entirely separate from American literary modernism as characterized by T. S. Eliot and Ezra Pound. This interpretation seems blind to the nature of New Negro cultural production. Many writers of the Harlem Renaissance emphasize artistic experimentation and resistance to conventional forms and ideas in their work—which is what literary modernism was all about. More recent revisionist work in this area has categorized Hughes and Larsen in the "second generation of US modernists," a group that also includes Ernest Hemingway, F. Scott Fitzgerald, and William Faulkner, all of whom "came of age during the second wave of Jim Crow and the racial segregation of urban space" (Smethurst, *Modernism* 190). From this perspective, race was a central aspect of society in the modernist era, and this group of modernists certainly included it in their work in more or less unconventional and confrontational ways.

Much of modernist writing is concerned with the search for "true" representation and the "refusal of socially defined conventions," and Harlem Renaissance writers were no exception (Kuenz 508). They wanted to be "both authentically black and authentically modern" and did not see these terms as mutually exclusive. The problem was how to avoid the constant lurking fear of inauthenticity. Some authors emphasize "the instinctive gift of the folk spirit" and "ancient" African heritage in their characters (Locke 51), but to uncritically locate an identity essence in a "primitive" past plays into racial stereotypes. To focus on an expression of a "modern self," one "not exclusive to black Americans" (Dawahare 23), might mean caving in to the "false, 'spurious' culture of mass marketing" (Kuenz 509). Both Larsen and Hughes portray the "folk" and a cosmopolitan black middle class in their work, at times and in various ways engaging in critiques of both.

Hughes's well-known salvo against middle-class inauthenticity appears in his 1926 essay "The Negro Artist and the Racial Mountain," published in the *Nation*. As Henry Louis Gates Jr. and Anthony Appiah note, Hughes "had no peer as an internationalist . . . and yet his cosmopolitanism, rare for any American in his time, never displaced his passionate engagement with and commitment to African-American vernacular culture" (*Langston Hughes* ix). In his essay, Hughes paints an unflattering portrait of an artist growing up in a middle-class home that only participates in white cultural forms; it would be "difficult" for

ducation and through spirituality, and she feels at home with
so sharply alienated from the "inconsequential chatter" of the
rgeoisie as well as their racial politics.

Helga's inability to find a "home" or a fixed identity is a lens through
which not only this novel but Larsen's life itself has been viewed. Lars-
en was considered the most accomplished black novelist of her generation after *Quicksand* was published—she won second place in the Harmon Foundation awards in 1928 and was the first African American
woman writer to win a Guggenheim in 1930. However, by the 1960s,
she had disappeared from accounts of the Harlem Renaissance.[3] One
reason for this is that Larsen had been described by biographers as
"fickle and unsettled" and a "delicate and unstable" person (McDowell ix, x), characterizations that seem to reflect Helga's character more
than Larsen's. Indeed, critics have often viewed *Quicksand* through
a biographical lens, and biographers have used to the novel to provide information about Larsen. Biographers have also used incorrect
biographical information to claim that Larsen routinely lied about her
life story. Unlike the biographers who preceded him, George Hutchinson corrects these rumors and falsehoods with new historical research
about her life in *In Search of Nella Larsen* (2006). Nevertheless, such
descriptions of Larsen as unstable damaged her literary reputation irreparably while she was still alive.

When *Quicksand* first appeared in March of 1928, however, it received fairly positive reviews. Du Bois loved it, calling it the "best
piece of fiction since the heyday of Chesnutt" in a 1928 review in *Crisis*, and reviewers admired the complexity of her characters (qtd. in Tate
237). One white reviewer praised the novel for being "wholly free from
the curse of propaganda" and applauded Larsen for being "aware that a
novelist's business is primarily with the individuals and not with classes" (Tate 237). White reviewers tended to focus on Helga's psychology and sexuality, while reviewers for African American periodicals
recognized Larsen's "frequent protests against racial discrimination"
and "identified with Helga's efforts to define herself independently of

racial restrictions" (238). In the 1970s and 1980s, critics ten
cus on "the 'tragic mulatto' image in readings of *Quicksand*" (Ro
782 n16), which was a typical image in postslavery fiction by wh
and blacks. Interpretations of Larsen's work were quite varied, the
seemingly determined by the political positions and motivations of the
critic.

Similarly, Hughes has been viewed as a poetic genius, the unoffi-
cial poet laureate of the Harlem Renaissance, but also as a poet whose
work was "trashy" and simplistic. He won a number of major awards
and honors, including *Opportunity* magazine's literary contest for
"The Weary Blues," the Spingarn contest, the Harmon gold medal for
his first novel, *Not without Laughter*, and a Guggenheim (Woods 25).
He has been praised for "daringly" enacting the "modernist challenge
to 'make it new'" (Hokanson 61), but his work has also been called
"old-fashioned" and static (Smethurst, *New Red* 144). In his review
of *Selected Poems* (1959), James Baldwin wrote, "Every time I read
Langston Hughes I am amazed all over again by his genuine gifts and
depressed that he has done so little with them" (37). African American
critics in particular were frequently disgusted by his working class–focused work; they designated his poems about mulattos "unsanitary" and
"degenerate," stating that "Hughes had [revealed] the 'secret' shame of
their culture" by "pandering to the tastes of whites for the sensational"
and had "betrayed his race" (Rampersad 61). Hughes responded by
saying that these reviewers must still believe that "we should display
our 'higher selves'—whatever they are" (qtd. in Rampersad 65). Critiques of Hughes's work, like those of Larsen's, have been based on
unstated ideologies related to race, class, and social status; moreover,
reviews of the same work can quite dramatically depend on the decade
in which the reviewers are living.

The "tragic mulatto" figure intersects the work of Larsen and
Hughes—a section of Hughes's poem "Cross" is the epigraph to
Quicksand. As Rampersad notes, "the mulatto theme—and its tran-
scendence—is one of the most prominent" themes in Hughes's work

(58), and the mixed-race individual is significant to Larsen's novels as well. While the mulatto figure in "Cross" is quite different from Helga Crane in a number of ways, both authors disrupt the common understanding of the tragic mulatto in their work. Hughes begins his poem with a suggestion of the speaker's "tragic mulatto" status as defined by his parentage, a white man and a black woman, and one expects from this—and from the title, "Cross," which suggests crucifixion—that the poem will uncover the essence of the mulatto, the reasons for his tragic life. But the poem resists this. Certainly, lines three through eight suggest that the speaker has become alienated from both parents during their lives, possibly cursing both parents in anger (or while "cross"), presumably for producing a child whose life would be painful and difficult. However, these lines simultaneously suggest that the speaker has worked through such anger and is "sorry" for the "evil wish" that his mother would go to hell (lines 6–7). The speaker now wishes the mother "well" (8), which suggests that she is alive and could conceivably be happy. Readers do not know at this point but will find out in lines nine and ten that the mother died (and thus presumably lived) in a "shack" and that the father died in a "big fine house"; the opening lines use only the modifiers "old" and "white" or "black" to describe the parents, hiding their immense class difference.

The speaker's working through of his anger might be the result of the parents' deaths rather than the achievement of psychological balance of any kind. To "wish her [the mother] well" (line 7) now seems to indicate a hope that she ended up in heaven and that the curse failed, which to an extent mitigates the sincerity of his apology for cursing her. In the final section (11–12), the speaker expresses "wonder" at the location of his own death, "being neither white nor black." Here he indicates a lack of a fixed location in society and a lack of racial identity. He is not both, but neither—not fixed, but placeless. These qualities could have condemned him to a life of invisibility and loneliness, or they could have freed him from racial categories. He either is irreparably damaged by his racial identity and obsessed with his own death, in typical tragic mulatto fashion, or is going about a relatively stable life, one hidden from the reader, idly wondering about his own death, given those of his parents.

Henry Louis Gates might have readers believe in the latter interpretation. In *Signifying Monkey*, he states that "the 'finding of the voice' of the speaking subject in a language in which blackness is the cardinal sign of absence is the subject of so much of Afro-American discourse" (qtd. in Jarraway 824). In "Cross," the protagonist's racially mixed heritage shows the falsity of the "notion of a pure self" (Jarraway 832), but given Gates's interpretation, it also indicates that black identity cannot be boiled down to an essence even when "unmixed" with white heritage. This can more clearly be seen in a poem like "Theme for English B," which explodes the notion of racial essence, whether biological or social. In the white teacher's request that the "page" the student writes "come out of you— / Then, it will be true" (lines 4–5), readers see a request for an individual essence. The student/narrator replies, "I wonder if it's that simple?" (6) and "Me—who?" (20). He argues that his identity is always contingent upon the identities of others, even of his white instructor, who is "a part of me, as I am a part of you [the instructor]" (32). In this poem, and in "Cross," human identity is indeterminate and contingent and boundaries are fluid. Hughes's poems do not work to homogenize aspects of black identity, but instead promise an "infinitely revolving subjectivity" (Jarraway 834), a diverse, changeable, and unknowable self.

Helga Crane does not fit the "tragic mulatto" pattern on the level of parentage, because her mother is a Danish immigrant from a middle-class background who became impoverished after marrying her poorer African American father. Her subjectivity, however, is similarly a work in progress, and the tragic ending of her life is based on her inability to understand this as a more flexible way of being. In this sense, the modernist understanding of identity in the novel is unavailable to its protagonist. At the point when she is contemplating a more nomadic lifestyle, she makes a sudden decision to fix herself in one place through marriage. Most critics approaching this novel have attempted to answer two related questions: why does Helga marry the Reverend Pleasant Green, and in Helga's words, "what was the matter with her? Was there, without her knowing it, some peculiar lack in her? . . . Why couldn't she be happy, content, somewhere?" (Larsen 81).

Typically, critics answer these questions by looking either to social institutions or to psychology. Either Helga's alienation is just a "state of consciousness, a frame of mind" that could be changed (with psychoanalysis, perhaps), or it is "produced by existing forms of social [and economic] relations and therefore subject to elimination only by a change in those social relations" (Carby 168). Claudia Tate uses a psychoanalytic lens that takes into account Helga's experiences as a woman and as a mixed-race individual, while still looking at the traumas inflicted on Helga by her racist white family during her childhood. This trauma manifests as an "intense self-loathing" that Helga represses but that emerges in moments of revulsion and confusion in moments of "pleasure" (Tate 249–50). Tate explains Helga's inexplicable marriage to Reverend Pleasant Green as connected to the traumatic abandonment by first her black father and then her white father, which has driven Helga throughout her life; the ending, in which Helga loses faith in religion, constitutes what Tate calls "a severe indictment of Western culture" and its "master plots of hegemonic desire that have defined her social identity" (253). The appropriateness of a psychoanalytic interpretation is well supported in the text, I argue, and in fact, its use is a kind of radical insistence on the interior depth and immeasurable complexity of the cosmopolitan African American woman, a modernist counterargument against the white supremacist ideology displayed in Thomas Jefferson's *Notes on the State of Virginia*.

An interpretation focused on Helga's reaction to social institutions makes a different kind of modernist protest. Critic Karin Roffman states that "*Quicksand* is an aesthetic meditation on how social problems become institutionalized through the very structures that seem also to have the greatest potential to help solve them," such as the educational system, the public library, and religion (754). In this analysis, which forms a critique of social forces, Helga's unconventional background and perspective force her outside of institutional structures and lead her to form implicit and explicit critiques of them. She marries Green because she believes that her husband and his small-town Alabama flock form a simple kind of social institution, one she can both embrace and control. She does not take seriously the fact that the Green's parishioners see her as a "scarlet woman," a "jezebel," and a "poor erring sister" (Larsen 112) and that she will never truly be accepted as one of them. She also underestimates the strength and power of the institutions of domesticity and maternity, which eventually overpower her. As Roffman notes, "the novel suggests that the desire for individual and intellectual freedom requires . . . resisting all institutions, all systems, and all statements (even one's own)" (776). In other words, Helga's pattern of restless mobility and withdrawal from situations in which she feels her identity being fixed (usually by men) are a potent form of resistance, one that partakes in modernist conceptions of African American subjectivity as always in process.

Despite the wildly varying views of their critics over the years, Langston Hughes and Nella Larsen were both highly innovative writers who found creative ways to challenge ideologies of race, class, and gender. While they focused most of their energies on protagonists from different classes, their incisive critiques of social ideology and conventional literary forms and approaches combine modernist forms with political protests in a way that is ultimately characteristic of the New Negro arts movement.

Notes

1. For more information on this, see Hodes.
2. For more about eugenics, see "Eugenics Movement Reaches Its Height: 1923" on the PBS site *People and Discoveries: A Science Odyssey.*
3. One reason for her disappearance from literary history was that her literary career came to an end after a scandal in which she was accused of plagiarizing a

short story. While the publication in which her story appeared (the *Forum*) vindicated her of the charges, she never published her third novel or any other literary work. Equally devastating was the breakup of her marriage at this time due to her husband's infidelity. Because she was a literary celebrity, various rumors about her sanity began to circulate, which further alienated her from her former colleagues and friends.

Works Cited

Baldwin, James. "*Selected Poems* (1959)." Gates and Appiah 37–38. Print.

Carby, Hazel V. *Reconstructing Womanhood: The Emergence of the Afro-American Woman Novelist*. New York: Oxford UP, 1987. Print.

Christian, Barbara. *Black Women Novelists: The Development of a Tradition*. Westport: Greenwood, 1980. Print.

Dawahare, Anthony. "The Gold Standard of Racial Identity in Nella Larsen's *Quicksand* and *Passing*." *Twentieth Century Literature* 52.1 (2006): 22–41. Print.

English, Daylanne. "W. E. B. DuBois's Family Crisis." *American Literature* 72.2 (2000): 291–319. Print.

Ernstmeyer, Phillip. "On 'The Cat and the Saxophone.'" *Modern American Poetry*. Ed. Cary Nelson and Bartholomew Brinkman. Dept. of English, U of Illinois at Urbana-Champaign, 2006. Web. 7 Jan. 2013.

"Eugenics Movement Reaches Its Height: 1923." *People and Discoveries: A Science Odyssey*. WGBH/Public Broadcasting Service, 1998. Web. 7 Jan. 2013.

Fraser, Nancy. "Rethinking Recognition: Overcoming Displacement and Reification in Cultural Politics." *Recognition Struggles and Social Movements: Contested Identities, Agency, and Power*. Ed. Barbara Hobson. New York: Cambridge UP, 2003. 21–34. Print.

Gates, Henry Louis, Jr., and Anthony Appiah, eds. *Langston Hughes: Critical Perspectives Past and Present*. New York: Amistad, 1993. Print.

Hodes, Martha. "The Sexualization of Reconstruction Politics: White Women and Black Men in the South after the Civil War." *Journal of the History of Sexuality* 3.3 (1993): 402–17. Print.

Hokanson, Robert O'Brien. "Jazzing It Up: The Be-Bop Modernism of Langston Hughes." *Mosaic* 31.4 (1998): 61–80. Print.

Hughes, Langston. *The Big Sea: An Autobiography*. New York: Hill, 1993. Print.

___."Cross." *The Collected Poems of Langston Hughes*. Ed. Arnold Rampersad and David Roessel. New York: Knopf, 1994. 58. Print.

___. "Hughes's 'The Negro Artist and the Racial Mountain' (1926)." *Nation*, 1926. *Modern American Poetry*. Ed. Cary Nelson and Bartholomew Brinkman. Dept. of English, U of Illinois at Urbana-Champaign, n.d. Web. 7 Jan. 2013.

Hutchinson, George. *In Search of Nella Larsen: A Biography of the Color Line*. Cambridge: Harvard UP, 2006. Print.

___. *The Harlem Renaissance in Black and White*. Cambridge: Harvard UP, 1995. Print.

Jarraway, David R. "Montage of an Otherness Deferred: Dreaming Subjectivity in Langston Hughes." *American Literature* 68.4 (1996): 819–47. Print.

Kuenz, Jane. "Modernism, Mass Culture, and the Harlem Renaissance: The Case of Countee Cullen." *Modernism/Modernity* 14.3 (2007): 507–15. Print.

Larsen, Nella. Quicksand *and* Passing. Ed. Deborah E. McDowell. New Brunswick: Rutgers UP, 1986. Print.

Lerner, Gerda. *Black Women in White America*. New York: Vintage, 1973. Print.

Locke, Alain. "Negro Youth Speaks." *The New Negro: Voices of the Harlem Renaissance*. Ed. Locke. New York, Simon, 1997. 47–53. Print.

McDowell, Deborah E. Introduction. Quicksand *and* Passing. By Nella Larsen. New Brunswick: Rutgers UP, 1986. ix–xxxi. Print.

Rampersad, Arnold. "Hughes' *Fine Clothes to the Jew*." Gates and Appiah 53–68. Print.

Roffman, Karin. "Nella Larsen, Librarian at 135th Street." *Modern Fiction Studies* 53.4 (2007): 752–87. Print.

Smethurst, James E. *The African American Roots of Modernism: From Reconstruction to the Harlem Renaissance*. Chapel Hill: U of North Carolina P, 2011. Print.

___. *The New Red Negro: The Literary Left and African American Poetry, 1930–1946*. New York: Oxford UP, 1999. Print.

Tate, Claudia. "Desire and Death in *Quicksand*, by Nella Larsen." *American Literary History* 7.2 (1995): 234–60. Print.

Tracy, Steven C. "On 'The Weary Blues.'" *Modern American Poetry*. Ed. Cary Nelson and Bartholomew Brinkman. Dept. of English, U of Illinois at Urbana-Champaign, n.d. Web. 7 Jan. 2013.

Woods, Katherine. "*The Big Sea* (1940)." Gates and Appiah 23–26. Print.

The Meaning of Rape in Richard Wright's *Native Son*

Kimberly Drake

As many influential critics have noted, Richard Wright's novel *Native Son* (1940) permanently changed not only black consciousness and black literature but also American culture (Kinnamon 127). In one of the earliest reviews of the novel, Clifton Fadiman states in the *New Yorker* that while it may be "the finest novel as yet written by an American Negro," as Henry Seidel Canby claimed in his book jacket comment, it is also "the most powerful American novel" since John Steinbeck's *Grapes of Wrath* (6). Early reviewers called for it to win "all the prizes," and *Native Son* was in fact a "serious contender for a Pulitzer prize" (Kinnamon 126). Margaret Walker Alexander argues that Wright's text inspired a group of writers to draw upon his protest mode, among these James Baldwin, Ralph Ellison, Chester Himes, Willard Motley, and Ann Petry ("Richard Wright" 201). In the "fiction of the Twentieth Century in Black America," she adds, "we can mark or date everything before and after Richard Wright" (201). June Jordan agrees with this assessment, considering *Native Son* to be the "prototypical, Black, protest novel," inaugurating "many, many followers" (86–87). As Henry Louis Gates notes, "never had the brute force of racism's crushing impact upon a black consciousness been revealed before in fiction, certainly never with such starkness. . . . The effect was like nothing before in the history of American letters" (xii–xiii). Ellison saw Wright's early work as revealing the author's "attainment of a new sensibility" and *Native Son* in particular as promising to "carry over a whole tradition" that will result in the "merging" of Negro literature "into the broad stream of American literature," a movement promising eventual social change ("Recent" 17).

Wright's fiction declined in popularity at the end of the 1940s for a combination of reasons. During the Cold War era, "McCarthyist hysteria" and "racial complacency" (Kinnamon 127) made the leftist

---

politics of protest literature more risky to support (Butler, Introduction xxx). Writers who had taken up Wright's form of the protest novel, Petry being a shining example, moved away from this form for those and other reasons. Former friends Ellison and Baldwin produced scathing criticism of Wright's work, Ellison revising his earlier praise to consider Wright a "very limited 'protest writer' whose 'harsh naturalism' was outdated and artistically thin" (xxx). Contemporary critics now view such statements less as objective examinations of Wright's work and more as challenges to Wright's substantial "place in African-American letters" between the late 1940s and early 1960s (xxx).[1] Certainly, the work Wright produced after moving to Paris was less critically acclaimed, although whether that is because it was more existential than naturalist in philosophy or because critics actually did want to see him repeat what he had achieved in *Native Son* is anyone's guess. The fact that "after a long eclipse and a decade after his death," Wright became "the favored ancestor of a great many new black writers" who "feel much akin to his militant spirit" and "reject" writers such as Baldwin and Ellison demonstrates that at least some of the negative criticism of his post–*Native Son* writing was a matter of context and perspective (Dickstein 119). The various conferences that occurred all around the world in honor of the centennial of his birth in 2008 are testaments to the staying power of his body of work to the present day.

What led Wright to produce this novel and thus spark a literary tradition? Although he was a childhood writer of stories and poetry and a rebellious young man,[2] his biographers agree that it was his "voracious" reading that led him to "the mode of representation familiarly known as naturalism" (Gates xi). Naturalism is a turn-of-the-century mode of realism, practiced by authors such as Stephen Crane, Theodore Dreiser, and Sinclair Lewis, that focuses "scientifically" on the ways in which social forces determine and control the lives of impoverished and socially marginal characters.[3] Wright felt drawn to this kind of literature because it denaturalized racism and poverty and allowed him a liberating view of society. Reading Lewis's *Main Street*,

---

Critical Insights

Dreiser's *Sister Carrie*, and Crane's *Maggie*, Wright derived a clear sense of the "narrow limits" that regulated the thoughts and actions of those around him, including, as he notes in his autobiography, *Black Boy*, people such as his "boss" (Fabre, "Beyond Naturalism?" 40). He wrote a work of classic naturalist fiction, the novel *Lawd Today!*, in 1935,[4] but the novel was not published during his lifetime.[5] In his subsequent work, he would discard various aspects of naturalism, particularly those that encouraged a great psychic distance between readers and characters. To naturalism's focus on the documentary realism of setting and characters who stand in for particular types of people, then, Wright would add a coercive narrative style, one in which the narrative point of view is limited to a protagonist living through an excruciating, traumatic, and often violent phase of life, forcing readers to live it along with him (most of his protagonists were male). Wright would use those aspects of naturalism that helped him create an excruciating reading experience designed to further his literary goal: to move readers to the "acceptance of a new consciousness" about the effects of racial and economic discrimination (Fabre, "Beyond Naturalism?" 53). After Wright began to attend meetings of the Chicago chapter of the John Reed Club, a literary organization for young communists, and joined the Communist Party in 1933 (Dolinar 85), he gained a coherent vision, an "organized search for truth" that "intellectually stabilized him in a world that seemed to be falling apart" (Butler, *Native Son* 6). It extended and developed the vision of the world he had been given by various works of naturalist literature and allowed him to grasp the theoretical bases for that vision, one he would never lose despite severing ties with the Communist Party in the early 1940s.

Although he had published poetry and stories in leftist publications, Wright's literary career took off in the mid-1930s with the publication of his story "Big Boy Leaves Home" in *The New Caravan* in 1936, to some critical acclaim. He began to develop a literary reputation and to win awards, eventually becoming one of the first African American writers to support himself solely through his writing. A year after "Big Boy Leaves Home" was published, Wright moved to New York, continuing his work for the Writers' Project by transferring to the New York branch, and completed the stories that would appear in *Uncle Tom's Children* (1938). To Wright's dismay, *Uncle Tom's Children* made "daughters of bankers" cry with sympathy at the plight of its characters (Fabre, *Unfinished Quest* 183). Wright hoped to make his next novel, *Native Son*, a tool to "destroy all the accepted ideas" about race relations, an "ideological bomb" in case it was "his last chance to speak out" (183). He appears in this statement to be fully aware of the risks he tended to take in his fiction, and certainly, the phrase "ideological bomb" is a fitting description of the impact of *Native Son*. However, he was wrong about how people would react to that book. The novel's record-breaking sales amounted to more than 200,000 copies in under three weeks (Fabre, *Unfinished Quest* 180); "in its first printing, the novel was sold out within three hours of publication" (Butler, *Native Son* 13). There were, predictably, negative reviews. Writing for the *Atlantic Monthly* in May 1940, David Cohn infamously labeled the novel a "blinding and corrosive study in hate," suggesting as well that blacks' lives were not as desperate and limited as Wright portrayed them (Butler, *Native Son* 13–15). Lillian Johnson, an African American critic, wrote in the *Baltimore Afro-American* that Wright had written not "a book that will do anything constructive for his people as a race" but rather one that could "do a great deal of harm"; she wished "the book had one intelligent colored person in it," and she wondered why Bigger had "to desire the white girl, even though he did not like her" (qtd. in Rowley 192–93). These and many other negative reviews show a profound misunderstanding of Wright's protagonist Bigger Thomas and of the portrayal of the white characters. Both kinds of misunderstanding can be attributed, in some cases, to Wright's use of the third-person limited point of view, which forces readers to see the textual world only through Bigger's consciousness.

By the time these reviews were published, Wright had already decided that the third-person limited point of view was in fact too limiting.

As noted in a 1939 letter to Paul Reynolds, his literary agent, in *Native Son*, he "gave the picture of the world from the point of view of Bigger alone and the unreality of the white characters was part of the movement of the story, that is, they formed the motive for Bigger's acting towards them in such a strange way" (qtd. in Fabre, *Unfinished Quest* 188–89). He adds, "I felt, when I first started writing, a sort of personal need to do this, a need which I don't feel now" (189). Wright seems to suggest that the reader's forced identification with Bigger is in some way undesirable, so he justifies it as his "personal need." White characters, Wright goes on to indicate, are rendered less "real" in this limited point of view—because that is how Bigger sees them. His references to Bigger's "acting" in a "strange way" and to "feel[ing]" a "personal need" are suggestive here, and they lead us to one of our two critical lenses through which to interpret the novel. By deploying coercive narration and forcing readers to identify with someone who acts in a "strange way," and by tracing this deployment to a "personal need," Wright practically calls for a psychoanalytic reading of the novel, if not of himself.

Interestingly, in this letter, Wright describes his next novel, later entitled *Little Sister*, a study of a college-educated black woman who passes for white in order to accept a job. Wright intended this novel to be "a study of the feminine personality in general" (Fabre, *Unfinished Quest* 190). We might want to read his plan for this next novel, coming after *Native Son*, as an awareness that his female characters were inadequate, especially his African American female characters, and consider that he felt, perhaps, a "personal need" to work through them in a novel-length treatment. At any rate, the idea behind *Little Sister* seems a great departure from the idea behind *Native Son*, in which Bigger accidentally kills Mary, the daughter of his employer, and then rapes and kills his girlfriend, Bessie, simply to prove that he has, in fact, chosen to kill as a route to power in his limited society. Wright must have realized during the writing of this novel that Bessie's death could be repugnant to readers, as he debated this plot point with a close female friend;

during the argument, he apparently began to shout, "I have to get rid of her. She must die!" (Fabre, *Unfinished Quest* 171). Such stories have not endeared Wright to feminist readers of his work.

The following of *Native Son* with *Little Sister*[6] seems to call out for a feminist literary critical perspective, but in the first few decades after the publication of *Native Son*, reviews did not mention the portrayal of his female characters as a negative aspect of the book. Wright's colleague and close friend Margaret Walker penned an early feminist critique of the novel in her biography of Wright, asking, "Why this negative treatment of Bessie? Of Bigger's mother? and the half-sister Vera?" and "Why such violence and brutality" toward Mary and Bessie? (*Richard Wright* 147). Her questions are still among the most relevant questions asked about this novel, which is still read and taught all over the world. Barbara Christian has noted that in Wright's novels, "women are seldom seen except in the role of a slightly outlined mama or as a victim" (qtd. in Davis 68). Farah Jasmine Griffin has recounted that "for years" she struggled with her "discomfort over Wright's portrayal of women," but she continued to include *Native Son* on her syllabi because of her "conviction that the novel was significant as a literary and cultural text" (75). Griffin's response to the novel's treatment of women is a common one for critics concerned with gender issues, but the issue of Wright's female characters has not been the central focus of most criticism.[7]

Critics interested in the portrayal of women first began to respond to the issue in scholarly articles published in the 1970s and early 1980s, and what these early articles share, I would argue, is a judgment about Richard Wright the person and the writer. A number of these critics seem to believe that Wright was fundamentally an unsophisticated, emotional writer and thus look to his biography to explain his work, as if all of his work were directly autobiographical. Michel Fabre, Wright's biographer and one of his most prolific critics, provides the basis for such a reading when he states that "we ought to remember" that Wright is "an emotionally powerful creator who writes from his guts," not "primarily a thinker but a novelist, and therefore, that whatever may be characteristically naturalistic in his fiction is more likely to have resulted from his personal experience as a poor black American" ("Beyond Naturalism?" 40). For Fabre, the aspects of Wright's fiction that are the most realistic and authentic are simply transcriptions of his experience. This is a common argument in the criticism of minority and women writers, one of many ways to resist taking their work seriously (thus it is surprising that Fabre admits to this perspective, since he built a career on Wright's work). Fabre's ideas, shared by other reviewers and critics, created a common viewpoint that early feminist readings built upon. Sherley Anne Williams, for example, states matter-of-factly, "Wright seldom loved his black female characters and never liked them, nor could he imagine a constructive role for them in the black man's struggle for freedom" (396). Williams presumes a simplicity in Wright's work that allows us a window into his mental and emotional processes about it.

The "Wright as simple, emotional writer" thesis provides the basis for other reviews that nevertheless attempt to complicate the argument that Wright is a misogynist. The novel's "careless misogyny" can be traced back to its author, as Barbara Johnson does in her essay about *Native Son*, but not directly (Johnson 153). If, as some critics claimed, the misogynistic acts of the characters "are not fully repudiated by the novel" (Smethurst 35), we might fault Wright but look for an artistic or political reason for his choices. In agreement with a number of feminist critics of her era, Valerie Smith notes that Wright "is especially judgmental with regard to black women, since his plots tend to recapitulate the cultural association of women with domesticity and socialization" (*Self-Discovery* 69). In Smith's reading, Wright shares the views of his protagonists (all of whom have "parallel" experiences to those of "young Richard") about women, but these views derive from the damaging ideologies of racial oppression, ideologies that Smith would presumably understand Wright to be mostly critiquing ("Alienation" 446).

Those who do not buy the "emotional Wright" thesis refute both the view of Wright's female characters and the view of Wright's unsophisticated writing. Thus the portrayal of Bigger can be seen a "nuanced critique of patriarchy" (Higashida 397), especially compared to the misogyny of leftist and black nationalist politics of the time (Irr 196). This statement can seem like a rationalization, but it raises an important issue: to what extent do Wright's protagonists represent Wright's views about women, and to what extent are the protagonists' views being held up to be examined? A number of critics have picked up on this issue in *Native Son* and commented on those who "mistakenly conflate the sexism of . . . Bigger with Wright's own stance" (Dawahare 12). Paul Gilroy censures critics who conflate "the brute machismo and uncomplicated misogyny" of the novel with Wright's "own attitudes and responses" (Introduction xiv). He questions those who dismiss Wright as "the purveyor of a crude, protest-oriented fiction that not only refuses to validate the dynamic, vital qualities of black culture but denies artistic and political legitimacy to the affirmative literary enterprises which are . . . endowed with feminine qualities," citing Zora Neale Hurston's work as one example of an "affirmative literary enterprise" (*Black Atlantic* 176–77). This argument is a more theoretically substantial and convincing one; it resists having to erase or defend Bigger's misogyny but clearly separates it from both Wright the person and Wright the artist. These critics have the benefit of writing more recently; we must acknowledge the fact that the feminist critics who responded so strongly to Wright's female characters in the 1970s and 1980s were not substantially different in their approach from other literary critics of the period and from those preceding them, and various schools of literary criticism at that time encouraged easy conflations of biography and text. Further, the feminist critics of the 1970s and 1980s were doing the valuable work of identifying an aspect of Wright's work that had been apparently invisible to critics and reviewers alike at the time of publication and in the three decades following.

Why did it take so long for a feminist perspective on this novel to become part of the critical literature? Perhaps because formal feminist literary criticism did not really begin, according to some critics, until the mid-1960s, when more women were hired to fill academic positions and could finally create a published reaction to the male-dominated world of literary studies. As "literature is one of the privileged sites for the congealing of notions" of gender and also the "site of their perpetual disturbance" (Weed 263), early feminist literary critics had plenty of work to do just to pick out literary constructions of gender roles and female characters' modes of acceptance of or resistance to them in texts by male writers, constructions that had often received little notice in published criticism until that point. They were also, of course, engaged in bringing to critical attention overlooked texts by women writers. However, as Deborah McDowell notes, early "practitioners" of feminist literary criticism were "largely white females who, wittingly or not, perpetrated against the Black woman writer the same exclusive practices they so vehemently decried in white male scholars" (153). For this reason, black feminist criticism, emerging in its current form in the late 1960s and early 1970s, had even more corrective work to do.[8] Through the 1980s and 1990s, feminist criticism continued to develop a "complex and diverse set of discourses" that intervened in cultural constructions of not only gender but also race, class, sexuality, and ability (Plain and Sellers 102).

One example of a discourse incorporated by feminist literary criticism was psychoanalysis. Psychoanalysis lends itself well to literary criticism because its methodology appears to mirror that of the literary critic, who, like a psychoanalyst, must work to construct an interpretation of a text's meaning, knowing that it is always partial and contingent. As Sigmund Freud himself knew, "there is no unconscious to be discovered, only the unconscious effects seen in dreams and jokes . . . and symptoms," and furthermore, "even these effects can never be apprehended directly" (Weed 263). Since the unconscious of a person or text cannot be directly apprehended, it is the role of the interpreter to look at pieces of the text where meaning might make itself visible.

Psychoanalytic criticism does not lend itself quite so easily to literary criticism focused on gender, race, class, and other socially constructed aspects of identity, however, because these critics always examine the textual individual in the context of normative social forces depicted in the text. On the other hand, classic psychoanalysis looks to the individual, to that person's family relationships, and to regulatory reactions to those relationships in its analysis of the patient's "issues." Mary Helen Washington represents the views of many when she states, "The psychoanalytic mode leads only to the individualistic self" (167). Put another way, early formulations of psychoanalysis "at once universalize[d] and transhistoricize[d] such phenomena as the Oedipus complex, the castration complex, repression, and the contents of the unconscious" (Forter and Miller 4), which suggests that one's particular sociopolitical status and constellation of group identities were irrelevant to one's psychological issues. The consequences of such beliefs are serious. As Jane Gallop argues, the "worst tendency, the inherent constitutional weakness of psychoanalysis, is to be apolitical (which is to say, to support the institutions in power)" (qtd. in Tuhkanen xvii); other critics have viewed psychoanalysis as "an inherently colonial project, a form of 'empire-building'—what [Gilles] Deleuze and [Félix] Guattari in *Anti-Oedipus* call 'the analytic imperialism of the Oedipus complex'" (Tuhkanen xvii). Left in its original formation, psychoanalysis is potentially colonizing whether as a clinical practice or as a literary critical tool; Freud's early accounts of his intrusive and damaging treatment of women diagnosed with hysteria (particularly Frau Emmy Von N) provide ample evidence of this.[9]

Nevertheless, African American writers and intellectuals grew interested in psychoanalytic concepts as early as the turn of the century[10] and became "obsessed" with Freud's theories in the 1920s, believing that "the new science could further the cause of racial inclusion" (Ahad 2). Because the "denial of full rights of citizenship was indelibly linked to the denial of black humanity, and more specifically, black interiority"—which we find stated most clearly in Thomas Jefferson's *Notes on the State of Virginia* (1785)—psychoanalysis could "create a productive space for the expression of black interiority" (Ahad 3, 5–6). It is in fact psychoanalysis's reliance on universalized constructions of normative subjectivity, and its idea that "abnormal" states of mind could be traced back to childhood events (and thus not to inferior biology) and cured through therapy, that made African Americans so interested in psychoanalysis as both a therapy and an analytic tool.

Although his most direct engagement with psychoanalysis seems to have occurred after *Native Son*'s publication, Wright was an avid reader of Freud and extremely interested in the "psychology of anger" (Rampersad 141; Tuhkanen xii). His interest was well timed, because during the late 1930s and 1940s, "social psychiatry" was on the rise, eventually diverging from "classic" psychoanalysis. Practitioners of social psychiatry worked to link "one's social environment" to one's "psychological state," the goal being to "lessen emotional suffering" through social analysis and thus social change (Ahad 83). Wright was interested in this activist version of psychoanalysis, and he worked very closely with psychiatrists Benjamin Karpman and Fredric Wertham in the 1940s to facilitate a connection between minority communities and psychoanalytic therapies that might revolutionize both entities. While his relationship with Karpman disintegrated after a couple of years, Wright and Ellison later collaborated with Wertham to establish a mental health clinic in Harlem.

This clinic was not entirely successful, partly because the issues faced by Harlem residents overwhelmed its resources but perhaps also because its doctors were to some extent working at cross-purposes with African American patrons Wright and Ellison (and perhaps with their own clients). Ellison and Wright hoped that psychoanalysis could "contextualize black folks within the project of modernity," showing that they were "integral to the formation" of the modern world "rather than antithetical to it" (Ahad 100). As Ellison notes in "Harlem Is Nowhere," the Lafargue Clinic had such potential. Its therapists were willing to "dispense with preconceived notions" and "accept the realities of

Negro" life in order to give the client "insight into the relation between his problems and his environment"; the therapist assured the client that his "personality damage" is not intrinsic but extrinsic, the result of a "denial of support through segregation and discrimination" (301–2). The clinic thus reframed psychoanalysis to allow for neurosis as an "ethically justifiable response to systematic forms of oppression," the indirect result of resistance to the white supremacist order (Ahad 95, 103). Ellison directs his analytical gaze not just at the psychological impact of oppression but also at the psychological impact of a universalized form of psychiatry. We see this meaning lurking in the phrase "preconceived notions," which may be both racial and psychoanalytic. We also see it here in his statement about why African American mental health issues have been ignored, if we substitute "psychoanalyst" for "whites": whites "impose interpretations upon Negro experience that are not only false" but also "a denial of Negro humanity" (301). Ellison's rhetoric here provides a critique of the pathologizing of blacks both in mainstream society and in psychoanalysis. Ultimately, though, it would seem that this rhetoric could not counteract the force of mainstream psychoanalysis, even upon the doctors at the Lafargue Clinic. Wertham himself may have contributed to the mainstream pathologizing of minority subjects as he attempted to achieve his professional goal, which was to "counteract the threat of [black] violence," by theoretically connecting violence, blackness, and sexual deviance (Ahad 107).[11] Lacking any examination of social factors, Wertham's research would only reinforce the dominant view of someone like Bigger.

Wertham did, however, collaborate with Wright in what may have been the first "psychoanalytic study of a literary creation"—Bigger Thomas—"based on analytic study of its author" (Ahad 92). The psychoanalytic examination of literary texts derived from analysis of the author (usually through biographical materials) has continued to be the practice of critics, especially in studies of minority and women authors, Wright in particular. Maria Mootry, for example, argues that "Wright's heroes" are "narcissistic," valuing the "company of men above all" and defining "themselves in opposition to women, either by using them" or "by perceiving themselves as being used by them" (118). She claims through analysis of *Black Boy* that "Wright himself indulged in this primary narcissism, although his self-centeredness reached a more subtle level" (119). As a way to understand Wright's treatment of his black female characters, Miriam DeCosta-Willis places passages from *Black Boy* alongside Wright's literary texts, reading those from *Black Boy* through a psychoanalytic lens in order to support a psychoanalytic reading of the literary works. She concludes that "Wright's view of the mother as an ambivalent object of desire and fear" was shaped "exclusively by his traumatic experiences with the women of his family" (DeCosta-Willis 551). Such criticism performs a misguided psychological reading that conflates Wright's fictional and autobiographical texts and assumes both to reflect Wright's authentic self.

They also, however, tend to use psychoanalytic tools uncritically. As Claudia Tate notes, practitioners of cultural studies must "further develop psychoanalytic theory" by "destabilizing its hegemonic analytical models in order to make them instructive methodologies for examining minority as well as majority cultural discourses" (236). In part, this is necessary because most African American novels are engaged in promoting what Hortense Spillers calls a "sociopolitical engagement of the utmost importance": the "*process* of self-reflection" (400). These novelists in particular ask "black readers to project the neurosis and psychosis of racism outside of themselves" (Tate 18–19)—onto characters who are clearly made neurotic by the racist institutions surrounding them. Without critically engaging psychoanalytic theory, we allow it to function as "a master discourse" that simply will not allow for such therapeutic reading strategies (Tuhkanen xxii). If, as philosopher Michel Foucault claimed, what the Lacanian revision of Freudian concepts achieved was "a theory of the subject" (Forter and Miller 7–8), then further revision of psychoanalyst Jacques Lacan's theories is necessary in order to fit this theory to the minority subject. W. E. B. Du Bois revised William James's and other classic psychoanalytic constructions of the split self in his version of double consciousness, deliberately adding racism as the cause of the "doubled" consciousness as well as making this state an ongoing one that could, in fact, prove to have beneficial effects. In a similar fashion, Wright revises Freudian psychoanalysis, "ceaselessly repurposing" aspects of psychoanalysis so that they applied to African American experiences in the modern world (Stringer 106).

I want to suggest ways in which the tools of psychoanalysis could be combined with those of feminist literary criticism in order to examine some of the most problematic aspects of *Native Son*. These include Bigger's violent treatment of his friend Gus, murder of Mary and claim that he had "metaphorically raped" her, and subsequent rape and murder of Bessie; the novel's treatment of white characters, particularly Mary, Jan, the Daltons, and Max; the extent to which Max's speech represents Wright's communist-inspired views of Bigger's life; Bigger's level of intelligence and consciousness as a character; and, finally, the disturbing concluding conversation between Max and Bigger. Psychoanalytic and feminist readings give us ways to understand what seems inexplicable in the novel and thus change our views of Wright's project in this novel and the extent to which it was successful.

It is important first to note that in a classic iteration of psychoanalysis, the psychoanalyst is working to elicit memories of a traumatic event that has been repressed and that has been producing varieties of nonnormative behavior in the analysand (the person being analyzed). Trauma theory presumes that because the trauma was too disturbing to be understood fully, it is "simultaneously experienced and not experienced," which means that the "psychic life of the traumatized individual is infected by belatedness" (Elmer 768; see also Caruth). The trauma victim frequently reenacts versions of the original trauma without any intent to do so, repetitions that function as that individual's "possession" by "a sort of fate" (Caruth 2). In *Native Son*, I would suggest, the original trauma is lynching, and Bigger's "fate" is to repeat the crime (sexual contact with a white woman) that would have been seen by whites as the cause of a lynching. No lynching takes place in the novel, yet it seems quite likely that Bigger is struggling with the overwhelming trauma of such events, as his own father is said to have been killed "in a riot," presumably by whites (Wright, *Native Son* 515). Bigger is well aware that he is not in control of his own actions on a number of occasions in the novel: "He hated himself at that moment. Why was he acting and feeling this way?" (489).

Readers ask the same questions about many of Bigger's actions, and psychoanalytic readings have the most potential to answer them. Furthermore, feminist readings have the potential to answer questions that Bigger does not think to ask himself, such as those concerning his treatment of Bessie. He may not consider interactions with his mother, sister, and Bessie to be important because his interactions with whites are far more "strange" to him (and possibly to readers). We see signs of this strangeness early in the text. In what we can read as a glimpse of his repressed trauma, Bigger tells Gus that the white folks live "in my stomach" so that he can "hardly breathe," as if "somebody's poking a red-hot iron down my throat" (Wright, *Native Son* 463). Bigger is trying to indicate that he has internalized whites' violent gaze, which then interferes with his ability to breathe and speak naturally. Yet his figurative description suggests as well a metaphoric rape by whites, one taking the form of oral penetration and impregnation. In the psychoanalytic understanding of repression, a repressed memory of trauma is stored in an inaccessible part of the psyche and periodically leaks into the conscious mind in the form of reactions that can take the form of hyperventilation, fainting, and other losses of physical control. The word "hysterical" is used a number of times in reference to Bigger, but it is a psychoanalytic term that refers originally to the disorders of women patients and was made popular in accounts of Freud's work (Weed 263).

As an alternative to the powerlessness that a "hysteric" experiences in moments when traces of the trauma leak into the psyche, Bigger "repeats" the traumatic invasion by inflicting it on those closest to him,

Gus and Bessie. When Bigger attempts to blame Gus for ruining their chances of robbing a deli, Gus sees through Bigger's projection and "reads" him in front of the gang. Bigger is humiliated and lashes out at Gus, eventually forcing Gus to lick the blade of his knife and using the knife to trace a circle around Gus's "belly button," which he threatens to "cut . . . out" (Wright, *Native Son* 481). When this tense moment is over, Bigger is momentarily paralyzed and confused, suggesting that he was "possessed" by some force he does not understand. As Marlon Ross notes, work by African American feminists demonstrates that historically, rape signifies not only "men's domination over women" but also a less gender-specific domination of African Americans through "sexualized violence from the period of slavery forward" (306). One could argue that Bigger has been indirectly traumatized by this sexualized violence (through the ever-present threat of lynching), something that not only makes him a rape victim but also makes him act as a rapist toward his friend Gus, who has just emasculated him.[12]

A version of Ross's redefinition of the term "rape" is later explicitly used by Bigger, when he decides to claim that he had, in fact, raped Mary. This can be confusing to readers, who typically see the contact between Bigger and a drunken Mary to be sexual in nature but not involving sexual penetration. What Bigger means, however, is that "rape was not what one did to women" but instead a feeling he experiences when he feels "as he had felt that night"—as if his life were being threatened by "the pack," meaning whites (Wright, *Native Son* 658). "Rape," then, refers not only to actual physical penetration but also to the emasculating penetration of the white gaze, which carries with it the threat of (sexualized) violence. Bigger certainly experiences the feeling of being penetrated and "contaminated" by Mary and her boyfriend, Jan, at various moments during their evening together.

As Ross notes, however, once rape begins to operate "in the discourse on race and gender" as both a "sign of the materiality of racial torture" and a "sign of the psychology of racial torture," the actual rape of black women comes to seem "exceptional" or nonexistent (307).

Bigger's view of Bessie replicates the rape-like penetration he has experienced from whites and that he repeats in his attack on Gus. He splits her into two Bessies, a body and a face, and he states that he would like to "blot out, kill, sweep away the Bessie on Bessie's face and leave the other helpless and yielding before him"; he would then place Bessie's body "in his chest, his stomach, some place deep inside him, always keeping her there . . . to have and hold" (Wright, *Native Son* 575). Specifically, he would like to silence Bessie, to use her "yielding" body as he chooses, and finally to internalize her in his stomach, the same place where whites live, the same area he wanted to cut open on Gus's body. When he decides he must kill Bessie because she might be "a dangerous burden" to him in his flight (577), he actually does use her body for his own sexual release, silences her by beating her head in with a brick, and then throws her body down an airshaft. By the time of his trial for Mary's murder, he has "forgotten" (repressed) her (882).

In the term "rape," then, we see references to physical attacks against women as well as to physical and psychological attacks against men, Bigger included. The fact that Bigger has been traumatized by the threat of lynching prior to the action of the text should be understood as not only a trauma that he has repressed but also a stereotype whose damaging presence he feels in a partly conscious way. The "rapist" stereotype that he claims when he decides that he did rape Mary functions as a form of trauma itself, as Jonathan Elmer notes:

> The double power of the stereotype to function as both cause and result of the subject's repetitions is the very subject of Wright's novel and the reason for his vexed place in literary history. . . . While many will say Bigger never is realized as a "living personality," perhaps this is because the aim of the novel is to present him as never having been one, but instead an individual perennially mortifying himself, or being mortified, into the crudest of symbols. (775–76)

Elmer here manages to defend Wright's project as far more conscious and complicated than critics such as Fabre would have us believe, and he also explains Bigger's problematic character (including his relations with and views of the women in his life) in such a way as to weaken substantially, in my opinion, the charges that the novel is misogynist. (Whether Wright himself was a misogynist is another matter entirely, and the relation of that issue to the novel is not only quite fraught but also outside the scope of literary criticism, it seems to me.)

A psychoanalytic perspective developed by Mikko Tuhkanen allows us to understand what motivates Bigger's interactions with white characters, particularly Mary, Jan, and Max. Tuhkanen presents Wright's coercive narration as not simply a narrative choice but an argument, one suggesting that "an acute appreciation of looking relations and of the way in which the subject is posited within visibility is critical to understanding the structures of subjection peculiar to African Americans" (xxii). Wright's form of narration highlights, in this view, the fact that racial violence is deeply connected to the visual perception of the embodied subject. In a world in which whites are considered racially "unmarked," and white men are the "ideal model of bodily abstraction," the "racially marked subject" is "coercively enveloped and immobilized within visibility, within a fixed perspective" (4). Not only does Bigger believe whites "live" in his "stomach," he also frequently thinks they are "looking inside of him" (Wright, *Native Son* 17). During such moments, he becomes paralyzed, or "fixed." His hysterical reaction to the entrance of Mrs. Dalton into Mary's bedroom, too, represents his fear that this blind woman might see him, that unless Mary is silenced, he will be "seen" as Mary's rapist and locked into the deadly fate that he has been trying to avoid.

However, when Bigger has successfully escaped from the scene of the crime "unseen," he realizes that white people are in fact unable to see him at all. Looking back at Jan and Mary's interactions with Bigger, we know Bigger is correct in his perception of their blindness. To Mary and Jan, Bigger is a symbol of a "people," to use Mary's term, one whom they need to "know" better in order to "liberate" (or enroll in their plans for class-based revolution). They interpret his angry paralysis before their eager gazes as timidity, so they press ever closer to him, penetrating ever deeper into his world, "unable to see that their interventions only reiterate the very conditions of Bigger's subordination" (Tuhkanan 19). Those investigating Mary's death also see Bigger as a timid, unintelligent servant, a stereotype from the era of slavery. Bigger exploits this form of "structural blindness" in whites to avoid being accused of Mary's murder (20). Even Max, Bigger's lawyer, fails to see him as an individual, misinterpreting Bigger in his closing argument at the trial. In that argument, Bigger represents a certain demographic—"every [male] Negro in America"—symbolizing the victim of racist violence (24). While Bigger does not fully understand (or even listen to) Max's argument, he seems to realize that Max has failed to see the meaning of his murderous actions, and in their last conversation, he attempts to break through Max's blindness to communicate this meaning: "What I killed for must have been good! . . . I didn't know I was really alive in this world until I felt things hard enough to kill for" (Wright, *Native Son* 849). The murders, Bigger argues, represent what he "wanted" and who he is. Max's terrified reaction to this statement is another clear symptom of his failure to understand Bigger on his own terms.

It would thus seem that only with the interpretive tools of feminist literary criticism and psychoanalysis (revised to include social forces as causes of psychic damage and as determining the nature of resistance to that damage) do particular explanations of this novel become visible. Whether Wright's novel was successful in exploding the racial consciousness of his 1940s readership is up for debate. I would suggest, though, that using more sophisticated approaches unavailable in that era, we can understand the complexity of Wright's project and appreciate the way in which coercive narration both illuminates and hides the meaning of Bigger Thomas's short life as well as the lives of the women he could not finally see.

Notes

1. Henry Louis Gates goes so far as to credit Wright with the successes of Baldwin and Ellison: Wright was responsible for the "shaping of a literary modernism" by inspiring Ellison and Baldwin toward their own experimental works, purely as a reaction to his protest fiction (Gates xiii).

2. As Valerie Smith notes, in *Black Boy*, Wright "describes ways in which the black family, operating as an agent of the majority white culture, suppresses all signs of individuality and power in its youth in order to fit them for their subordinate position in the Jim Crow system. Willful, perceptive, and creative, young Richard refuses to internalize the restrictions of either his black or his white oppressors" (66).

3. It is more helpful to consider a naturalist writer's "scientific" approach to a text as a dedication to authentic, documentary-style exactness in the details of setting and conflict rather than as an "objective" consideration of how setting affects character.

4. Originally entitled *Cesspool*, this novel follows postal worker Jake Jackson in a highly detailed fashion through one dismal day in Depression-era Chicago, beginning and ending with Jake's violence toward his wife and his (physical and political) unconsciousness.

5. Rampersad claims that this was because the Depression-era publishing industry was hesitant to commit to first novels as well as to experimental material, and Wright's novel certainly took risks, including innovative punctuation, capitalization, and usage as well as sexual content (17).

6. A long draft of this novel was written, but it was never finished or published.

7. Robert Stepto certainly does not defend Wright's treatment of his female characters, but he manages to credit Wright with the "recent fiction" of "black women authors" such as Petry, Toni Morrison, and Alice Walker, who wrote, he claims, to "revise and redeem" Mrs. Thomas and Bessie (208). He suggests that the rise of "a feminine and sometimes feminist voice in contemporary Afro-American fiction may be directly related to the narrow and confining portraits of black women in earlier modern fiction, including that of Wright" (209).

8. African American women (including black women authors) had been writing about black women's literature long before the current body of critical knowledge was developed (Keizer 154).

9. In particular, I am thinking of his "erasure" of Frau Emmy's memories and the resulting damage to her sense of self as he worked to remove the sources of her anxiety (rather than work with her to manage them).

10. Pauline Hopkins's novel *Of One Blood; or, The Hidden Self* (1903) deploys the concept of the unconscious, and W. E. B. Du Bois's *The Souls of Black Folk* (1903) adapts the psychoanalytic term "double consciousness" to refer to a kind of racial trauma.

11. Wertham's work was socially productive in other ways; his study of children at the Lafargue Clinic proved that segregation "created a massive public health problem" and "an unsolvable conflict" in the minds of children, and it also

established the idea of internalized racism, which refutes "popular and long-standing scientific" claims of "black inferiority" (Ahad 170 n25).

12. Ross goes on to discuss the fact that "just as black women are displaced by black men as the proper victims of race rape, so the taboo threat of male-male penetration is displaced by the proper, less palpable, less disturbing threat of 'emasculation,'" in other words, repressing "same-sexuality" and the very real castrations of black men during lynchings (316).

Works Cited

Ahad, Badia Sahar. *Freud Upside Down: African American Literature and Psychoanalytic Culture*. Chicago: U of Illinois P, 2010. Print.

Butler, Robert. Introduction. *The Critical Response to Richard Wright*. Ed. Butler. Westport: Greenwood, 1995. xxv–xxxix. Print.

___. *Native Son: The Emergence of a New Black Hero*. Boston: Twayne, 1991. Print.

Cappetti, Carla. "Sociology of an Existence: Richard Wright and the Chicago School." *The Critical Response to Richard Wright*. Ed. Robert Butler. Westport: Greenwood, 1995. 81–93. Print.

Caruth, Cathy. *Unclaimed Experience: Trauma, Narrative, and History*. Baltimore: Johns Hopkins UP, 1996. Print.

Davis, Jane. "More Force than Human: Richard Wright's Female Characters." *Obsidian* 1.3 (1986): 68–83. Print.

DeCosta-Willis, Miriam. "Avenging Angels and Mute Mothers: Black Southern Women in Wright's Fictional World." *Callaloo* 28 (1986): 540–51. Print.

Dickstein, Morris. "Wright, Baldwin, Cleaver." *New Letters* 38.2 (1971): 117. Print.

Dolinar, Brian. "The Illinois Writers' Project Essays: Introduction." *Southern Quarterly* 46.2 (2009): 84–89. Print.

Du Bois, W. E. B. *The Souls of Black Folk*. New York: Penguin, 1982. Print.

Ellison, Ralph. "Harlem Is Nowhere." *Shadow and Act*. New York: Vintage, 1964. 294–301. Print.

___. "Recent American Negro Fiction." Rev. of *Native Son*, by Richard Wright. *New Masses* 11.6 (1941): 22–26. Rpt. in Gates and Appiah 11–18.

Elmer, Jonathan. "Spectacle and Event in *Native Son*." *American Literature* 70.4 (1998): 767–98. Print.

Fabre, Michel. "Beyond Naturalism?" *Richard Wright*. Ed. Harold Bloom. New York: Chelsea, 1988. Print.

___. *The Unfinished Quest of Richard Wright*. Chicago: U of Illinois P, 1993. Print.

Fadiman, Clifton. Rev. of *Native Son*, by Richard Wright. *New Yorker* 2 Mar. 1940: n. pag. Rpt. in Gates and Appiah 6–8.

Forter, Greg, and Paul Allen Miller, eds. *Desire of the Analysts: Psychoanalysis and Cultural Criticism*. Albany: SUNY P, 2008. Print.

Gates, Henry Louis, Jr., and Kwame Anthony Appiah, eds. *Richard Wright: Critical Perspectives, Past and Present*. New York: Amistad, 1993. Print.

Gilroy, Paul. *The Black Atlantic: Modernity and Double Consciousness*. Cambridge: Harvard UP, 1992. Print.

___. Introduction. *Eight Men*. By Richard Wright. New York: HarperPerennial, 1996. xi–xxi. Print.

Griffin, Farah Jasmine. "On Women, Teaching, and Native Son." *Approaches to Teaching Wright's* Native Son. Ed. James A. Miller. New York: MLA, 1997. 75–80. Print.

Higashida, Cheryl. "Aunt Sue's Children: Re-viewing the Gender(ed) Politics of Richard Wright's Radicalism." *American Literature* 75.2 (2003): 395–425. Print.

Irr, Caren. "The Politics of Spatial Phobias in *Native Son*." *Critical Essays on Richard Wright's* Native Son. Ed. Keneth Kinnamon. New York: Hall, 1997. 196–212. Print.

Johnson, Barbara. "The Re(a)d and the Black." Gates and Appiah 149–55.

Jordan, June. *Civil Wars*. Boston: Beacon, 1974. Print.

Keizer, Arlene. "Black Feminist Criticism." Plain and Sellers 154–68.

Kinnamon, Keneth. "How *Native Son* Was Born." Gates and Appiah 110–31.

McDowell, Deborah. "New Directions for Black Feminist Criticism." *Black American Literature Forum* 14.4 (1980): 153–59. Print.

Mootry, Maria K. "Bitches, Whores, and Woman Haters: Archetypes and Typologies in the Art of Richard Wright." *Richard Wright: A Collection of Critical Essays*. Ed. Richard Macksey. Englewood Cliffs: Prentice-Hall, 1984. Print.

Plain, Gill, and Susan Sellers, eds. *A History of Feminist Literary Criticism*. New York: Cambridge UP, 2009. Print.

Rampersad, Arnold. "Too Honest for His Own Time." *New York Times Review of Books* 29 Dec. 1991: 3+. Print.

Ross, Marlon B. "Race, Rape, Castration: Feminist Theories of Sexual Violence and Masculine Strategies of Black Protest." *Masculinity Studies and Feminist Theory: New Directions*. Ed. Judith Kegan Gardiner. New York: Columbia UP, 2002. 305–43. Print.

Rowley, Hazel. *Richard Wright: The Life and Times*. New York: Holt, 2001. 191–94. Print.

Smethurst, James. "Invented by Horror: The Gothic and African American Literary Ideology in *Native Son*." *African American Review* 35.1 (2001): 29–40. Print.

Smith, Valerie. "Alienation and Creativity in the Fiction of Richard Wright." Gates and Appiah 433–48.

___. *Self-Discovery and Authority in Afro-American Narrative*. Cambridge: Harvard UP, 1987. Print.

Spillers, Hortense. "'All the Things You Could Be by Now, If Sigmund Freud's Wife Was Your Mother': Psychoanalysis and Race." *Black, White, and in Color: Essays on American Literature and Culture*. Chicago: U of Chicago P, 2003. 376–428. Print.

Stepto, Robert. "'I Thought I Knew These People': Richard Wright and the Afro-American Tradition." *Chant of Saints: A Gathering of Afro-American Literature, Art, and Scholarship*. Ed. Stepto and Michael S. Harper. Urbana: U of Illinois P, 1979. 195–211. Print.

Stringer, Dorothy. "Psychology and Black Liberation in Richard Wright's *Black Power* (1954)." *Journal of Modern Literature* 32.4 (2009): 105–24. Print.

Tate, Claudia. *Psychoanalysis and Black Novels: Desire and the Protocols of Race.* Oxford: Oxford UP, 1998. Print.

Tuhkanen, Mikko. *The American Optic: Psychoanalysis, Critical Race Theory, and Richard Wright.* Albany: SUNY P, 2009. Print.

Walker Alexander, Margaret. "Richard Wright." *New Letters* 38.2 (1971): 182–202. Print.

___. *Richard Wright: Daemonic Genius.* New York: Warner, 1988. Print.

Washington, Mary Helen. "Barbara Johnson, African Americanist: The Critic as Insider/Outsider." *Differences* 17.3 (2006): 167–76. Print.

Weed, Elizabeth. "Feminist Psychoanalytic Literary Criticism." *The Cambridge Companion to Feminist Literary Theory.* Ed. Ellen Rooney. New York: Cambridge UP, 2006. 261–82. Print.

Williams, Sherley Anne. "Papa Dick and Sister-Woman: Reflections on Women in the Fiction of Richard Wright." *American Novelists Revisited: Essays in Feminist Criticism.* Ed. Fritz Fleischmann. Boston: Hall, 1982. 394–415. Print.

Wright, Richard. "How 'Bigger' Was Born." *Richard Wright: Early Works.* Ed. Arnold Rampersad. New York: Lib. of Amer., 1991. 851–82. Print.

___. *Native Son. Richard Wright: Early Works.* Ed. Arnold Rampersad. New York: Lib. of Amer., 1991. 443–850. Print.

CRITICAL READINGS

Radical and Nationalist Resistance in David Walker's and Frederick Douglass's Antislavery Narratives____

Babacar M'Baye

Introduction

Both David Walker and Frederick Douglass were revolutionary abolitionists who made tremendous contributions to the African American struggle for freedom, equality, and justice in the United States. As a forerunner of Douglass, Walker initiated radical forms of protest against oppression that resonated with those of his successor. In spite of the particular times and places out of which their lives and works evolved, Walker and Douglass shared a radical resistance against bondage and a staunch critique of the inhumane ways in which African Americans were treated during slavery. Walker had a strong influence on Douglass's antislavery resistance. This influence is apparent in Douglass's emphasis on the slaves' right to gain freedom and equality by rising against their masters, which is an idea that Walker had already stressed in his writings.

Focusing on *Walker's Appeal, in Four Articles; Together with a Preamble to the Coloured Citizens of the World, but in Particular, and Very Expressly, to Those of the United States of America* (1829) and Douglass's *Narrative of the Life of Frederick Douglass, An American Slave, Written by Himself* (1845), this chapter will examine Walker's and Douglass's similar radical protests against the racist subjugation of American blacks during slavery. As this chapter shows, Walker and Douglass were pioneers of a radical tradition that fiercely resisted the disenfranchisement of blacks in the United States in the nineteenth century. Yet Walker's *Appeal* is unique in this radical tradition, since, unlike Douglass's *Narrative*, it calls for slave uprisings. Moreover, unlike Walker, who directly represents slave owners as tyrants, Douglass lets his narrative speak for him by revealing the tyranny through the horrible actions of individual planters against slaves. However,

Douglass's representation of slavery is no less radical and nationalist than Walker's, since it also emphasizes the cruelty of bondage in order to create public disgust and solidarity against slave owners.

Defining Black Radicalism

"Black radicalism" refers to the subversive, unyielding, subaltern, and selfless ways in which various black communities from around the world resist oppression by representing themselves as a part of the world population that has been dispossessed, objectified, and demonized through bondage, imperialism, colonialism, and other forces of Western capitalism. Representing black radicalism as the complex African "negation of Western civilization," Cedric J. Robinson argues, "It is a specifically African response to an oppression emergent from the immediate determinants of European development in the modern era and framed by orders of human exploitation woven into the interstices of European social life from the inception of Western civilization" (73).

A crucial part of black radicalism is black nationalism, which is the solidarity that black populations whose ancestors were both enslaved and colonized by Europeans developed in order to resist such tyranny. Thus, black nationalism is a broad concept that includes many things. Tommie Shelby explains:

> Black nationalism, as an ideology or philosophy, is one of the oldest and most enduring traditions in American political thought. Black nationalists advocate such things as black self-determination, racial solidarity and group self-reliance, various forms of voluntary racial separation, pride in the historic achievements of those of African descent, a concerted effort to overcome racial self-hate and to instill black self-love, militant resistance to antiblack racism, the development and preservation of a distinctive black ethnocultural identity, and the recognition of Africa as the true homeland of those who are racially black. (665)

In this sense, black nationalism is a multifaceted movement that deserves more critical attention than it has so far received. Even if this movement has been the subject of numerous books, it remains misunderstood since people mainly associate it with the African American resistances against racism during the 1960s and 1970s, neglecting its roots in the black radicalism that both Walker and Douglass reflect in their antislavery resistances and protests.

Walker's *Appeal*

Walker's *Appeal* is the work of an African American revolutionary whose life was a perpetual quest for knowledge of and freedom from slavery. Although Walker was born in Wilmington, North Carolina, the exact date of his birth is unknown; current research suggests that it occurred in either 1796 or 1797 (Hickey 569). It is certain that Walker's father was a slave who died before his child's birth and that his mother was a free woman. As Sean Wilentz points out, "under the laws of slavery, he [Walker] was born free" since his mother was not a slave (viii). As he was born free, Walker traveled across the South with his mother and developed an early awareness of the horrors of slavery. Walker's early familiarity with the terrors of slavery also stemmed from the fact that he lived in Charleston, South Carolina, from around 1815 to 1820, where a literate and organized black community read about such matters in abolitionist papers and tracts, publications that southern legislators disliked.

Walker's familiarity with slavery strengthened his literacy. He had been able "to read and write at an early age" (Ready 84), and such precocious literacy inspired him to travel north in an attempt to become more aware of the plight of blacks in the United States. Sometime in the 1820s, Walker moved to Boston, where his reading and writing skills and knowledge of slavery allowed him to observe and understand the condition of blacks living in the northern part of the United States. Yet Walker might have had other reasons for relocating to the North, because on February 23, 1826, he married Eliza Butler, who, as

Rufus Burrow Jr. argues, could have been a slave woman with whom he fell in love before he moved to Boston (20).

Like Charleston, Boston was a city where an increasingly literate and worldly black community existed in the early nineteenth century, giving Walker the opportunity to widen his knowledge of racial injustices and live, however humbly, in a city known for its revolutionary past. Walker's connections with Boston are discussed in the book *The Struggle for Freedom: A History of African Americans* (2007), in which Clayborne Carson, Emma J. Lapsansky-Werner, and Gary B. Nash write that in Boston, "Walker became a used clothing dealer, a worshiper at the black Methodist church, and an agent for the country's first black newspaper, *Freedom's Journal*" (167). Walker's radicalism began 1827 when, as Sterling Stuckey recounts in a 1975 study of black nationalism, Walker and a small group of other "people of colour" gathered "under his roof" to promote a publication entitled *Freedom's Journal*, which aimed to denounce slavery and racism ("David Walker" 25). According to Stuckey, the gathering was "a sign that they [Walker and his group] were aware of the seriousness of the problems facing people of African ancestry; for that paper, from its inception, had made clear its opposition to slavery and racism and had opposed those forces which would hold back the advance of African peoples in the ancestral home and in the diaspora" (25). The gathering was a seminal moment in black radicalism since it occurred about the time Walker started to write his *Appeal*. Carson, Lapsansky-Werner, and Nash point out that it was "one of the nineteenth century's most provocative and prophetic essays" to be written in Boston, "in the shadow of Bunker Hill, where an early battle for American independence had raged" (167).

Walker's *Appeal* became a sensational publication in many parts of the United States where it was distributed and read by blacks and whites alike, earning the book the distinction of being "the most widely circulated work that came from the pen of an American Negro before 1840," as Vernon Loggins described it (qtd. in Chapman 23). Such a success was not without consequence; it was met with harsh resistance,

ally from planters who viewed both the book and its author as ~~ats~~ to the social and economic order of slavocracy. According to Wilentz, "legislators in Georgia and Louisiana became so alarmed that they enacted new harsh laws restricting black literacy," while "horrified Northern journalists joined in denouncing what a Boston editor called 'one of the most wicked and inflammatory productions ever issued from the press'" (vii). These white defenders of slavery dismissed Walker's *Appeal* because they were afraid of the book's radicalism and viewed it as encouragement for slaves to kill their masters. Such a fear was justified since Walker's *Appeal* was published in 1829, when the slave rebellion that began in August 1791 in Saint-Domingue (the colonial name of present-day Haiti) was still fresh in the minds of both blacks and whites in the United States.

The Saint-Domingue revolution was the consequence of political developments in Haiti that culminated one night in August 1791 when a group of slave gangs led by Dutty Boukman killed their masters and burned their plantations. Describing this uprising, C. L. R. James recounts in *A History of Pan-African Revolt* (1938) how "each slave-gang murdered its masters and burnt the plantation to the ground." Yet, as James argues, "On the whole, they [the Haitian slaves] never approached in their tortures the savageries to which they themselves had been subjected" (39). The Haitian slaves' rebellion was important since it was one of the first instances of black nationalism and radicalism in the Americas. By rising against their masters, the Haitian slaves demonstrated their capacity to unite for the common goal of liberating themselves and other blacks from bondage. This kind of united violent rebellion was the main thing slaveholders were trying to prevent with all of their terror tactics through the decades. Coming together allowed these slaves to organize their emancipation and show their ability to form a strong nationalism and solidarity that transcended the ethnic, linguistic, and ideological differences that existed among them.

The revolt of Haitian slaves against their masters influenced Walker's *Appeal*, which alludes to the importance of solidarity in the

formation of black radicalism. The book invokes a messianic fo...
appears to be no other than Toussaint L'Ouverture, who was o...
the instigators of the Haitian Revolution. As Laurent Dubois argue...
L'Ouverture was the "master of the crossroads" of the Haitian Revolution (176–77). Even if he does not mention L'Ouverture by name,
Walker seems to be aware of his role in the Haitian rebellion, which
was successful only because slaves worked together under his leadership to resist their French masters' tyranny. While the success of the
Haitian Revolution could be credited to Boukman, François Makandal,
Georges Biassou, Jean-Jacques Dessalines, and other enslaved men
who also resisted the French, these men regarded L'Ouverture as the
major architect of their uprising.

Walker's familiarity with L'Ouverture is visible in the statement
in which he tells American slaves, "The person whom God shall give
you, give him your support and let him go his length, and behold in
him the salvation of your God. God will indeed, deliver you through
him from your deplorable and wretched condition . . . I charge you
this day before my God to lay no obstacle in his way, but let him go"
(20). Walker's assertion suggests his conception of black nationalism
as a radical resistance that a slave community develops by choosing
a leader that liberates them from bondage. In this sense, Walker perceived Haitian slaves' unity around L'Ouverture as an important model
of black nationalism for American slaves. The Haitian Revolution,
which he considered as an example of solidarity and organized rebellion that American slaves could emulate, inspired Walker's philosophy
of black nationalism. Moreover, Walker perceived Haitian blacks as
an important influence on the fate of American slaves. He describes
the "Haytians" as the "brethren" who, "according to their word, are
bound to protect and comfort us" (56). Walker's statements convey his
attempt to link the Haitian Revolution with the struggle of blacks in the
United States against injustices and harsh conditions, achieving what
James Brewer Stewart describes as an "African American view of history's moral direction set in transatlantic terms" (111). This perspective

considers the liberation struggles of blacks living on the opposing sides of the Atlantic Ocean as parts of the same history. In this sense, Walker perceived the Haitian nationalism as a movement that would influence African Americans to hope for a day when they too would stand together and liberate themselves from slavery.

Yet Walker's invocation of Haiti is not always positive because it also serves as a warning against the danger of disunity among blacks. Writing his *Appeal* about twenty-six years after the end of the Haitian Revolution, Walker had witnessed the disunity among the blacks that L'Ouverture had saved from French colonialism. He feared a similar disunion among blacks in the United States, believing that they would remain enslaved if they were fragmented. He writes: "O my suffering brethren ! remember the divisions and consequent sufferings of *Carthage* and of *Hayti*. Read the history particularly of Hayti, and see how they were butchered by the whites, and do you take warning" (20; ital. in orig.). Through these examples, Walker suggests that black radicalism becomes an ineffectual form of a resistance when it is deprived of unity. This vision is apparent in Walker's representation of Hannibal, a Carthagian commander and politician who led an army against Rome during the Second Punic War (218–202 BCE), as "that mighty son of Africa" who could have completely and permanently conquered the Italian city if he had the full backing of his people. According to Walker, "Had Carthage been well united and had given him [Hannibal] good support, he would have carried that cruel and barbarous city by storm" (20).

Walker might have regarded L'Ouverture as another black leader whose radicalism was finally marred by racial colonialism and lack of solidarity. Soon after L'Ouverture led Haitians to freedom, the French general Napoléon Bonaparte arrested him and locked him in a squalid and cold cell in Fort de Joux, where he died on April 7, 1803 (Coupeau 33). Although Jean-Jacques Dessalines, L'Ouverture's principal lieutenant, immediately carried the torch of the Haitian Revolution, the movement was hampered by the lack of solidarity among blacks. Thus,

Lennox Honychurch writes, "Haiti had gained its freedom, but Toussaint's dreams of an orderly, educated and commercially thriving society were lost in the anarchy which resulted from lack of unity" (34). Walker recognizes this decline in Haiti's nationalism when he represents the island as a glorious nation that fell into chaos when the blacks that L'Ouverture freed ceased to come together and believe in themselves after their leader died. He describes Haiti as the island where "the glory of the blacks and terror of tyrants . . . is enough to convince the most avaricious and stupid wretches" of the need for black unity and says that it is "plagued with that scourge of nations, the Catholic religion" (21). This statement reveals Walker's bias against Catholicism, which he regards as less adequate for slaves than the Protestant faith, and suggests his perception of religions in general as forces that disunite blacks through miseducation.

In this vein, Walker describes "ignorance and treachery one against the other" as "a servile and abject submission to the lash of tyrants" (21). For Walker, miseducation is a tool of control that allows slave owners to influence blacks into oppressing their own people. For instance, Walker describes how miseducation led some free blacks to see themselves as superior to enslaved blacks. He writes:

These are some of the productions of ignorance, which he [the careful observer] will see practised among my dear brethren, who are held in unjust slavery and wretchedness, by avaricious and unmerciful tyrants, to whom, and their hellish deeds, I would suffer my life to be taken before I would submit. And when my curious observer comes to take notice of those who are said to be free, (which assertion I deny) and who are making some frivolous pretentions to common sense, he will see that branch of ignorance among the slaves assuming a more cunning and deceitful course of procedure.—He may see some of my brethren in league with tyrants, selling their own brethren into *hell upon earth*, not dissimilar to the exhibitions in Africa, but in a more secret, servile and abject manner. (22; ital. in orig.)

Here Walker represents miseducation as a colonial tool that created internalized oppression among blacks whom the masters tricked into believing they were superior to enslaved members of their race. Denouncing such ignorance, Walker berates free blacks who were repulsed when slaves killed slaveholders and slave drivers, whom he calls "*murdering* men" and "*notorious wretch*[es]" (24–25; ital. in orig.). Walker mentions an article of the *Columbian Centinel*, dated September 9, 1829, in which a "colored woman" depicted a group of slaves who rebelled against slave drivers and slave catchers as murderers (24). Walker berates the woman's description of events, in which a black slave driver from Kentucky named Gordon, "who had purchased in Maryland about sixty negroes, was taking them, assisted by an associate named Allen and the wagoner who conveyed the baggage, to the Mississippi" (23). The "colored woman" described how the slave rebellion evolved: "The neighborhood was immediately rallied, and a hot pursuit given—which, we understand, has resulted in the capture of the whole gang and the recovery of the greatest part of the money.— Seven of the negro men and one woman, it is said were engaged in the murders, and will be brought to trial at the next court in Greenupsburg" (23–24). Protesting against the descriptions of the rebellion, Walker argues that the real "*murdering men*" were the masters who held slaves in bondage (24–25). He writes:

> Here is a set of wretches, who had SIXTY of them in a gang, driving them around the country like *brutes*, to dig up gold and silver for them . . . Should the lives of such creatures be spared? Are God and Mammon in league? What has the Lord to do with a gang of desperate wretches, who go *sneaking about the country like robbers*—light upon his people wherever they can get a chance, binding them with chains and hand-cuffs, beat and murder them as they would *rattle-snakes*? Are they not the Lord's enemies? Ought they not to be destroyed? (25; ital. in orig.)

This text conveys Walker's validation of the slaves' strong will to be free and their cognizance of the inevitable, irrevocable, and bloody life-and-death battle that a revolution against the institution of slavery would take. Walker's belief that the "wretches" who kill people like "*robbers*" and "*rattle-snakes*" must be "destroyed" signifies his radical conception of antislavery as a determined resistance and protest for the retrieval of the slaves' confiscated liberty. Such antislavery resistance is nationalist since it urged slaves to unite in an attempt to recover their God-given freedom that American slavery had taken away.

Walker's radical theory of rebellion against servitude is also apparent in the passage of the *Appeal* where he exhorts slaves to rise against their captors. Couching his support for this rebellion in a statement in which he ironically quotes Jefferson's *Notes on the State of Virginia* (1787), Walker asserts:

> The blacks, once you get them started, they glory in death. The whites have had us under them for more than three centuries, murdering, and treating us like brutes; and, as Mr. Jefferson wisely said, they have never *found us out*—they do not know, indeed, that there is an unconquerable disposition in the breasts of the blacks, which, when it is fully awakened and put in motion, will be subdued, only with the destruction of the animal existence. (25)

The passage reinforces Walker's conception of uprising as a demonstration of black people's disposition to fight for their freedom. Such a statement reveals Walker's radical and nationalist protest against slavery, apparent in his lamentation of the violence and abuse whites perpetrated against blacks for centuries, as well as in his call for slaves to resist this oppression. Moreover, the passage also reveals Walker's conception of nobility, an idea that Thomas Jefferson ascribed mostly to Native Americans, as a virtue that blacks also possess, as is noticeable in Walker's celebration of the slaves' willingness to die for their liberty.

Encouraging slaves to physically resist the tyranny of their oppressors was a radical form of protest against slavery that whites could not accept since it threatened their ways of life. In this sense, Herbert Aptheker argues, Walker's *Appeal* conveys an idea of African American "moral superiority" to whites "which shook the slaveholders to their boots when it appeared in 1829" (340). Another idea that might have shaken "the slaveholders to their boots" was Walker's depiction of resistance as the slaves' reclamation of their right to be free. This idea would have been dangerous to white readers, who could not help imagining the possibility of bloody upheaval among slaves and the likely consequences of such events for the institution of slavery, including the loss of material gains and slave labor. By writing a story that provides bloody scenes of resistance against slavery, Walter became, in the eyes of proslavery whites, a traitor who represented dissident and dangerous forms of protest that deserved the same kind of punishment that was laid on Nat Turner and his followers. William Loren Katz explains, "His [Walker's] message was simple: if you are not given your liberty, rise in bloody rebellion. When copies of his *Appeal* were found in Southern cities from Virginia to Louisiana, slaveholders panicked. They offered a reward for Walker's capture, dead or alive" (164–65).

Due to the publication of his *Appeal*, Walker received death threats at the same time that new laws against black freedom were being enacted throughout the United States. In his essay entitled "Slaves Virtually Free in Ante-Bellum North Carolina," John Hope Franklin writes, "A law against the circulation of books and papers that tended to 'excite insurrection, conspiracy or resistance in the slaves or free Negroes' was passed at the next session of the Legislature [of North Carolina]. Another law was passed which prohibited 'all persons from teaching slaves to read and write, the use of figures excepted'" (289). Franklin also states, "The increase of free Negroes in every part of the State and the provocations by such individuals and groups as David Walker and the Vermont Legislature caused the passage of a law, in 1830, carefully regulating the manumission of Negro slaves" (289). The above passage show the attempts of whites in many states to use the uproar against Walker's *Appeal* as an opportunity to nip potential slave uprisings in the bud through the passage of restrictive slave laws.

Such restrictive legislations resonate with the kind of fear that Jefferson expressed in *Notes on the State of Virginia*, some forty years before Walker's *Appeal* was published. In query 18 of the book, Jefferson, who by 1787 was torn by the paradox of being both a slave owner and a defender of freedom and equality, attempted to resolve his anxieties through a treatise on the nature and future of blacks in the United States. Like Walker, Jefferson believed that God would not let the oppression of one group remain unpunished and that such domination weakens the tormentors' power and freedom. In *Notes*, he asks,

> Can the liberties of a nation be thought secure when we have removed their only firm basis, a conviction in the minds of the people that these liberties are of the gift of God? That they are not to be violated but with his wrath? Indeed I tremble for my country when I reflect that God is just: that his justice cannot sleep for ever: that considering numbers, nature and natural means only, a revolution of the wheel of fortune, an exchange of situation, is among possible events: that it may become probable by supernatural interference! (163)

Jefferson's allusion to "a revolution of the wheel of fortune" indicates his fear of the unpredictable change that God could bring to the lives of whites in colonial America without warning. Yet Jefferson's statement also suggests something more dreadful in his eyes, which is the chaos that could occur if God and nature were to lead the subjugated slaves to rebel against their oppressors. Jefferson believed that such divine intervention was possible since logic proved its inevitable realization. In this vein, Jefferson argues that nobody wants to labor indefinitely for the enrichment of another person. He writes, "For if a slave can have a country in this world, it must be any other in preference to that in which he is born to live and labour for another: in which he must lock up the faculties of his nature, contribute as far as depends on his individual endeavours to the evanishment of the human race, or entail his own miserable condition on the endless generations proceeding from him" (163). Jefferson's assertion reflects a deep-seated fear of slave resistance that nevertheless underscores his recognition of the slave's agency and human rights. In this sense, Jefferson was a hypocritical intellectual since he defended slavery when he knew and acknowledged that slaves had a burning desire to be free and that they might violently wrest this liberty from their white oppressors when the opportunity arose.

Unable to resolve this paradox, Jefferson remained a supporter of slavery who came up with the deceptive scheme of advocating the emigration of blacks from the United States to Africa. Jefferson's fear of slave rebellion was so strong that he could not bear the presence of blacks in the United States. His apprehension led him to argue that removing blacks to a different land would prevent the justifiable anger of the slaves from expressing itself in the form of a national disaster. He writes, "Deep rooted prejudices entertained by the whites; ten thousand recollections, by the blacks, of the injuries they have sustained; new provocations; the real distinctions which nature has made; and many other circumstances, will divide us into parties, and produce convulsions which will probably never end but in the extermination of the one or the other race" (Jefferson 138). These words suggest Jefferson's fear of the rancor that American slaves had toward whites who had enslaved them for centuries. Knowing that a similar resentment had led Haitian slaves to rise against their masters, Jefferson anticipated a comparable revolt in the United States. In an attempt to prevent such a revolt from occurring, he supported an amendment recommending that all slaves "born after passing the act" be emancipated and later "colonized to such place as the circumstances of the time should render most proper" (138–39). The "place" that Jefferson had in mind might have been Liberia, since this was the settlement where the American Colonization Society, of which he was a member, relocated many free blacks during the 1820s.

Yet Jefferson's plan to remove American blacks to Africa was part of a larger plan that Walker denounces in the *Appeal*. Jefferson was not the only proponent of black emigration; many white leaders made the same proposition. Bruce Rosen traces the black emigration ideology to either 1816 or 1817 in Washington, DC, when Henry Clay, who was a new politician from Kentucky, and other white Americans formed the American Society for Colonizing the Free People of Color in the United States, also known as the American Colonization Society (177). The ACS is often described as an organization that attempted to protect slaves from violence. Merton L. Dillon argues that the ACS's mission was to reduce the mortality of slaves and "to lessen the likelihood of slave unrest by removing the slaves' most obvious allies" (109). The evidence suggests that the ACS did not necessarily work in favor of slaves, since its emigration proposal was a racist attempt to rid the United States of its free black populations. The removal of free blacks from the country deprived slaves of the social, political, and economic leadership that could sustain their freedom struggle and made them more vulnerable to the abuse of whites. Since he was aware of these inconsistencies, Walker presents in his *Appeal* evidence that opposes the emigration plan. Speaking about Clay, who later supported the passage of the Fugitive Slave Act of 1850, Walker asks in the *Appeal*:

Do you believe that Mr. Henry Clay, late Secretary of State, and now in Kentucky, is a friend to the blacks, further, than his personal interest extends? Is it not his greatest object and glory upon earth, to sink us into miseries and wretchedness by making slaves of us, to work his plantation to enrich him and his family? Does he care a pinch of snuff about Africa— whether it remains a land of Pagans and of blood, or of Christians, so long as he gets enough of her sons and daughters to dig up gold and silver for him? If he had no slaves, and could obtain them in no other way if it were not, repugnant to the laws of his country, which prohibit the importation of slaves (which act was, indeed, more through apprehension than humanity) would he not try to import a few from Africa, to work his farm? Would he work in the hot sun to earn his bread, if he could make an African work for nothing, particularly, if he could keep him in ignorance and make him believe that God made him for nothing else but to work for him? (50–51)

In a similar vein, Walker disparages the views of Elias Caldwell, another supporter of the ACS, who was a clerk of the Supreme Court of the United States. In his emigration proposal, Caldwell writes, "Surely, Americans ought to be the last people on earth, to advocate such slavish doctrines, to cry peace and contentment to those who are deprived of the privileges of civil liberty, they who have so largely partaken of its blessings, who know so well how to estimate its value, ought to be among the foremost to extend it to others" (qtd. in Walker 52). Responding to Caldwell's arguments, Walker declares, "The real sense and meaning of the last part of Mr. Caldwell's speech is, get the free people of color away to Africa, from among the slaves, where they may at once be blessed and happy, and those who we hold in slavery, will be contented to rest in ignorance and wretchedness, to dig up gold and silver for us and our children" (52).

Jefferson's proposal to relocate blacks to Africa also stemmed from his fear that the Haitian Revolution might lead American slaves to rise against their masters. He was not the only white slaveholder who felt this way. According to Winthrop D. Jordan, since 1791, white Americans had viewed Saint-Domingue as a threat to their security, and when the colony's legislature requested armed assistance to quell the uprising that year, South Carolina's governor Charles Pinckney forwarded the plea to President George Washington. Governor Pinckney urged action, lest Haiti become "a flame which will extend to all the neighboring islands, and may eventually prove not a very pleasing or agreeable example to the Southern States" (Jordan 386–87).

In a similar fashion, Jefferson considered the Haitian rebellion as a matter of security for the United States. According to Jordan, in December 1793, "Jefferson wrote to warn the governor of South Carolina of two mulattoes coming from St. Domingo [*sic*] to incite insurrection. Jefferson never lost his conviction that St. Domingo might easily fall as a spark in the tinder box of the South" (381). He was afraid that the Saint-Domingue uprising would spill over the United States and lead blacks to fight for their freedom. When, at the dawn of the nineteenth century, "many nations had reason to dread Toussaint's revolutionary army, with its record of retribution" (Adams 21), Jefferson wrote to an abolitionist friend, "We shall be the murderers of our own children" (qtd. in Adams 22). Jefferson's fear of slave rebellions was justified because such revolts did occur in the United States during the early nineteenth century. These rebellions include Gabriel Prosser's plot of 1800, the Denmark Vesey insurrection of 1822, and the Nat Turner revolt of 1831. The Denmark Vesey rebellion is particularly pertinent here since it occurred seven years before Walker published his *Appeal* and might have influenced the author's representation of American slaves uprising.

According to Lerone Bennett, the Denmark Vesey conspiracy was "one of the most elaborate slave plots on record," involving "thousands of Blacks in Charleston, S.C. and vicinity" (455). Yet this rebellion failed when it was disclosed to whites before it occurred. As Walter C. Rucker relates, the plot "of a planned revolt in Charleston" was discovered on May 25, 1822, and "included between 6,600 and 9,000 slaves divided into six attack groups" who planned on "killing all whites they found" (159). When the plot was discovered upon the confession of a house slave, thirty-seven blacks were hanged and Vesey and five of his followers were executed at Blake's Landing in Charleston, South Carolina (Bennett 474–75). The Vesey conspiracy is important to the current discussion since, as Sterling Stuckey suggests in *Slave Culture*, he united slaves who had recently arrived from Haiti and Africa with those who were already in the United States in order to create a strong slave rebellion (43–53). This resistance was a form of black radicalism since it aimed to uplift the conditions of blacks in both Africa and the New World. As Franklin and Alfred A. Moss argue, "He [Vesey] believed in equality for everyone and resolved to do something for his slave brothers and sisters" (146).

Vesey's radical fight against injustice might have inspired Walker's resistance to oppression. Evidence presented by Peter P. Hinks in *To Awaken My Afflicted Brethren: David Walker and the Problem of Antebellum Slave Resistance* (1997) shows that Walker attended a camp meeting of slave revolutionaries in South Carolina around the time of the Vesey conspiracy and trials (29). Moreover, as Marion D. Kilson suggests, like Vesey, Walker had traveled extensively and was aware of the success of the Haitian Revolution and the Missouri Compromise Debate (175–87). The Missouri Compromise Debate was the series of arguments that occurred in the US Senate between January and February 1820 that led to Congress's agreement to admit Missouri as a slave state and Maine as a free state and bar slavery from all the remaining Louisiana Purchase lands. Walker's awareness of this Missouri debate at a time when he was privately involved in secret slave revolutionary meetings reveals his strong commitment to black liberation in the United States and his desire to see the American slaves rise against whites just as their Haitian counterparts did in the late eighteenth century. Though Vesey's rebellion took place seven years before the publication of the *Appeal*, it anticipated Walker's belief that dominated groups eventually rise up against their oppressors.

Walker's *Appeal* is a radical narrative that loudly urged African slaves in the United States to rise against slaveholders and slave owners. The *Appeal* took unique positions on the issues around the social and economic conditions of blacks in the United States and Africa in the early nineteenth century, when the idea of establishing colonies in Africa for African Americans had created many controversies in the United States.

Frederick Douglass's *Narrative*

Frederick Douglass's slave narrative remains a neglected topic in the study of early black nationalism in the United States because critics tend to regard Douglass merely as a patriotic African American author who vehemently denounced slavery. What critics overlook is the radical quality of Douglass's antislavery protest. By studying the radical nature of Douglass's denunciation of slavery, one can understand both Douglass's protest strategies and their connections with Walker's. Moreover, one can understand how Douglass consistently reveals a blend of radicalism and nationalism by showing interdependency between his quest of personal freedom and his struggle for the liberty of all American slaves.

Douglass was an African American orator, journalist, editor, and author of the most influential nineteenth-century slave narrative. Douglass was born a slave in 1818 in the place that he describes in his narrative as "Tuckahoe, near Hillsborough, and about twelve miles from Easton, in Talbot County, Maryland" (Andrews 225). According to his own account, Douglass was the son of his white master. In the book, Douglass writes, "My father was a white man. He was admitted to be such by all I ever heard speak of my parentage. The opinion was also whispered that my master was my father" (*Narrative* 255–56). Yet Douglass had no memory of his mother, since they were separated at his birth. He states, "My mother and I were separated when I was but an infant—before I knew her as my mother" (256). Despite this tragedy, Douglass had a few privileges over other slaves since he was the son of a white slave owner. The fact that his father was his master may be what kept him from being sold or treated worse than he was when he was a child. Douglass acknowledges that he was treated better than most child slaves at Colonel Lloyd's plantation were. He says that he was "seldom whipped" by his master there and notes that in Baltimore, he "was much better off" in terms of food "than many of the poor white children in the neighborhood" (271, 278). Yet Douglass's privileges were temporary since they did not prevent him from being at risk of being sold when he was a teenager. Such was the case when, after Captain Anthony died, Douglass was made to return to the home plantation to be part of an evaluation of property, though he was returned to

Baltimore when, "thanks to a kind Providence," he fell to Mrs. Lucretia Auld's portion (282–83). In another fortunate situation, Douglass was sent back to Baltimore rather than being sold or executed after he attempted to escape.

In 1826, Thomas Auld, the son-in-law of Douglass's master, sent the slave boy to the home of his brother Hugh in Baltimore, where "he was taught to read by his master's wife, Mrs. Hugh Auld" (Emanuel and Gross 12). In 1832, Douglass returned to St. Michael's, Maryland, to live with Thomas, who later lent him to Edward Covey (Douglass, *Narrative* 225). Douglass's relocation to Baltimore gave him privileges that slaves did not have. One of such privileges was the instruction that Mrs. Auld gave him in how to read and write. Douglass states, "She very kindly commenced to teach me the A, B, C. After I had learned this, she assisted me in learning to spell words of three or four letters" (274). Although it was disrupted when Mr. Auld "forbade Mrs. Auld to instruct me further" (274), this education benefited the slave child by instilling in him a strong love of learning and a relentless desire to write as well as a white person could. Douglass describes how he secretly copied what Mr. Auld wrote in his "copy-book" until he "finally succeeded in learning how to write" (281).

Providence rescued Douglass again in 1836, when, as a young adult, he was sent to Baltimore to learn about the caulking trade. After three years of escape attempts, Douglass finally reached his goal in 1838 when he disguised himself as a sailor and went first to New York City, then to New Bedford, Massachusetts. According to Carson, Lapsansky-Werner, and Nash, Douglass "married Anna, a free woman he had met in Baltimore, where she was a domestic servant" (186). Anna was instrumental in Douglass's freedom. As C. James Trotman points out, "she became a major influence for encouraging him in his plans to escape and helping to make it happen by financing his escape to freedom" (28).

Another person who played a major role in Douglass's freedom was the leader of the American antislavery movement, William Lloyd

Garrison. According to Carson, Lapsansky-Werner, and Nash, Douglass worked with Garrison, who sent him to England for two years while the American abolitionists raised funds to buy his freedom (186). When he gained his freedom in 1845, Douglass toured with abolitionists to speak against slavery. Yet, as Emanuel and Gross remark, in 1847 Douglass ended "his antislavery connections with William Lloyd Garrison" and embarked upon "an independent career in journalism with his own weekly, *The North Star*, and continued it until 1863 through his subsequent *Frederick Douglass' Paper* and *Douglass Monthly*" (12–13). Douglass's separation from Garrison suggests his radicalism since it allowed him to break with a white leader who did not recognize his intellectual autonomy. Severing himself from Garrison allowed Douglass to freely recount his experiences as both a slave and a freedman and disseminate his views about racism, inequality, democracy, and other issues. Such views appear in Douglass's books *My Bondage and My Freedom* (1855) and *Life and Times of Frederick Douglass* (1881).

Douglass's portrayal of bondage is radical since it reveals the inhumane ways in which the institution oppressed American slaves. Such radicalism is apparent early in his *Narrative*, where he depicts the horrible manner in which slaveholders separated mothers from their babies in an attempt to prevent contact between them. He states, "It is a common custom, in the part of Maryland from which I ran away, to part children from their mothers at a very early age. . . . For what this separation is done, I do not know, unless it be to hinder the development of the child's affection toward its mother, and to blunt and destroy the natural affection of the mother for the child" (*Narrative* 256). This statement conveys Douglass's radicalism because it portrays slavery as a barbaric system that severely oppresses slaves. On the one hand, slavery dehumanizes the slave child by severing his or her relationship with the mother; on the other, it dehumanizes the slave mother by breaking her "natural affection" for her child. In depicting slavery in such ways, Douglass foreshadows his radical representation of the institution as the most inhumane and cruel form of oppression he ever witnessed.

Early in the second chapter of his *Narrative*, he describes the horrid conditions that confronted blacks on the plantation where his master was "the overseer of the overseers" of Colonel Edward Lloyd (259). Here, Douglass describes the systemic way in which the plantation served as a colony that allowed the slaveholders to amass wealth from the hardship of slaves who were brutally treated. According to Douglass, even if the slaves raised a "great abundance" of "tobacco, corn, and wheat" (259), they were usually beaten and poorly fed. He writes that "if a slave was convicted of any high misdemeanor, became unmanageable, or evinced a determination to run away," he was "severely whipped, put on board the sloop, carried to Baltimore, and sold to Austin Woolfolk, or some other slave-trader, as a warning to the slaves remaining" (260). Douglass's statement is both radical and nationalist since it reveals his incrementally bold opposition to the inhuman institution. Douglass expresses radicalism by using this unflinching exposure of the horrors of slavery to show that his individual freedom depended on the liberation of all slaves. Further, his radicalism is nationalistic, stemming from his perception of slaves as individuals whose fates are tied with his destiny. Such a mutuality between Douglass's personal freedom and the liberty of all slaves is apparent in the fact that Douglass did not fully enjoy the limited freedom that he had in 1845, when his *Narrative* was first published, because he selflessly perceived himself as a member of a black community that was still enslaved.

During his adolescent years, Douglass himself experienced similar cruelty, especially from Mr. Edward Covey, whose abuse he describes as follows: "Mr. Covey gave me a very severe whipping, cutting my back, causing the blood to run, and raising ridges on my flesh as large as my little finger" (*Narrative* 290). As Mr. Covey's beatings continued, Douglass began to resist his master's abuse in radical terms that recall the bondman's opposition to his owner in Georg Wilhelm

Friedrich Hegel's master-slave dialectic. In this dialectic, both the slave and the master dwell in an eternal psychological and physical battle to diminish each other. In his 1807 book, *Phenomenology of Spirit*, Hegel writes, "Each seeks the death of the other . . . Thus, the relation of the two self-conscious individuals is such that they prove themselves and each other through a life-and-death struggle. They must engage in this struggle, for they must raise their certainty of being *for-themselves* to truth" (632; ital. in orig.). Yet, even if they are caught in an endless combat, the slave and the master know that their survival depends on their partial recognition of each other's consciousness and power.

The master-slave dialectic in Douglass's *Narrative* is visible in the passage where Douglass radically opposes Mr. Covey by physically fighting against him on one particular occasion. Douglass writes, "He [Mr. Covey] asked me if I meant to persist in my resistance. I told him I did, come what might; that he had used me like a brute for six months, and that I was determined to be used so no longer" (*Narrative* 298). This statement suggests Douglass's direct and unyielding protest against slavery to such an extent that his master ends up fearing his consciousness about his own right to be free. Douglass is aware of the change in Covey's attitude toward him; during the six months following their fight, he says, Covey "never laid the weight of his finger upon me in anger. He would occasionally say, he didn't want to get hold of me again. 'No,' thought I, 'you need not; for you will come off worse than you did before'" (298). In putting up such a staunch resistance against Mr. Covey, Douglass developed a radical form of protest that resonated with the subversive agency of the bondman in Hegel's master-slave dialectic.

Unfortunately, not everyone believes that the slave has the strong power to resist the master's authority. For instance, Hegel did not believe that the slave could be victorious in the dialectic struggle against the master. According to Vincent B. Leitch, "Hegel imagines that each individual would prefer to guarantee continued recognition from the other, while not extending that recognition in turn," and visualizes the slave and the master as two individuals engaged "in a battle that ends when the Slave grants recognition and service to the Master in return for continued life" (627). As Leitch points out, "both the Master and Slave stake their life in the battle, but the loser becomes a slave by choosing a life of servitude over death at the hand of the victor" (627). By representing the master as the tacit winner of his dialectic with the slave, Hegel downplays the agency that the bondsperson underscores by developing a self-reflexive consciousness. In response to Hegel's dismissal of the slave's agency, Paul Gilroy argues that "it is the slave rather than the master who emerges from Douglass's account possessed of 'consciousness that exists for itself,' while his master becomes the representative of a 'consciousness that is repressed within itself'" (60). From this perspective, Mr. Covey stops beating Douglass not because he has magnanimity but because his slave has put up a radical rebellion that has bent his master's authority. By threatening to resist Covey's future tyranny, Douglass has compelled the master to negotiate with his slave and validate his humanity. Douglass gains a tremendous self-consciousness from this resistance that allows him to ascertain his manhood by radically opposing Mr. Covey's hegemony. He describes his fight with Mr. Covey as "the turning-point in my career," which "rekindled the few expiring embers of freedom, and revived within me a sense of my own manhood" (*Narrative* 298). Therefore, radical resistance against Mr. Covey allows Douglass to establish his humanity and right to be treated as the equal of any other man.

Douglass's newfound freedom spirit leads him to invoke the radical and nationalist theory of unmitigated freedom from tyranny by any necessary means that Walker had used earlier. Douglass reclaims this philosophy when he affirms the resolve of the American slaves who run away from their owners to regain their liberty at any cost. He says, "In coming to a fixed determination to run away, we did more than Patrick Henry, when he resolved upon liberty or death. With us it was a doubtful liberty at most, and almost certain death if we failed. For my part, I should prefer death to hopeless bondage" (*Narrative* 306). Such a desperate attempt to escape from slavery by any necessary means is a radical form of resistance, since it is founded on the slaves' absolute readiness to die than to remain in bondage. Running through woods full of reptiles, infested swamps, and brutal kidnappers, slaves continued their escape attempts even when they were at risk of being caught and sent back to their plantations. Revealing the plight of runaway slaves, Douglass writes in his *Narrative*:

> At every gate through which we were to pass, we saw a watchman—at every ferry a guard—on every bridge, a sentinel—and in every wood, a patrol. We were hemmed in upon every side. Here were the difficulties, real or imagined—the good to be thought, and the evil to be shunned. . . . When we permitted ourselves to survey the road, we were frequently appalled. Upon either side we saw grim death, assuming the most horrid shapes. Now it was starvation, causing us to eat our own flesh;—now we were contending with the waves, and were drowned; now we were overtaken, and torn to pieces by the fangs of the terrible bloodhound. (306)

This passage reveals the unending agony that runaway slaves experienced as they worried about the possible failure of their escape attempts, even if they resolved to complete their long journey. Douglass recognizes the hardship that runaway slaves faced, describing escapees who were compelled to eat their own flesh for fear of starvation. By depicting the runaway slaves' predicament in such gruesome ways, Douglass provides a radical portrayal of slavery that reflects the brutal nature of the system. Such a representation of slavery is radical since it exposes the tremendous degrees to which the institution oppressed African Americans by dehumanizing and depersonalizing them. As a nationalist, Douglass perceived himself as a part of these enslaved blacks that America tremendously oppressed. His identification with the enslaved blacks allowed him to empower his radical depiction of and opposition to slavery by letting abolitionist sympathizers know that his primary allegiance lay with the subjugated blacks from whom he came. By identifying with these blacks and depicting their predicament in touching ways, Douglass developed a radical protest tradition that could influence white abolitionists to oppose slavery. His heartbreaking imagery of the evil institution reinforces his abolitionist struggle while empowering his relentless denunciation of human servitude.

Douglass's antislavery protest is also apparent in the speeches that he gave between the 1830s and the late nineteenth century. Many of these speeches—including an address that Douglass gave at the World's Temperance Convention in Covent Garden Theater, London, on August 7, 1846—appear in *Life and Times*. In the speeches included in this book, Douglass depicts slavery as an institution that deprived blacks of their American citizenship and patriotic rights. In order to illustrate this seclusion and disenfranchisement of blacks, Douglass represents himself as a person who could not be a delegate at the World's Temperance Convention, because the blacks who could have voted for him to become a United States public official were disenfranchised. In one of the speeches included in a chapter of *Life and Times* entitled "Impressions Abroad," Douglass says, "I am not a delegate to this convention. Those who would have been most likely to elect me as a delegate could not, because they are to-night held in abject slavery in the United States" (249). Having shown the United States' obliteration of the slaves' rights to elect him as a foreign ambassador, Douglass then depicts slavery as the usurpation of the slaves' citizenship. He continues, "The three million slaves are completely excluded by slavery, and four hundred thousand free colored people are almost as completely excluded by an inveterate prejudice against them on account of their color" (249).

Douglass's speech had a strong impact on his international (and mostly white and abolitionist) audience, since it was strategically designed to generate repulsion toward the immorality of slavery. Such a strategy is evident in the four words—"Cries of 'Shame! Shame!'"—that follow the above passage, a way of inciting the reprobation and disgust the participants of the international antislavery movement expressed toward slavery. Such a strategy reveals not just Douglass's rhetorical skill but also his capacity to pinpoint the discrepancy between America's ideal of liberty and its disenfranchisement of blacks during slavery. As Richard Newman, Patrick Rael, and Philip Lapsansky argue, "Douglass's gift was not so much his originality as his ability to concisely and vibrantly express moral outrage—the outrage due a nation which lauded itself on its commitment to freedom while denying liberty to people of African descent" (214). In this sense, Douglass's nationalism was as radical as Walker's was, since it denounced the hypocrisy of a Jeffersonian American democracy in which blacks were denied liberty.

Douglass illustrates this American paradox in a letter to President Andrew Johnson, dated February 7, 1866, in which he subtly protests how the president was about to be swayed by the malicious attempts of former slaveholders to disenfranchise free slaves on the pretense of enduring black enmity toward whites. Douglass replies to this issue by representing this supposed enmity as the result of a "divide both to conquer each" strategy, asserting, "Those masters secured their ascendancy over both the poor whites and blacks by putting enmity between them" (*Life and Times* 383). As a skilled logician, Douglass then urges President Johnson to avoid contradicting his promise to give blacks freedom by not yielding to "slaveholding and slave-driving" attempts to reshackle blacks through legislation that would allow their disenfranchisement, whipping, denial of welfare, and other abuses (384). By warning Johnson about the dangers of reempowering former slave masters and overseers over the freed slaves, Douglass urges the president to let blacks gain their freedom. In this sense, Douglass was, like Walker, an intellectual who radically refused to take anything less than the liberty that American owed to blacks. Eric J. Sundquist writes in *Blacks, Jews, Post-Holocaust America* (2005), "As Walker, Douglass, and other abolitionists argued, moreover, it was blacks, in their quest for freedom, who were chosen to bear the special burden of repairing the flawed design of the revolutionary fathers" (105). Like Walker, Douglass understood that America's principles of equality, liberty, and justice would remain mere ideals unless the nation's underprivileged populations received them and participated in the concretization and improvement of the country's democratic notions.

Furthermore, Douglass was similar to Walker because he, too, staunchly opposed the attempt of the American Colonization Society to move African Americans to Africa. Douglass's rejection of the emigration plan is apparent in his letter to Harriet Beecher Stowe, dated March 8, 1853, in which he reveals his disapprobation of this plan. In the letter, Douglass says, "The truth is, dear madam, we are *here*, and here we are likely to remain. Individuals emigrate—nations never. We have grown up with this republic, and I see nothing in her character, or even in the character of the American people, as yet, which compels the belief that we must leave the United States" (*Life and Times* 286–87; ital. in orig.). This passage suggests Douglass's rejection of the emigration scheme on the ground that it would remove American blacks from the homeland they knew and helped transform as a nation. Douglass viewed America, not Africa, as the homeland of African Americans and the place where they should conduct their struggle. As Waldo E. Martin Jr. writes, "Douglass always insisted that 'the native land of the American Negro is America. His bones, his sinews, are all American,'" showing that he was part of the "integrationists [who] remained more firmly convinced of their fundamental Americanness, refusing to leave the land so inextricably bound with their sense of self and their history" (71).

Douglass preferred to be perceived as a quintessential American who rejected racial categorizations and preferred to see himself as a black man fighting for freedom in a diverse country. Showing discomfort about racial classifications, Douglass writes in *Life and Times*:

I have often been bluntly and sometimes very rudely asked, of what color my mother was, and of what color was my father? In what proportion does the blood of the various races mingle in my veins, especially how much white blood and how much black blood entered into my composition? Whether I was not part Indian as well as African and Caucasian? Whether

I considered myself more African than Caucasian, or the reverse? . . . How is the race problem to be solved in this country? Will the Negro go back to Africa or remain here? Under this shower of purely American questions, more or less personal, I have endeavored to possess my soul in patience and get as much good out of life as was possible with so much to occupy my time; and, though often perplexed, seldom losing my temper, or abating heart or hope for the future of my people. (513)

The passage shows that Douglass was troubled not only by the emigration project but also by the American obsession with categorical group identity. Douglass sometimes refused to be labeled as either African or Caucasian because he believed that such classifications revive the enduring American fixations on essential identities that can be understood only by people "profoundly versed in psychology, anthropology, ethnology, sociology, theology, biology, and all the other ologies, philosophies and sciences" (512–13). Douglass's statement reveals his promotion of a unique kind of nationalism that would allow African Americans to embrace the multiple ethnic and geographic identities out of which their ancestors came and become one united and self-reliant black community that would serve as a model of development for the rest of American society. Douglass's nationalism celebrates African American freedom and self-determination within the context of an independent and self-reliant American society. In this sense, Douglass's nationalism was more open than Walker's, since it aimed at integrating African Americans into American society instead of just giving them autonomy and freedom within this culture. However, in spite of the difference between Walker and him, Douglass was also both a radical and a nationalist, since he, too, stressed African Americans' indisputable right to be free and prosper as equal citizens of the United States.

Conclusion

In their narratives, both Walker and Douglass represent slavery, disenfranchisement, and socioeconomic oppression as justifiable reasons for radical rebellion by American slaves. By celebrating the slaves' preference for death over servitude, the two authors were pioneers in a long, subversive black radical tradition that developed in the United States during slavery. Both were radical and nationalist intellectuals who viewed outward resistance and protest against the barbarism of slaveholders and overseers as tools that could dismantle slavery. The two intellectuals also perceived such tools as effective means for enslaved blacks to achieve freedom in an American society that would remain incomplete and unjust until slavery was abolished and the freedom and equality for which the nation stands were extended to blacks.

Works Cited

Adams, Jerome R. «Pierre François Dominique Toussaint L'Ouverture: Commander of a Slave Army, 1743–1803 (Haiti)." *Liberators, Patriots, and Leaders of Latin America: 32 Biographies.* Jefferson: McFarland, 2010. 14–24. Print.

Andrews, William L. "Douglass, Frederick (1818–1895)." *The Oxford Companion to African American Literature.* New York: Oxford UP, 1997. 225–26. Print.

Aptheker, Herbert. "Afro-American Superiority: A Neglected Theme in the Literature." *Phylon* 31.4 (1970): 336–43. Print.

Bennett, Lerone, Jr. *Before the Mayflower: A History of Black America.* 1961. New York: Penguin, 1988. Print.

Burrow, Rufus, Jr. *God and Human Responsibility: David Walker and Ethical Prophecy.* Macon: Mercer UP, 2003. Print.

Camic, Charles. *Experience and Enlightenment: Socialization for Cultural Change in Eighteenth-Century Scotland.* Chicago: U of Chicago P, 1983. Print.

Carson, Clayborne, Emma J. Lapsansky-Werner, and Gary B. Nash. *The Struggle for Freedom: A History of African Americans.* New York: Pearson, 2007. Print.

Chapman, Abraham. Introduction. *Black Voices: An Anthology of Afro-American Literature.* Ed. Chapman. New York: Mentor, 1968. 21–49. Print.

Coupeau, Steeve. *The History of Haiti.* Westport: Greenwood, 2008. Print.

Davis, David Brion. *The Problem of Slavery in Western Culture.* New York. Oxford UP, 1966. Print.

Dillon, Merton L. *Slavery Attacked: Southern Slaves and their Allies.* Baton Rouge: Louisiana State UP, 1990. Print.

Douglass, Frederick. *The Life and Times of Frederick Douglass, Written by Himself.* 1881. New York: Collier, 1962. Print.

___. *Narrative of the Life of Frederick Douglass, an American Slave. The Classic Slave Narratives.* Ed. Henry Louis Gates Jr. New York: New Amer. Lib., 1987. 245–331. Print.

Dubois, Laurent. *Avengers of the New World: The Story of the Haitian Revolution.* Cambridge: Harvard UP, 2004. Print.

Eiselein, Gregory. "David Walker." *The Concise Oxford Companion to African-American Literature.* Ed. William L. Andrews, Frances Smith Foster, and Trudier Harris. New York: Oxford UP, 2001. 415–16. Print.

Emanuel, James A., and Theodore L. Gross, eds. *Dark Symphony: Negro Literature in America.* New York: Free, 1968. Print.

Fanon, Frantz. *The Wretched of the Earth: A Negro Psychoanalyst's Study of the Problems of Racism and Colonialism in the World Today.* 1963. New York: Grove, 1966. Print.

Franklin, John Hope. "Slaves Virtually Free in Ante-Bellum North Carolina." *Journal of Negro History* 28.3 (1943): 284–310. Print.

Franklin, John Hope, and Alfred A. Moss Jr., eds. *From Slavery to Freedom: A History of African Americans.* 1947. New York: McGraw, 1994. Print.

Gilroy, Paul. *The Black Atlantic: Modernity and Double Consciousness.* Cambridge: Harvard UP, 1992. Print.

Gray, T. R. "To the Public." *The Confessions of Nat Turner.* By William Styron. 1967. New York: Bantam, 1983. xiii–xiv. Print.

Hegel, Georg Wilhelm Friedrich. "From *Phenomenology of Spirit.*" *The Norton Anthology of Theory and Criticism.* Ed. Vincent B. Leitch. New York: Norton, 2001. 630–36. Print.

Hickey, Kevin M. "Walker, David." *Encyclopedia of African American History.* Ed. Leslie M. Alexander and Walker C. Rucker. Vol. 2. Santa Barbara: ABC-CLIO, 2010. 569–72. Print.

Hinks, Peter P. *To Awaken My Afflicted Brethren: David Walker and the Problem of Antebellum Slave Resistance.* University Park: Pennsylvania State UP, 1997. Print.

Honychurch, Lennox. *Book 3: The Caribbean People.* Cheltenham: Nelson, 1995. Print.

James, C. L. R. *A History of Pan-African Revolt.* 1938. Chicago: Kerr, 1995. Print.

Jefferson, Thomas. *Notes on the State of Virginia.* 1787. Chapel Hill: U of North Carolina P, 1995. Print.

Jordan, Winthrop D. *White over Black: American Attitudes toward the Negro, 1550–1812.* Chapel Hill: U of North Carolina P, 1968. Print.

Katz, William Loren. *Eyewitness: The Negro in American History.* 1967. New York: Pitman, 1971. Print.

Kilson, Marion D. deB. "Towards Freedom: An Analysis of Slave Revolts in the United States." *Phylon* 25.2 (1964): 175–87. Print.

Leitch, Vincent B. "Georg Wilhelm Friedrich Hegel, 1770–1831." *The Norton Anthology of Theory and Criticism.* Ed. Leitch. New York: Norton, 2001. 626–30. Print.

Levine, Robert S. "Road to Africa: Frederick Douglass's Rome." *African American Review* 34.2 (2000): 217–31. Print.

Martin, Waldo E., Jr. "Frederick Douglass: Humanist as Race Leader." *Black Leaders of the Nineteenth Century.* Ed. Leon Litwack and August Meier. 1988. Urbana: U of Illinois P, 1991. 59–84. Print.

Moses, Wilson Jeremiah. Introduction. *Classical Black Nationalism: From the American Revolution to Marcus Garvey.* Ed. Moses. New York: New York UP, 1996. 1–42. Print.

Newman, Richard, Patrick Rael, and Philip Lapsansky, eds. *Pamphlets of Protest: An Anthology of Early African American Protest Literature, 1790–1860.* New York: Routledge, 2001. Print.

Owens, Joseph. *Dread: The Rastafarians of Jamaica.* Kingston: Sangster's, 1976. 18. Print.

Ready, Milton. *The Tar Heel State: A History of North Carolina.* Columbia: U of South Carolina P, 2005. Print.

Robinson, Cedric J. *Black Marxism: The Making of the Black Radical Tradition.* Chapel Hill: U of North Carolina P, 2000. Print.

Rosen, Bruce. "Abolition and Colonization, the Years of Conflict: 1829–1834." *Phylon* 33.2 (1972): 177–92. Print.

Rossiter, Clinton, ed. *The Federalist Papers.* 1787–88. New York: New Amer. Lib., 1961. Print.

Rucker, Walter C. *The River Flows On: Black Resistance, Culture, and Identity Formation in Early America.* Baton Rouge: Louisiana State UP, 2005. Print.

Shelby, Tommie. "Two Conceptions of Black Nationalism: Martin Delany on the Meaning of Black Political Solidarity." *Political Theory* 31.5 (2003): 664–92. Print.

Stewart, James Brewer. "Boston, Abolition, and the Atlantic World, 1820–1861." *Courage and Conscience: Black and White Abolitionists in Boston.* Ed. Donald M. Jacobs. Bloomington: Indiana UP, 1993. Print.

Stuckey, Sterling. "David Walker and the Ideological Origins of Black Nationalism." *African Themes.* Ed. Ibrahim Abu-Lughod. Evanston: Northwestern U, 1975. 25–46. Print.

___. *Slave Culture: Nationalist Theory and the Foundations of Black America.* New York: Oxford UP, 1987. Print.

Sundquist, Eric J. *Blacks, Jews, Post-Holocaust America.* Cambridge: Belknap, 2005. Print.

Trotman, C. James. *Frederick Douglass.* Santa Barbara: ABC-CLIO, 2011. Print.

Walker, David. *David Walker's Appeal, in Four Articles; Together with a Preamble, to the Coloured Citizens of the World, but in Particular, and Very Expressly, to Those of the United States of America.* 1829. Ed. Sean Wilentz. Rev. ed. New York: Hill, 1995. Print.

Wilentz, Sean. "Introduction: The Mysteries of David Walker." *David Walker's Appeal, In Four Articles; Together with a Preamble, to the Coloured Citizens of the World, but in Particular, and Very Expressly, to Those of the United States of America.* By David Walker. Ed. Wilentz. Rev. ed. New York: Hill, 1995. vii–xxiii. Print.

Wright, Donald R. *African Americans in the Colonial Era: From African Origins through the American Revolution.* Wheeling: Davidson, 1990. Print.

The New Woman Chafes against Her Bonds_____

Adeline Carrie Koscher

Effective protest literature promotes, even generates, a zeitgeist of change. The New Woman novelist at the fin de siècle emboldened masses of women to recognize within themselves that alienated woman, the "new" woman. The end of the nineteenth century saw the emergence of a new breed of women who challenged and rejected many of the accepted rituals and mores imposed upon them in the preceding Victorian era. Some were leaders—forerunners who inspired transformation in others—while some women quietly rejected the earlier dictates for their sex. The behaviors and ideology of these New Women included adopting rational dress (rejecting the corset), fighting for rights within marriage, rejecting a sexual double standard, insisting on a woman's right to education, and continuing to agitate for women's suffrage. Had these women existed before? Certainly, but they were growing in numbers and in volume. They were more difficult to dismiss and ignore. "The label 'New Woman' signaled new, or newly perceived, forms of femininity which were brought to public attention in the last two decades of the nineteenth century" (Richardson and Willis 1). Novelists presented this New Woman in her daily life—suffering, struggling, resisting tradition. According to Ann Ardis in *New Women, New Novels: Feminism and Early Modernism*, more than one hundred such novels were written between 1883 and 1900 (4). Many female readers sympathized with this character, recognizing in her a piece of their own experience. This recognition of self as represented by the New Woman protagonist promoted a sense of unity with other like-minded women, even though readers felt isolated in their own communities.

The New Woman had been made foul and detestable by the conservative press,[1] but New Woman writers[2] presented a conflicted heroine with whom the late Victorian woman sympathized. These novelists received letters of praise from their contemporaries, ranging from those of social prominence to those of little social significance. Readers claimed that these authors created a human voice that spoke a truth readers had known. One woman said of *The Story of an African Farm* by Olive Schreiner, "I read parts of it over and over," and she claimed the heroine's struggle was one familiar to many women: "I think there is hundreds of women what feels like that but can't speak it, but she could speak what we feel" (qtd. in First and Scott 121).

New Woman authors Charlotte Perkins Gilman and Kate Chopin, among others, protested the accepted institutions of marriage, motherhood, and sexuality. Through their polemical writing and their fiction, they challenged the status quo for women and engaged society to do the same. Some were journalists, public speakers, politicians, but it was their writing—primarily their fiction—that persuaded the populace to change its way of thinking about women and gender politics. It is often most difficult for those without power to let go of what they have been persuaded to believe is safe, but those without power—without a voice in the ruling bodies of government—are often the most in need of change. Through fiction, a stealthy means of persuasion, these writers invited their readers to trade safety for the promise of change.

Stylistically the authors vary: some embrace realism, others naturalism, still others utopianism. The area where the authors consistently find their strength is the New Woman character herself, inspiring sympathy through the voice of a human being who is not self-righteous or all-knowing but is in a struggle for self-actualization. She aims to uncover an authentic female self and determine who she is as an individual. The New Woman novelist suggests that no meaningful change can take place until a woman makes this essential discovery. New Woman heroine Lyndall in Schreiner's *The Story of an African Farm* makes the comparison to the practice of foot-binding: "We fit our sphere as a Chinese woman's foot fits her shoe . . . In some of us the shaping to our end has been quite completed. . . . [Others of us] wear the bandages, but our limbs have not grown to them; we know that we are compressed, and chafe against them" (135–36). The inevitable chafing Lyndall describes resounded more than Lyndall recognizes in her analogy. Many women at the fin de siècle were chafing against their "bandages." The New Woman writer wrote of the inevitable resistance against social constraints and of the determination for the foot to be a foot and not a malformed, crippled representation of itself.

As the twentieth century approached, feminists felt compelled to move for change. The role of woman as wife and mother, as angel of the house, was becoming less readily accepted by women. The nineteenth-century ideals and institutions that ensconced women were openly questioned, challenged, and rejected by some. An opportunity was opening, and the New Woman saw the glimmer of possibility for significant change for women. They sought not only to reform laws and access, but to transform the perception of woman—who she was and the person she was capable of being. The New Woman novelist wrote her as she was: full of potential and willing to explore it. The 1890s, and to some extent the surrounding two decades, saw a surge in the assertion of women's voices insisting on changes to the fabric of society—legal, institutional, and behavioral. Critic Margaret Morgan-roth Gullette asserts the significance of the 1890s in suggesting that "the energies expended in that decade, the incredible expansion of discourse about women *by women*, the revolutionary changes in fiction that occurred, and the long-term effects of that expansion" were so novel and experimental that they symbolically represent the "starting point of the wider modern movement," both the women's movement and literary modernism (495).

To combat her growing influence, the New Woman's opponents launched an assault on her. As Angelique Richardson and Chris Willis point out in *The New Woman in Fact and Fiction*, one of the fictive New Women of the fin de siècle was the one found on the pages of the periodical press. "Journalists and cartoonists played a significant part in establishing the cultural status of the New Woman. . . . As far as her opponents were concerned, the more startling and vivid the picture, the better" (Richardson and Willis 13). As Richardson and Willis elaborate, "The 'journalistic myth' . . . simplified and satirized the New Woman's real concerns over social and moral issues" (24). Patricia Marks suggests that the caricature of the New Woman is "as all caricature and satire are, an exaggeration," not so much an exaggeration of the New Woman's character but of the New Woman as one who is "the embodiment of multifold fears about change itself" (205). In these desperate attempts to preserve the women of the Victorian era, the New Woman caricatures and satires "tried to represent the unthinkable" and "invert[ed] the characteristics by which women were superficially identified" (Marks 206). Marks suggests that the jabs of the satire focused more on what the satirist valued than on the values of the object of ridicule.

The rebellious woman who rejected her role, who challenged the mores of her society earned the title "new woman." The categorization was shifty, and the connotation depended entirely on who was using the term. Love her or hate her, society could not ignore her. She insisted on acknowledgement. "In the guise of a bicycling, cigarette-smoking Amazon," the New Woman is identified by twenty-first-century critics Angelique Richardson and Chris Willis as "a cultural icon of the *fin de siècle*" (12). The New Woman was denigrated as an unfit mother who would bring about the fall of humankind. She was tagged as a sexual deviant and femme fatale on one day, and bluestockinged, monocled, and masculine the next day. She was seen as a hysterical, disobedient wife and a dangerous, rebellious daughter. Lyn Pykett summarizes the contradictions in the portrayal of the New Woman:

> The New Woman was by turns: a mannish amazon and a Womanly woman; she was oversexed, undersexed, or same sex identified; she was anti-maternal, or a racial supermother; she was male-identified, or manhating and/or man-eating, or self-appointed saviour of a benighted masculinity . . . she was radical, socialist or revolutionary, or she was reactionary and conservative. (xii)

Those who sought to turn the New Woman into a caricature found an audience who already sympathized with such portrayals. The satire also discouraged some women from seeking public association with the New Woman. The more representative portrayal of the New Woman offered by the New Woman novelist also had wide appeal and had power. Lucy Bland notes, "Many of these novels by women are today unknown, but at the time they sold in their millions" (144). The popular success of these authors was valued primarily as large-scale communication and education since "these female 'new woman' writers thought of their fiction as didactic in intent and as a political contribution to the women's 'cause'" (Bland 144).

The conservative opponents' devotion to preserving nineteenth-century ideals for women was matched by the conviction and commitment of the New Woman novelist. Describing Charlotte Perkins Gilman, her friend Harriet Howe wrote, "Nothing daunted her. Nothing could daunt her" (qtd. in Ceplair 3). Of her own work Gilman asserted that "literature" was not her primary goal, stating, "I have never made any pretence of being literary" (*Living* 284). Rather, social reform was her objective through her fiction. According to Carol Farley Kessler in her examination of Gilman's "progress toward utopia," a comprehensive study of Gilman's writing, Gilman "believes that literature can enact social changes, can function as social action, can convey alternative versions or visions of human action" (43). Kessler explains this approach to fiction as "a position of clear self-consciousness regarding literary didacticism. The cultural work central to Gilman's utopian fiction is a 're-presentation' of alternative possibilities for being female or male" (43). Gilman's commitment to social change was focused on women: "I know women best, and care more for them. I have an intense and endless love for women—partly in reverence for their high estate, partly in pity for their blind feebleness, their long ages of suffering" (qtd. in Ceplair 8).

Readers did not merely consume these novels; they responded to them. The authors' aims were successful and the means by which the writers accomplished their goal was the New Woman heroine, a fictional representation of the new, odd, strange woman who existed in society. This fictional representation challenged the authenticity of the New Woman presented by her opponents, and it rang true for many readers. Most significantly, the readers whose comments have been preserved suggest that the novelists brought forth a being unlike any that readers had previously encountered in fiction—a *new* woman. "At last the likeness of a new woman has been caught and committed to paper with audacity, fidelity, and literary skill" (qtd. in Small xxv). W. T. Stead notes the distinction of the New Woman novelists' depiction of female experience in his review of Ella Hepworth Dixon's *The Story of a Modern Woman*. Stead highlights the newness and importance of this rendering of character: "The Modern Woman novel is not merely a novel by a woman, or a novel written about women, but it is a novel written by a woman about women from the standpoint of Woman" (64). The novelty of writing by, about, and from the standpoint of a woman might seem commonplace to the twenty-first-century reader, but it was not so to the reader—male or female—of the late nineteenth century.

Stead aptly recognizes Dixon's successful rendering when he states Dixon "has studied her [woman], painted her, and analysed her as if she had an independent existence, and even, strange to say, a soul of her own" (64). Stead's "strange to say" is at the heart of the matter. There is a tone of a shamefaced embarrassment for his society at being surprised by a presentation that identifies a woman as having a soul of her own. In a letter responding to Gilman's short story "The Yellow Wall-paper," a medical doctor wrote, "When I read 'The Yellow Wall Paper' I was much pleased with it; when I read it again, I was delighted with it, and now that I have read it again I am overwhelmed with the delicacy of your touch and the correctness of portrayal" (qtd. in Dock 93). The public was startled by the New Woman novelists' heroines, by the authenticity of the presentation of their voices and their souls. Some were comforted by this presentation, some discomforted by it, but these New Woman heroines struck a chord that rang true to many readers.

Once she had a fair rendering of the New Woman and had the attention of her audience, what did the New Woman novelist do with these? She put her heroine in the world. The New Woman novelist made commentary through her heroine's experience, identifying that which would stifle or suppress her potential—her great offering. New Woman novelists did not all agree on the content of that offering, but they agreed that it was profound and should not be squandered. The institutions of marriage and motherhood as defined by society were first on the chopping block.

"Marriage for love is the beautifullest external symbol of the union of souls; marriage without it is the uncleanliest traffic that defiles the world," says Lyndall, Olive Schreiner's New Woman heroine (*African Farm* 156); so say most of the New Woman novelists as they enter into the marriage debate, validating a heterosexual union while simultaneously invalidating the institution of marriage that exists in their society. New Woman perspectives on marriage ranged from viewing marriage as the noblest profession to seeing it as the figurative "iron cage, wherein women are held in bondage, suffering moral starvation, while the thoughtless gather round to taunt and insult their lingering misery" (Caird, "Marriage" 192–93).

Subtlety was not their aim, nor was pessimism—their commentary was critical, but their vision was optimistic. Despite resistance, Schreiner remained hopeful. In her letters she writes, "I see . . . the possible regeneration of the race in that new union of friendship between man and woman: it must and will come at last, our dreams *are* not delusions but the forerunners of the reality" (Schreiner, *Letters* 84; emphasis in orig.). Envisioning an ideal was essential to the process of achieving a new order. Mona Caird asserts, "First of all we must set up an ideal, undismayed by what will seem its Utopian impossibility" ("Marriage" 196). What was the reality that these writers so desperately wanted to transform and what inroads were these radicals making?

Bland outlines that "feminists had been criticizing marriage . . . in terms of its injustices: a woman's economic dependency, loss of legal and political rights, an unequal divorce law, and, above all, the assumption of a husband's *ownership* of his wife" (124; italics in orig.). In her study of marriage and sexuality in relation to the early British feminists of the turn of the century, Bland notes that this criticism of marriage, though met with much adversity, made inroads for women, both legal and social.[3] Despite the legal successes, feminists were frustrated by "the condition of a married woman as legally under the 'protection' of her husband, with her legal existence subsumed within his" (Bland 125).

As marriage was evolving, so too was divorce in relation to the laws associated with it and social attitudes toward it. Many agitators for change, including radical male lawyers and feminists, moved for divorce to be made a less expensive endeavor that was also more accessible to women, one that "place[d] both sexes on an equal footing with respect to grounds for divorce" (Bland 184). They sought to significantly expand the grounds for divorce to include grounds that would protect women, such as "abuse of conjugal 'rights'" and "the communication of venereal disease" (184, 185). Some were successful, and marriage and divorce laws changed, though slowly.[4] The concept of alimony was also introduced at this time and applied to a deserter, regardless of sex (Richardson and Willis 7). The introduction of alimony was crucial to developing women's financial independence. Even when women did find employment, it was not likely to be lucrative.[5] Women who chose marriage as a profession and whose marital endeavor failed due to desertion would not be quite so financially destitute with the introduction of alimony.[6]

However, there was a lingering awareness that embedded in marriage was the understanding of the ownership by one man of one woman. A society that allowed for such an institution would be one in which women would always remain subordinate to men. Most agreed on this on both sides. Feminists believed such an approach to marriage would keep society from progressing; stunted, subordinate women could bring men down, be a burden, and create degenerate children.

New Woman novelists posited that the old version of marriage had to be discarded and a new version had to be created. Utopian fiction allowed society to recognize the promise of something entirely new. In her study of feminist utopias, Francis Bartowski explains, "Feminist fictions are the 'places' where women speak the desires that frame the anticipatory consciousness of utopia made concrete, bringing the not-yet into the here and now" (162). If New Woman novelists restricted themselves to writing realistic fiction, they would find themselves hampered by their realities, and they often did. In utopian writing, the possibilities for women, their social roles, and identities were endless. Charlotte Perkins Gilman imagined a whole new world in which to reinvent marriage.

On occasion Gilman has been rebuked by critics, even dismissed as a female separatist. This is primarily because of her novel *Herland*, in which she imagines a nation of women that, prior to the action of the plot, through catastrophe and miracle, becomes a single-sex, self-sustaining society. Into this world fly three American male interlopers: Vandyck Jennings, Jeff Margrave, and Terry O. Nicholson. The novel is commonly categorized as utopian. When interpreted in its truest form, utopia is a place that does not exist; therefore, Herland fits this category. As a perfect place—as the term "utopia" has come to be used—Gilman herself would not admit to Herland's utopian status. The central goal of the Herlanders is to find a way to coexist peacefully with men again, to love men and be loved by them, to work together in harmony, and to propagate the ancient way—that is, sexually. They want this "miracle of union in life-giving" for connection and heterosexually shared parenthood (Gilman, *Herland* 119). The women of Herland are asexual in their reproduction and raise the children of the community together. They are not looking to change the structure of their rearing and raising of children. They are looking to include men in the process. One of the most significant fears highlighted in this text is that the women of Herland and the male explorers from the United States are too far apart in their separate evolutions, social and genetic, to reunite in the desired manner. Gilman suggests that the American man of the early twentieth century has much evolving to do before he can reap the benefits of living with these New Women.

The goal of Gilman's novel is the central goal of the novelists examined in this study. They primarily sought to uncover and reclaim a woman's true nature, though that was only the first step. To accomplish that would be impossible given the existence of the institution of marriage. The argument was not that women who were freed from the constraints of marriage would automatically succeed in uncovering what lay deep within. However, even if they could catch a glimmer of that nature, a society that continued to support marriage in its current form would smudge out that glimmer with its thickest smog. Individual escapes from the institution would not suffice; the institution had to be torn down and rebuilt. Most agreed that it should be rebuilt in some form or another and that a union of the sexes was desirable.

New Woman novelists saw the loss of identity for a woman when entering into a marriage as devastating, not merely in a symbolic manner but literally as well. Without independent identity, her liberty to leave the union was hampered despite the inroads the courts were slowly making with respect to women and divorce.

Related to the difficulty for a woman to leave came the problem of legal ownership of the wife by her husband, further clouding the connection between the woman and man. This legal ownership was taken to the extent of owning the wife's physical person: "Given that marital rape went unrecognized in law, the slavery of marriage was sexual as well as economic" (Bland 132).

The primary concern for the New Woman and the New Woman novelist was the identification and distillation of female self-identity. Historically, marriage was the transfer of ownership of and responsibility for a woman from her father to her husband, changing her name and familial associations. This history was detrimental to the female self-identity. In Victorian marriage, the wife defines herself by her husband: by his profession, his name, his ancestral background, his money, and his reputation. An independent identity was not possible for an ideal Victorian wife. She might have hobbies, do humanitarian work, have accomplishments, but primarily she was Mrs. So-and-So, wife and eventually mother. In *Herland*, Gilman has her hero Vandyck suggest about "the marriage tradition of our general history" that it "relates the woman to the man" (120). Vandyck explains, "He goes on with his business, and she adapts herself to him and to it. Even in citizenship, by some strange hocus-pocus, that fact of birth and geography was waved aside, and the woman automatically acquired the nationality of her husband" (120–21). The suggestion that a woman's alliances and associations were transmuted by marriage implies that her primary allegiance is to her homé, her primary duty is to her home, and her primary source of identity is determined by her home. And her "home" is her husband, symbolized by his ring, his name, his house, his family, and his children. All these become representative forms of oppression because of their symbolic associations with oppression and possession by the husband of his wife.

Vandyck relates the shock and surprise of the women of Herland at the concept of "wife" and that of name taking:

> As to the names, Alima, frank soul that she was, asked what good it would do.
>
> Terry, always irritating her, said it was a sign of possession. "You are going to be Mrs. Nicholson," he said, "Mrs. T. O. Nicholson. That shows everyone that you are my wife."
>
> "What is a 'wife' exactly?" she demanded, a dangerous gleam in her eye.
>
> "A wife is a woman who belongs to a man," he began.
>
> But Jeff took it up eagerly: "And a husband is the man who belongs to a woman. It is because we are monogamous, you know. And marriage is the ceremony, civil and religious, that joins the two together—'until death do us part,'" he finished, looking at Celis with unutterable devotion. (Gilman, *Herland* 117)

Despite the fact that the two men and the two relationships are different, Jeff reveals his ignorance of a woman's economic dependence on
a man in a marriage in his society. He is also unaware of the inability
for a man to equally belong to a woman as a woman does to a man in
marriage as he knows it. Through an attempt to balance and idealize
this joint ownership, his quick defensive explanation does not address
the name issue, and so the Herlanders press it:

> "Do your women have no names before they are married?" Celis suddenly
> demanded.
> "Why, yes," Jeff explained. "They have their maiden names—their fa-
> ther's names, that is." (118)

Still somewhat baffled, the Herlanders continue to question the men
about the loss of "maiden" names:

> "And what becomes of them?" asked Alima.
> "They change them for their husbands', my dear," Terry answered her.
> "Change them? Do the husbands then take the wives' 'maiden names'?"
> (118)

The faulty logic of the patriarchal culture is lost on the Herlanders who
cannot make the connection because there is none to make unless the
men explain the cultural context in which this system of adopting new
names is used. But betraying their culture's flaws, juxtaposing them to
this Herland culture's successes, is not the approach these Americans
ever take. It is, however, the approach Gilman takes.

> "Oh, no," he laughed. "The man keeps his own and gives it to her, too."
> "Then she just loses hers and takes a new one—how unpleasant! We
> won't do that!" Alima said decidedly. (118)

And they don't! The Herland women are willing to pacify the men with whom they plan to enter into a union on levels that they feel are harmless, but a loss of identity, however symbolic and benign it might be in Herland, is not an adjustment they are willing to make. The representation by Gilman that this symbolic loss of identity is significant to a woman in society is suggestive of an issue far more deeply rooted. It represents the dangerous loss of self a woman experiences in marriage and the detrimental effects this has on her psyche, as revealed in Gilman's short story "The Yellow Wall-paper." In *Herland*, with humor, understatement, and gentle mockery, Gilman adeptly writes her commentary on this social ill in succinct dialogue that is convincing even by twenty-first-century standards.

In Gilman's Herland, the "marriages" are entered into to appease the men; the Herlanders allow this symbolic nod to the institution. The Herlanders recognize marriage as insignificant and antiquated, but they understand that it is an aspect of the men's former lives that they are not yet willing to abandon entirely. Because it carries neither history for the women nor any legal or traditional suggestion of bondage in Herland, Gilman implies that the union is soluble. She illustrates this when one of the "husbands" attempts rape on his "wife," at which time the bonds of matrimony are not even considered, and the "husband" faces perpetual anesthesia or exile.

"'Might as well not be married at all,' growled Terry. 'They only got up that ceremony to please us . . . They've no real idea of being married'" (Gilman, *Herland* 124). The offending Terry is quite right: the Herlanders have no understanding of the concept of "being married" in the traditional sense. Giving up the self to be possessed by a husband and entering into an ironclad union are concepts beyond the capacity of a Herlander to understand.

In the nineteenth century, the Victorian chivalric code protected an unmarried woman's right to her own body in that a man could not legally rape her. Once a wife, the tables turned. Committing to a husband included committing to his sexual appetites and whims regardless of her own. Struggle or scream though she might, he had a right to his wife's body whenever he so chose. In Britain, until the Clitheroe case in 1887, a husband had a right to own his wife's person, entitling a man to custody of his wife (Bland 136). As extreme as these statements might seem to a twenty-first-century reader, the general acceptance of this established a tone for the marriage relationship between a man and a woman. This standard was what New Woman novelists attacked— what they aimed to destroy. In agreement with each other on this issue, New Woman novelists asserted that no relationship could be healthy if both partners are not of equal value to one another, if both partners are not on equal footing—sharing both burden and joy. If one partner can legally own the other, the suggestion was that the relationship would be hopelessly flawed. Thus, Schreiner's most frustrated feminist heroine, Lyndall, states, "I am not in so great a hurry to put my neck beneath any man's foot" (*African Farm* 131).

Kate Chopin's novel *The Awakening* establishes "the focus upon woman as captive wife and her recognition of that bondage" (Jacobs 81). In the opening chapters, Chopin's Edna acquiesces and holds out her hands to receive her wedding rings of which her husband has been in possession while she swam. Later, Edna tries to grind her wedding ring into the floor of her room in a fit of rebellion. "Edna could not help but think that it was very foolish, very childish, to have stamped upon her wedding ring" (Chopin 54). After the realization of the absurdity and futility of rebellion against the symbol of her oppression, Edna chooses genuine rebellion. "She was visited by no more outbursts, moving her to such futile expedients. She began to do as she liked and to feel as she liked" (54). This rebellion should be read as much as one against self as it is commonly read as a rebellion against her husband and marriage. Her self-disgust reveals this. Edna chooses marriage, like many of the heroines, as an escape from another kind of confinement, that of young maidenhood under the thumb of her father (18–19). She puts the ring on her own finger after swimming.

Edna chooses to leave the marriage, her husband, and her two sons to re-create herself in a society that is not yet capable of valuing Edna in her reformed state and that ultimately destroys her. For Edna, as with many of the heroines, the problem with her marriage has many roots, but the taproot leads to a loveless union. Chopin explains that "her marriage to Léonce Pontellier was purely an accident, in this respect resembling many other marriages which masquerade as the decrees of Fate" (18).

Outside of marriage, Edna discovers both emotional and sexual awakenings with men. Still, there is the subtle suggestion that if Edna were to enter into a marriage with Robert Lebrun, the man she believes she loves, or with Alcée Arobin, the man she had experienced "the first kiss of her life to which her nature had really responded" (Chopin 80), the love and the sexual longing would eventually die. In Edna's marriage, she experiences many flaws: meaningless existence, lack of meaningful labor, "sex parasitism," a sense of being owned by another. Léonce, Edna's husband, does not conceal that he views her as his property and that he can dictate her actions and thoughts. The reader's first introduction to Léonce is to see him "looking at his wife as one looks at a valuable piece of personal property" (4). In the following scenes, Léonce insists on certain behaviors from Edna, demanding that she come in from outdoors and not swim out too far. Like an obstinate child, Edna disobeys. Her rebellion initially is childish and representative of her pluck. When she eventually moves out of her husband's home, she is unsure why exactly she is so inclined. She tells Mademoiselle Reisz that it is because she does not like that the house is not hers, nor is it theirs, but it is her husband's. She is coming to understand that this economic reliance is a burden to her (76). She prefers to stay in a much smaller house that the fruits of her artistic labor afford. She prefers to feel love for Robert rather than emptiness toward her husband, and she prefers sexual pleasure from Alcée rather than the forced physical relationship she has with her husband.

Edna redefines what she wants in relationships with men after rejecting the experience of traditional marriage. The women of Herland accept marriage with the intruders only because they associate no negative connotations with it. Marriage to them holds only positive potential. They do not know marriage as Edna does or as Lyndall does, as a trafficking in women. They hope for and expect a genuine union of souls and the potential to procreate the old-fashioned way. As time passes in their wedded lives, they become acquainted with marriage as it is accepted by the "civilized" world off the plateau, and they resist specific constructs within it. What they oppose is what Gilman sees as marriage's greatest flaws—its greatest offenses to woman's nature. These flaws restrict marriage from becoming a healthy partnership between men and women. These include inequality of personal space, a lack of ownership over one's own body, and inequality in labor. Much to the surprise of the male protagonists, the women will not budge on these issues. When the men force the issue, particularly in the case of the attempted rape, the women of Herland come together in the defense of the endangered. The men are confined and then exiled. Even the union that the society of Herland has so longed for is not valued at the cost of sacrificing one woman. This is the great difference between the experience of marriage in Herland and that of the realistic fictions of the other authors in this study. Although the fictions differ from author to author, true for all is that union—as central as it is to the drive of these feminists—is not of more value than the individual soul of any one woman. When that soul is damaged, distorted, or sacrificed, the union is unworthy and no longer union. Rather, it is a usurpation of self and a devouring of one being to sustain the other. New Woman novelists agree this approach to marriage will destroy society as a whole. "We have in us the blood of a womanhood that was never bought and never sold; that wore no veil, and had no foot bound; whose realized ideal of marriage was sexual companionship and an equality in duty and labor" (Schreiner, *Woman and Labor* 148).

Gilman's short story "The Yellow Wall-Paper" presents a typical relationship between a husband and wife. Loosely based on her own experience, Gilman imagines the radical implications of such a relationship. Suffering from what critics generally interpret as postpartum depression, the narrator of the story is forced to "rest" in a single room with mesmerizing wallpaper. No mental stimulus, prescribes her doctor husband. In "The Yellow Wall-paper," Gilman's narrator discovers women trapped in the wallpaper and begins to live a double life. By day, the narrator and the women in the paper live under the guise of Victorian propriety, and by night, they escape those bonds. The knowledge of this escape excites the narrator of "The Yellow Wall-paper," but she will reveal nothing to anyone who might threaten to remove the opportunity for this escape:

> Life is very much more exciting now than it used to be. You see I have something more to expect, to look forward to . . .
>
> John is so pleased to see me improve! He laughed a little the other day, and said I seemed to be flourishing in spite of my wall-paper.
>
> I turned it off with a laugh. I had no intention of telling him it was *because* of the wall-paper . . .
>
> I don't want to leave now until I have found it out. (Gilman, "Yellow" 38)

Gilman writes into her narrator's character an unquenchable thirst for discovery parallel to that of the New Woman novelist's thirst for self-discovery. The woman behind the paper is the narrator, and the discovery is self-discovery. The New Woman novelist and the narrator of "The Yellow Wall-paper" are drawn to each other.

Once she has connected with it—the wallpaper, the woman behind it, the hundreds of women trapped inside of it—she cannot escape its lure. "The smell! . . . It creeps all over the house. . . . It gets into my hair" (Gilman, "Yellow" 38). The New Woman novelist takes this knowledge to a new level, beyond the personal, and she sees her duty to heal society with her new knowledge and to liberate other trapped women from the wallpaper that confines them. "As soon as it was moonlight and that poor thing began to crawl and shake the pattern, I got up and ran to help her" (40). By the end, when the narrator of "The Yellow Wall-paper" has peeled nearly all the wallpaper off, she sees "so many of those creeping women," and she wonders "if they all come out of the wall-paper as I did" (41). This scene represents the ironic feeling of isolation that the New Women experienced. They experience isolation in spite of their intense desire to enact change in the name of women and society.

Like the hero in the archetypal hero's journey, the New Woman heroine and novelist have gone into the abyss—behind the wallpaper. The New Woman heroine faces the challenges and obstacles there. Surviving these, she reaches atonement, at one with herself. Like the hero, she must return with her new knowledge to society in order to impart that knowledge to those who have not experienced her journey. However, she is not of the same constitution as the hero of Greek myth, and the gods are not on her side. Reflecting on this return, the narrator concludes, "I suppose I shall have to get back behind the pattern when it comes night, and that is hard!" (Gilman, "Yellow" 41). The validation and escape is liberating, but in order to make it worthwhile, the New Woman novelist must return her knowledge to society. The narrator of "The Yellow Wall-paper" opts not to: "It is so pleasant to be out in this great room and creep around as I please!" (41). Gilman relieves her of her duties to society and allows her the license to stay within the comfort of her personal liberation.

The narrator asserts that she will not go outside because outside it is green and not yellow. Inside there is a "smooch" in the wall where her shoulder fits so she "cannot lose [her] way" as she creeps (Gilman, "Yellow" 42). As with other female gothic fiction, the house becomes the domain of the woman and is often a symbol of the woman's body or of the woman herself. In "The Yellow Wall-paper," the narrator "creeping" along the "smooch" in the wall so as not to lose her way describes the New Woman novelist who is exploring the woman trapped behind the wallpaper of turn-of-the-century existence. Echoing the narrator's final words to her husband who represents what oppresses her, the New Woman novelist finds herself exclaiming, "I've got out at last," and she, too, has "pulled off most of the paper" so her jailer cannot "put her back" (42).

The final scene of Chopin's *The Awakening* presents Edna back at Grand Isle on the isolated beach facing the sea and her subsequent release and demise.

> For the first time in her life she stood naked in the open air, at the mercy of the sun, the breeze that beat upon her, and the waves that invited her.
>
> How strange and awful it seemed to stand naked under the sky! how delicious! She felt like some new-born creature, opening its eyes in a familiar world that it had never known.
>
> The foamy wavelets curled up to her white feet . . . The touch of the sea is sensuous, enfolding the body in its soft, close embrace. (108–9)

The two New Woman heroines, Edna and the narrator of "The Yellow Wall-paper," are caught with too much knowledge, too much insight and desire with no adequate outlet—no suitable partner and no purposeful existence. Society has no place for them and does not want them. They are in parallel predicaments and meet a similar fate—one that has been read as liberation or tragedy.

Though Chopin's language draws the reader optimistically to a return of woman to her nature, Edna is not emerging from the sea, reborn; she is returning to it and to death. One can read optimism, naturalism, or ethereal elevation into Chopin's closing scene, but one still cannot escape that it is the closing, the end of Edna's awakening, and the end of her progress. She dies, leaving unchanged the society that exiled her back to her natural roots. Her foil, Adèle Ratignolle, is not about to start agitating for the vote, and her mentor, Mademoiselle Reisz, will remain a recluse, for it is the only way she can survive in her society.

What the fictional voices reveal of ideals and desires, and the fictional beings attempt to accomplish in self-awareness and social acceptance, is remarkable and remarkably new. They slough the skin of their Victorian predecessors and, in so doing, make themselves vulnerable. Most ultimately fail, are miserable, and die young. So what good does it do to write the New Woman heroine into existence at all? Why liberate her from the bonds of nineteenth-century, middle-class sexuality, motherhood, and marriage only to force her to face the fact that there is no alternative for her but death, despair, or the knowledge that she is living a hypocritical life? New Woman heroines have their voices resonate, and all are heard and were heard from 1884 to 1915. They shook the foundations of the institutional structures that endeavored to confine them. Although they successfully influenced few in the fictional world they inhabited, they inspired discussion and change in the authors' real societies. Fear, debates, enthusiasm, and empathy were resounding responses to the lives and voices of the New Woman heroine.

Women's literature scholar Elaine Showalter admits, "*The Awakening* broke new thematic and stylistic ground as Chopin went boldly beyond the work of her precursors in writing about women's longing for sexual and personal emancipation" (*Sister's Choice* 65). Showalter also highlights that Chopin's voice is echoed by Mademoiselle Reisz, the artist and strange woman in the world of *The Awakening*, who claims that "the artist must possess 'the courageous soul that dares and defies'" (66). Each New Woman novelist in her way boldly "dares and defies." The authors have direction and purpose; they have a social and political agenda for change, and fiction is their most effective vehicle for enacting this change. Their effectiveness is in the representation of a new kind of woman attempting to affirm herself, to rise to her highest potential, and then to attempt to survive her society while clinging to her selfhood.

Mademoiselle Reisz might have claimed that the artist's soul is one "that dares and defies" (Chopin 61), but she is also afraid of the water. A pianist, she dares and defies in her music that society does not understand, and then she hides away, a hermit, a recluse, tortured by her solitude. The reader is led to believe that she lives an enlightened life internally, but her only release of this self is through her art, which is rarely understood—another level of isolation. Throughout *The Awakening*, Edna's learning to swim parallels her learning to be. It is described with a sensual language of liberation and discovery: "Edna plunged and swam about with an abandon that thrilled and invigorated her" (47). Chopin only allows Mademoiselle Reisz such abandon in her music; she avoids the water and avoids complete awakening. Mademoiselle Reisz, like other mentors in the New Woman novel, is a predecessor to the New Woman. She has survived because she has not gone in the water. The New Woman novelist suggests with her fiction that there can be no more avoidance of the water, and the heroines in many cases go even further than their creators.

Recognizing the existence of the New Woman novelist and her influence is critical. Showalter explains that the feminists "represent a turning point in the female tradition, and they turn inward" (*A Literature* 175). The New Woman novelists initially set out "with a sense of utility and a sense of mission, a real concern for the future of womanhood" (Showalter 175). They sculpted out of air and ideas a woman who was a new, realistic, and sympathetic character, who spoke of change and represented it, and who inspired transformation. "By refusing to accept definitions of traditional male and female roles and instead offering alternatives to mainstream expectations, Gilman forces readers to question boundaries defining behavior assumed acceptable on the basis of gender" (Kessler 43). Gilman and other New Woman novelists influenced society through these questions and presentations of possibilities. "Few recent historians have grasped the profundity of the social metamorphoses brought about by 'new women'" (Gilbert and Gubar 21).

Notes

1. *Cornhill Magazine* "presented her as a 'fast' woman pursuing an unwilling male prey" (Ledger 13). A series of images satirizing the New Woman's values were published in the British magazine *Punch* throughout the 1890s and are reproduced in *The New Woman in Fiction and in Fact*, edited by Angelique Richardson and Chris Willis.

2. Prominent New Woman writers include Sarah Grand, Mona Caird, Ménie Muriel Dowie, Ella Hepworth Dixon, Kate Chopin, Charlotte Perkins Gilman, Olive Scrheiner, and George Egerton, among others.

3. The Infant Custody Acts (1839, 1873), the Married Women's Property Acts (1870, 1882), and the Matrimonial Causes Act (1878) all contributed to a changing state of marriage in Britain.

4. The well-documented Married Women's Property Acts of 1870 and 1882 "eventually gave all married women the right to their own property, extending the equitable concept of married women's 'separate estate', while dispensing with the need for settlements and trustees" (Richardson and Willis 7).

5. Records of women's wages in Britain and the United States from this period indicate that women generally made one-third of the wages of a man in the same position (Faderman 185).

6. In addition to these legal advances, the British Court of Appeal's ruling on the Clitheroe abduction case began to establish that a man was not legally permitted to rape his wife. Though, as Lucy Bland notes, "reaction to the verdict was mixed" (136).

Works Cited

Ardis, Ann. *New Women New Novels: Feminism and Early Modernism*. New Brunswick: Rutgers UP, 1990. Print.

Bartowski, Frances. *Feminist Utopias*. Lincoln: U of Nebraska P, 1989. Print.

Bland, Lucy. *Banishing the Beast: Feminism, Sex and Morality*. New York: St. Martin's, 2002. Print.

Caird, Mona. *The Daughters of Danaus*. 1894. New York: Feminist, 1989. Print.

___. "Marriage." 1888. *A New Woman Reader: Fiction, Articles, and Drama of the 1890s*. Ed. Carolyn Christensen Nelson. Toronto: Broadview, 2001. 185–99. Print.

Ceplair, Larry. Introduction. *Charlotte Perkins Gilman: A Nonfiction Reader*. Ed. Ceplair. New York: Columbia UP, 1991. 1–8. Print.

Chopin, Kate. *The Awakening*. 1899. New York: Norton, 1994. Print.

Dixon, Ella Hepworth. *The Story of a Modern Woman*. London: Merlin, 1990. Print.

Dock, Julie Bates, comp. and ed. *Charlotte Perkins Gilman's 'The Yellow Wall-paper' and the History of Its Publication and Reception*. University Park: Pennsylvania State UP, 1998. Print.

Faderman, Lillian. *Surpassing the Love of Men*. 1985. London: Women's, 1997. Print.

First, Ruth, and Ann Scott. *Olive Schreiner: A Biography*. 1980. New Brunswick: Rutgers UP, 1990. Print.

Gilbert, Sandra M., and Susan Gubar. *No Man's Land: The Place of the Woman Writer in the Twentieth Century*. Vol. 2. New Haven: Yale UP, 1988. Print.

Gilman, Charlotte Perkins. *Herland*. 1915. *Herland, The Yellow Wall-paper, and Selected Writings*. Ed. Denise D. Knight. New York: Penguin, 1999. 1–143. Print.

___. *The Living Charlotte Perkins Gilman: An Autobiography*. 1935. Madison: U of Wisconsin P, 1990. Print.

___. "The Yellow Wall-paper." *Charlotte Perkins Gilman's 'The Yellow Wall-paper' and the History of Its Publication and Reception*. Comp. and ed. Julie Bates Bates. University Park: Pennsylvania State UP, 1998. 27–42. Print.

Gullette, Margaret Morganroth. Afterword. *The Daughters of Danaus*. 1894. By Mona Caird. New York: Feminist, 1989. 493–534. Print.

Jacobs, Dorothy. "*The Awakening*: A Recognition of Confinement." *Kate Chopin Reconsidered: Beyond the Bayou*. Ed. Lynda S. Boren and Sara deSaussure Davis. Baton Rouge: Louisiana State UP, 1992. 80–94. Print.

Kessler, Carol Farley. *Charlotte Perkins Gilman: Her Progress toward Utopia with Selected Writings*. Syracuse: Syracuse UP, 1995. Print.

Ledger, Sally. *The New Woman: Fiction and Feminism at the Fin de Siècle*. Manchester: Manchester UP, 1997. Print.

Ledger, Sally, and Scott McCracken, eds. *Cultural Politics at the Fin de Siècle*. Cambridge: Cambridge UP, 1995. Print.

Marks, Patricia. *Bicycles, Bangs, and Bloomers: The New Woman in the Popular Press*. Lexington: UP of Kentucky, 1990. Print.

Pykett, Lyn. Foreword. *The New Woman in Fact and Fiction: Fin-de-Siècle Feminisms*. Ed. Angelique Richardson and Chris Willis. Basingstoke: Palgrave Macmillan, 2002. xi–xii. Print.

Richardson, Angelique, and Chris Willis. Introduction. *The New Woman in Fact and Fiction: Fin-de-siècle Feminisms*. Ed. Richardson and Willis. Basingstoke: Palgrave, 2002. 1–38. Print.

Schreiner, Olive. *Olive Schreiner Letters: 1871–1899*. Vol. 1. Ed. Richard Rive. Oxford: Oxford UP, 1988. Print.

___. *The Story of an African Farm*. 1883. Mineola: Dover, 1998. Print.

___. *Woman and Labor*. New York: Stokes, 1911. Print.

Showalter, Elaine. *A Literature of Their Own: British Women Novelists, from Brontë to Lessing*. Rev. ed. London: Virago, 2009. Print.

___. *Sister's Choice: Tradition and Change in American Women's Writing*. Oxford: Oxford UP, 1994. Print.

Small, Helen. Introduction. *Gallia*. 1895. By Ménie Muriel Dowie. London: Everyman, 1995. xxv–xlii. Print.

Stead, W. T. "The Book of the Month: The Novel of the Modern Woman." Rev. of *The Story of the Modern Woman*, by Ella Hepworth Dixon. *Review of Reviews* 10 (1894): 64–74. Print.

The Solidarity of Song: Proletarians, Poetry, and the Public Sphere of the Lawrence Textile Strike of 1912

Tara Forbes and Mikhail Bjorge

> It is the first strike I ever saw which sang! I shall not soon forget the curious lift, the strange sudden fire of the mingled nationalities at the strike meetings when they broke into the universal language of song. (Ray Stannard Baker, "The Revolutionary Strike")

Ray Baker noticed this "strange sudden fire" during the Lawrence, Massachusetts, textile strike of 1912, during which song became one of the strike's defining features. In the face of vicious opposition from employers, the local and state governments, and the capitalist class itself, the workers of Lawrence fought back with strikes, pickets, meetings, speeches, and songs—and concomitant words—all under the revolutionary banner of the Industrial Workers of the World (IWW). Situating song as a form of direct proletarian praxis reveals how strikers were able to expose, analyze, and critique the wider society from their vantage. Moreover, contextualization and textual/socioeconomic analysis creates theoretical space for the multifaceted manifestation and role(s) of militant, radical, and revolutionary song and hence militant, radical, and revolutionary literature. Indeed, the song/strike dialectic was a mass and immediate manifestation of proletarian power distinctly within both the public sphere and class struggle itself; therefore, song was a significant facet of proletarian revolt, not merely a sideshow of niche interest.

Throughout the entire strike, the IWW furthered the strike effort with their organizational skills and song. Song was important to the IWW since its founding convention in Chicago. Both "The Marseillaise" and "The Internationale," two revolutionary workers' songs originating from European revolutionary struggles, were sung at the event. Richard Brazier, a Canadian militant transplanted to Spokane, noted, "What first attracted me to the IWW was its songs and the gusto with which its members sang them" (Green et al. 375). Perhaps a good thing too, as Brazier went on to become the founding voice behind *The Little Red Songbook—Songs to Fan the Flames of Discontent* (1908), the tome that became the secular hymnbook of the radical worker.[1] By the time of the Lawrence strike, the songbook was many editions deep and was greatly expanded. Revolutionary song, Brazier argued, was as important as that of written propaganda pamphlets and books. Indeed, he posited, "Songs are easily remembered but dull prose is soon forgotten" (qtd. in Brenner, Day, and Ness 108). Like a lengthy text, these songs were full of "anger and protest," calling "to judgment our oppressors and the profit system they have devised" (108), but in a much more jovial package, as "song tells the story simply" (Carter 365). Not merely educational but also dealing "with every aspect of the workers' lives," these songs were self-situated tools meant to "stir the workers to action" (Green et al. 381).

Song became an important part of the IWW's tactical arsenal. Lyrics and rollick brought workers to its cause, educated them on the basics of revolutionary theory, and gave voice to an often voiceless, faceless class.[2] The simple cadence allowed ease of singing and remembering for the many workers for which English was a new language. Indeed, when Salvation Army bands were sent to drown out IWW speakers on street corners, the workers would subvert the censorious attempt of the church by singing along, but with their own lyrics (Nolan and Thompson 4–5).[3] Furthermore, aligned with the radically democratic ethos of the IWW, the idea of "a useful tune" allowed proletarians to directly acknowledge their current social positions as laudable and full of militant agency. The nature of the IWW song suddenly made it "possible for workers to see themselves as agents and producers of wealth—potentially the saviors of society rather than as inevitable victims" (Furey 56).

The radical song was a manifestation of the IWW members' basic ethos: these songs, this militant and radical literature, materialized from a proletarian milieu of activity and struggle, emerging intrinsically from the bottom up, from the workers themselves.[4] Inclusive to the broader goal of the IWW, songs were often crafted in workers' own language, a direct refusal of the postliturgical notion of a canonical language. The goal of the self-constructed song-as-tool was not only "fanning the flames of discontent," but (re)constituting solidarity, education, and promotion of the organization while exerting a radical, militant worldview into the public sphere. Furthermore, mirroring the preamble of the IWW, by appropriating the sordidly hierarchical songs of capitalism, the state, and the church, workers were culturally "forming the structure of the new society within the shell of the old" (Kornbluh 12).

Noted Marxist philosopher Antonio Gramsci argued that "all men are intellectuals . . . but not all men have in society the function of intellectuals" (304) and further that "each man, finally, outside of his professional activity carries on some form of intellectual activity" (305). Through this intellectual activity, no matter how seemingly insignificant, people contribute to "sustain a conception of the world or to modify it, that is, to bring into being new modes of thought" (Gramsci 321). By engaging its members (called "Wobblies") as workers and intellectuals, the IWW created a public space in which proletarians could establish their own songs and exert them *meaningfully and performatively* on the foundation of class struggle. Hence the role of song would be to aid workers not only in the service of immediate gain on a picket line, meeting, or free speech fight, but constitutively in construction, performance, and (re)production in text for later use. Mary Heaton Vorse, a journalist covering the strike, stated:

> They [strikers] are learning history and economics translated into the terms of their own lives. Many of them suddenly find hitherto unsuspected powers. . . . The workers set off singing the songs they themselves have made up under the pressure of the strike. Like new blood these new talents flow through the masses of the workers. (12)

Song became a medium for the articulation of intelligence inherent to the human condition, so often seen by the capitalist as merely a tool for production and the extraction of surplus value.

Thus the radical song emerged as more than an educational tool, a recruitment tool, a signifier and public(ized) expression of solidarity, a way to boost spirits, strengthen pickets, or produce militancy: it became self-constructed intellectual work, manifest in real time and within the workers' struggle generally and the revolutionary program of the IWW specifically. On a picket line, on a march, in a parade, during a meeting, and in spontaneous outburst, the song became an avenue to exert a sense of militant ownership of space and to force a radically intellectual reenvisioning of the possible. In combination with organized action, the song shattered the silence of individual proletarians suffering in lonely isolation. Thus the song is more than just "radical literature": it is perhaps a prime example of how literature can actually *be* radical and how the voiceless and those lost to history can speak. These songs emerged from the bottom up and were in the service of not only the strikers' immediate needs but also of the social realm of the IWW, an organization that actively worked for proletarian revolution. In the hands of the manifold workers within the IWW, the song became a weapon and "every shout a cannon ball" (Giovannitti 30).

The IWW was a radical, militant, and revolutionary proletarian organization founded in Chicago, Illinois, in 1905. Although predominantly a union, the IWW involved itself in a myriad of struggles: advocating with and for the unemployed and the transient, advocating free speech for workers, and the struggle against war and militarism, among others. The assortment of people who met in 1905 to give life to a new organization included anarchists, socialists, and unionists. Although divided on many issues, they were united in several prominent beliefs. Their first concern was that their new organization needed to be a union organized along industrial lines.[5] Another was the first line of their constitution, namely that "the working class and the employing class have nothing in common. There can be no peace so long as hunger and want are found among millions of working people and the few, who make up the employing class, have all of the good things in life" (Kornbluh 12–13). For the IWW, the working class was expansive, including recent immigrants, women, the unskilled, and workers of all ethnolinguistic groups. The IWW was also opposed to the predominant umbrella labor organization in the United States at the time, the American Federation of Labor (AFL), and thought that it was ill suited to the task of uniting the proletariat into a class for itself, a class that could fight and eventually destroy capitalism.

In the early twentieth century, the AFL was essentially the only mass umbrella organization for unionized American workers. If one wanted to unionize, one's only significant option was an AFL affiliate. The emergence of the IWW changed this and, in doing so, shifted the realm of possibility for workers. Historian Howard Kimeldorf penned a series of juxtapositions in relation to the IWW and the AFL:

> Where the AFL broke up the working class into a multitude of tiny craft unions, the IWW envisioned "One Big Union." . . . Where the AFL's membership consisted mostly of native-born, skilled, white craftsmen, the IWW was committed to organizing almost everyone else, targeting in particular the unskilled, recent immigrants, women, and workers of color. Where the AFL monopolized employment opportunities for its current members by restricting union access . . . the IWW offered a true "communism of opportunity" based on mass recruiting, low initiation fees, and work sharing. And where the AFL advocated an industrial peace based on the sanctity of contracts, the IWW promised unrelenting class war, refusing as a matter of principle to sign labor agreements or any other such "armistice" until the working class had secured its final emancipation from capitalism. (2)

It should be added that whereas the AFL believed in the legalistic "grievance procedure" for handling problems between the employer and worker, the IWW believed in direct action. Furthermore, while the

AFL thought that workers should be organized and controlled from the top of the organization down, the IWW believed that the workers were the experts and the vast majority of job-related activity should be controlled from the bottom up. The most significant difference, however, between the IWW and the AFL was regarding the electoral-political realm and the necessary telos of proletarian action. The AFL believed that the ultimate goal of unionization should be to raise the wages and living conditions of certain workers and, in the political realm, to "reward our friends and punish our enemies" (Hayes 757)—"friends" and "enemies" to be determined by the leadership. The IWW, in stark juxtaposition, believed that, as one founding delegate put it, "dropping pieces of paper into a hole in a box never did achieve emancipation of the working class" (qtd. in Kornbluh 12). Furthermore, the IWW believed that the final goal of organizing was to conglomerate all workers into "one big union," call a general strike, and take over all industry in the interests of the proletariat itself, abolishing capitalism as well as the state that protects and preserves it.[6]

Although many of the songs sung on the Lawrence picket lines do not speak of violence, it was not a bloodless struggle. The workers were pitted against not only their bosses but against state mechanisms as well. However, the majority of the songs did not advocate for violence; rather, they advocated for power. In her book *On Violence*, theorist Hannah Arendt distinguishes between violence and power in terms of means to a goal, stating, "Since the end of human action, as distinct from the end products of fabrication, can never be reliably predicted, the means used to achieve political goals are more often than not of greater relevance to the future world than the intended goals" (4). In other words, because the product of the strike is unknown, the actions taken during the strike are of significance. Arendt avers that it is "a rather sad reflection on the present state of political science that our terminology does not distinguish among such key words as 'power,' 'strength,' 'force,' 'authority,' and, finally, 'violence'" (*On Violence* 43). "Force," as defined by Arendt, should "indicate the energy released by physical or social movements" (44–45). Indeed, this strike was part of a social movement, and it was a forceful one. The workers exerted their force as a class onto the bosses. Furthermore, "*power* corresponds to the human ability not just to act but to act in concert. Power is never the property of an individual; it belongs to a group and remains in existence only so long as the group keeps together" (44; italics in orig.). Thus the *force* of the social movement of the strike was due to the class-situated *power* of the strikers themselves. The theme of power as a group dynamic is seen in all of the Lawrence songs. The refrain of solidarity resonates strongly throughout every song discussed, and militant solidarity was the main reason for the success of the strike. These songs aided in forming a community of workers sharing the same struggle.

According to Arendt, the public sphere "gathers us together" (*Human Condition* 52). The mill workers in Lawrence (re)produced their struggle in the public sphere and, with the inclusion of song, planted it firmly. Song aided in creating a social environment through solidarity while educating and motivating the strikers and the public. Even though the outcomes of workers' struggle can be uncertain, the means to the goal are essential. In the case of Lawrence, the means produced a successful strike. Using song as a tool of struggle is substantial as "only where things can be seen by many in a variety of aspects without changing their identity, so that those who are gathered around them know they [here, the strikers] see sameness in utter diversity, can worldly reality truly and reliably appear" (Arendt, *Human Condition* 57). This manifestation of workers' power was immediate, and the songs' placement in the public sphere alongside the now very public reality of workers' struggle allowed the strike to gain not only national interest and a "reliable" representation, but it also shaped a solidarity among workers that was manifestly extraordinary.

Emma Goldman, an observer of the strike at Lawrence, links social change intimately with growing workers' movements and emphasizes the importance of solidarity:

So long as discontent and unrest make themselves but dumbly felt within a limited social class, the powers of reaction may often succeed in suppressing such manifestations. But when the dumb unrest grows into conscious expression and becomes almost universal, it necessarily affects all phases of human thought and action. (241)

This "conscious expression" became "almost universal" during the genesis of the strike in Lawrence. "Short Pay! Short Pay!" yelled some workers at the Everett Mill; "All out!" encouraged others (Moran 171; Watson 11). The place was the monstrous Everett Mill in Lawrence, Massachusetts, and the date was Thursday, January 11, 1912. The workers at the mill had just received their first paychecks following a change in labor law. This law required mill owners to move to a fifty-four-hour workweek from a fifty-six-hour one. The mill owners had largely paid off their mills and were issuing dividends to shareholders. Their profits were bolstered not only by rampant exploitation of their workers but by protective tariffs and government contracts. Nonetheless, the employers slashed the commensurate wages of those workers from whom they had reaped their massive profits, wages that "were already at the starvation point" (Flynn 117). Lawrence had a population of almost eighty-six thousand, and well over fifty thousand worked in, or depended on the wages from, the local mills. Although wages could be as low as a few dollars a week to as high as twelve dollars (Watson 75), the average week's pay for a worker in Lawrence was around six dollars (72). Their pay-cut constituted about fifty cents a week, or the price of ten loaves of bread, according to the strikers (Bureau of Labor 496–97); for families perpetually on the brink of starvation and eviction, this was an enormous hardship.

The workers from the Everett Mill expanded their action throughout the city the next day. Workers from Everett went into the mill to get any stragglers off their looms and onto the picket line. When some refused to leave, their machines were destroyed with whatever was at hand. From Everett, the strikers ran from mill to mill, growing in numbers as they went along. In the Wood Mill, the largely male strikers, accompanied by the "blowing of horns," cleared the mill of workers and, anticipating a long strike, sabotaged some machines (Moran 172). The machines went deathly silent, but the picket lines, marches, and meetings came alive.

It is fitting that "The Marseillaise" and "The Internationale" were sung at both the founding convention and on the picket lines at Lawrence, and they were in many ways foundational songs within the revolutionary tradition.[7] "The Marseillaise" was composed by Rouget de Lisle and became the French national anthem (Green et al. 56). De Lisle was a French army officer, and the song was dedicated to the French commander of the Army of the Rhine (Kornbluh 173). It has been used as a "revolutionary rallying cry across borders" by many socialist and communist organizations and groups and has appeared in numerous anthologies of union and leftist songs (Green et al. 56).

The workers on the picket lines would have known the lyrics to "The Marseillaise" in their own languages and would have been able to sing along with ease. Moreover, the lyrics offered the workers a sense of shared struggle that could easily be applied to battles of all kinds. "The Marseillaise," as published in both *Rebel Voices* and *The Big Red Songbook*, begins with a broad call to "Ye sons of toil" (line 1).[8] In the three English-language verses most commonly sung at Lawrence,[9] France is not mentioned and the content remains expansive. The first verse mentions "children" and "wives" (line 3), which fit into the textile strikes quite well: the majority of strikers were adolescents and women, and the song instructs the masses to "Behold their tears and hear their cries!" (4), demanding compassion along with solidarity. Creating a common enemy in the second verse strengthens this new-found solidarity:

> With luxury and pride surrounded,
> The vile, insatiate despots dare,
> Their thirst for gold and power unbounded,

To mete and vend the light and air.
Like beasts of burden, would they load us,
Like gods would bid their slaves adore,
But man is Man, and who is more?
Then shall they longer lash and goad us? (14–22)

The final verse is sung as a call to arms. It begins as a series of questions for its oppressed singers, attempting to solidify a common goal: "O, Liberty; can man resign thee" (23). The chorus, reiterated at the end, strengthens this call as it repeats "To arms! to arms!" (10).

"The Internationale" has many of the same qualities as "The Marseillaise" that enticed struggling workers to sing it, but "The Internationale" is more specifically applicable. "The Internationale" was written by Eugene Pottier, a transport worker from Paris (Kornbluh 174). "The Internationale" was an old standard in the IWW community, and the IWW adopted some of the lyrics for their own use, which were sung by the delegates to the first IWW convention held in 1905 (174). "The Internationale" begins in much the same tone as "The Marseillaise." The opening verse is positioned broadly and appeals to "ye prisoners of starvation" to "arise" (line 1). In contrast to "The Marseillaise," though, the IWW version of "The Internationale" takes its position as a workers' song as early as the chorus:

'Tis the final conflict,
Let each stand in his place,
The Industrial Union
Shall be the human race. (lines 9–12)

This emphasis on workers' struggle continues throughout the song. Indeed, the modified IWW version goes as far as to say, "Wage systems drain our blood" in the third verse (line 22).

"The Internationale" was widely considered the "anthem of European radicals" (Moran 192), and it was commonly known in a plentitude of languages. Reporter Al Priddy noted a musical version of the song on the picket lines at Lawrence: "They played the *Internationale*, and the vibrant, laughing men and women sang it in a Pentecostal merging of languages and dialects" (qtd. in Moran 193; italics in orig.). The workers at Lawrence, as diverse as they were in cultures and languages, all shared in the same struggle. They united behind songs written for other purposes, and they sang those songs in countless traditions, but they sang them in solidarity.

The strike in Lawrence and the songs surrounding it began to diverge from the male-dominated and generic "workingman" songs that were prominent, such as "The Marseillaise" and "The Internationale," and songs emerged that were written by the workers in their struggle for themselves, by themselves. Just as the strike was run from the bottom up, so were the songs. Old standards, while still relevant, were augmented with those songs created by the strikers for and by themselves. Although the generalized struggle songs like "The Marseillaise" and "The Internationale" were certainly unifying, they did not rally the workers around the pertinent and immediate struggle at hand, the textile strikes and the workers walking the picket lines. Songs such as "The Eight-Hour Song" by Richard Brazier began filling the gap. During the Lawrence strike, textile workers in Paterson, New Jersey, had formed the Eight-Hour League in solidarity, well before the textile labor unrest reached them in the form of a strike (Kornbluh 178), and Brazier's song emerged from this struggle.

"The Eight-Hour Song" is, yet again, very broad but emerged as a direct result of the textile workers' struggles for decent wages and hours. Brazier calls upon "workers young and old, / To organize against the shirkers" (lines 9–10), linking the younger mill workers with the older workers in Lawrence. Although the lyrics continue the tradition of being broad enough to apply to other struggles, one line is enough to link the song back to Lawrence and the struggle at hand: "Workers do you hear us calling, 1912, the first of May?" (7). The placement of 1912 in the middle of the song is subtle, but it reminds the reader (or singer) of the large and successful textile strike in Lawrence. "The Eight-Hour Song" reflected the struggle of the Lawrence textile workers, and this link is demonstrated through the lyrics, but the song remained broad enough to be applied to subsequent struggles in a variety of industries, thus carrying a message of militancy and solidarity throughout the working class.

By January 27, at least twenty-five thousand workers were off the looms and on the picket lines. Of these twenty-five thousand, a great many were women and children and truly international demographically. According to an IWW pamphlet from September of that year, the strikers consisted of "twenty-seven different nationalities, speaking forty-three different languages and dialects," and the strikers' committees were organized both out of these linguistic elements and by industrial classification of the workers themselves ("On the Firing Line"). For the IWW, differing language and ethnicity was only a minor barrier to organizing. As William "Big Bill" Haywood told the strikers, "There is no foreigner here but the capitalists. . . . Do not let them divide you by sex, color, creed, or nationality" (qtd. in Dubofsky 140). Furthermore, while the strike committee was largely male, the women of Lawrence were the backbone of the strike, as the IWW had no pretense of "proper" feminine roles. Although differing in ethnic origin, religion (or lack thereof), and language, one thing all mill workers shared was the poor working conditions and low pay and the decrepit condition of working life in Lawrence.[10] Despite this general commonality of living and working conditions, there were problems with picket lines being broken. This was reflected in the song "Few of Them Are Scabbing It."

"Few of Them Are Scabbing It," an anonymous song, appeared in the June 29, 1912, edition of *Solidarity* under the headline, "Songs Sung by the Workers on the Lawrence Picket Line" (Kornbluh 179). Arthur H. Lowe, president and director of the Lancaster Mills, is mentioned by name twice in "Few of Them Are Scabbing It," and he was one of Lancaster Mills' largest stockholders (179). The lyrics of the song focus on the scabs, or workers who cross the picket lines, at Lawrence: "Few scab weavers sneaking through the line, / They're the ones Mr. Lowe will fine, / They sneak in and get their measly pay" (lines 3–5). However, the attention is turned to Lowe as a predatory figure who preys upon scab workers who need the work. Although "Mr. Lowe says he will treat them well" (9), in reality, "after he's used them, he'll let them go to hell, / While the strikers cheerfully yell / Few of them are scabbing it!" (10–12). The workers are able to overcome language and ethnic barriers through organization and song in order to identify the cause of their poor working conditions and unlivable wages. The workers, and these songs, identified a common enemy and were able to create a militant labor movement based on the one thing they had in common, class.

The US Bureau of Labor report on the strike relayed that "some 23,000 employees had gone out on strike, and of these not over 2,800 belonged to organizations and were thus in position to be supported financially" (64). Although the IWW had been organizing in Lawrence since 1906, when the strike erupted, Lawrence IWW Local 20 had only a few hundred members. Therefore, the IWW had a difficult job feeding thousands of workers and their families, all now without income. The report continued that it was "a conservative estimate" to say that the total number of affected people was "some 50,000, out of a total population in Lawrence of approximately 85,000" (64). Some fifty differing ethnolinguistic communities combined with the organizational capacity of the IWW to coordinate the strike.

The strike committee swiftly came up with demands. They wanted a 15 percent wage increase, elimination of the hated premium system,[11] and a "no repercussion" clause for any action taken during the strike by the workers. Melvyn Dubofsky noted that there was no "mention of revolution," but there did not have to be for revolutionary ethos to be present (140–41). The IWW believed that the revolutionary struggle was dialectically created by organizing workers, as strikes would not only make proletarian life better under capitalism, but create the militancy and organization for the ultimate destruction of the capitalist system itself (Schmidt and van der Walt 133–39).[12] Before the revolution, however, the workers had to be fed and clothed, and the strike had to be won.

Centered in the Franco-Belgian Hall and Portuguese Hall, the IWW helped coordinate the allocation of food, coal, and shoes for the fifty thousand affected. Their ration cards allowed for the procurement of items not available at the many workers' kitchens set up at all of the major ethnolinguistic halls.[13] Indeed, it truly was a community strike. Barbers refused to cut the hair of scabs, landlords were told not to rent to the unsympathetic and to wait on rent for strikers, and everywhere strikers wore their buttons and armbands with the simple slogan Don't Be A Scab (Brenner, Day, and Ness 101).

Meeting halls found new life as places where groups once excluded politically and economically exerted their social power in a serious manner. The strike committee was led by "each major occupational group and each of the 16 major languages spoken" and was coordinated in a directly democratic fashion (Thompson and Bekken 48). At first the employers were unafraid of the strikers, mainly based on racist assumptions that the divisions of ethnic origins would divide the strikers and that differing factions could be used to rend the others asunder.[14] Their pernicious hopes quickly vanished. In a few short days, the city had become a commune of a sort, with all being fed and housed, either by the formal institutions facilitated by the IWW and local groups or by the informal networks that had precipitated elements of militancy within the communities themselves (Cameron 140). With the matter of interethnic solidarity largely cemented, there was still a strike to be fought and won, and winning strikes is a tough business.

Local 20 of the IWW quickly called in organizers to help lead the strike. In the first days, Joseph Ettor and Arturo Giovannitti, among others, came from New York. Ettor was fluent in English and Italian and had a grasp of Yiddish, Polish, and Hungarian, and while an able speaker, he was a master tactician. He was quickly elected to lead the strike committee. Giovannitti was the master orator, and his inspired "Sermon on the Common" at Lawrence is rightfully considered a labor classic (Pernicone 50). The gifted young leadership—they were twenty-six and twenty-eight—in combination with the militancy and organization of the strikers panicked the mill owners into crude action. A cache of dynamite was found near where Ettor got his mail, and he and Giovannitti were arrested for the alleged plot. The conspiracy quickly unraveled, and local businessman and politician John Breen was fined five hundred dollars for attempting to frame the leaders. With the conspiracy revealed, strikers quickly faced the combined might of state and capital within days of the picket's eruption.

Massachusetts governor Eugene Foss sent in the militia to augment the local police. Foss was a factory owner in his own right, and the state militia was openly hostile to the picketers.[15] With Lawrence being turned into something of an armed camp, strikers collectively decided to send many of their children away to live with sympathetic families in other cities. The Children's Exodus was designed to alleviate financial stress on the families, create good propaganda, and protect the children from the violence of the police and militia.[16] The exodus was quite successful and engendered a tremendous amount of sympathetic press coverage (Cameron 142–43). The authorities were unimpressed by the "scheme" and told the National Guard that no more children were to be let out of the city. Striking families challenged this order on February 24, when a group of children were chaperoned by their families to the train station. Just before they boarded their trains, over two hundred police, many on horseback, charged the group. As one organizer later described the scene, police "closed in on us [the crowd] with their clubs, beating right and left . . . The mothers and children were thus hurled in a mass and bodily dragged to a military truck and even then clubbed" (qtd. in Cameron 143).

Police violence was not limited to women and children, and the mass of armed men put their weapons to work in other ways. On January 29, the police attacked a peaceful march. During the police riot, striker Anna Lo Pizzo was shot and killed, almost assuredly by a police officer's bullet. The following day, John Ramey, an eighteen-year-old Syrian musician, was bayoneted twice in the back while fleeing from a group of militia with his band. He died of his wounds later that evening. Ramey was murdered for being an active musician on a picket line, speaking to the power of music and the manifest antipathy that power felt toward it. Capitalizing on the deaths, the authorities had Ettor, Giovannitti, and a local militant named John Caruso arrested for "indirect" responsibility for Lo Pizzo's murder (Pernicone 50), even though nineteen witnesses had seen Officer Beloit shoot her (Haywood 249). Denied bail, they sat in jail until well after the strike was won.

The brazen attempts to decapitate the IWW were a failed endeavor. The IWW quickly replaced Ettor and Giovannitti with, among others, Elizabeth Gurley Flynn and William "Big Bill" Haywood. Between ten thousand and fifteen thousand strikers met Flynn and Haywood on their arrival in Lawrence shortly before the arrest of Ettor and Giovannitti. The leaders marched with the reception committee to the main public park singing "The Internationale" the entire way (Haywood 247). Haywood was a seasoned orator and organizer, emerging from the tough world of Western mining strikes. Flynn was a young but tremendously talented speaker and was dearly loved by the strikers.[17] Although the strike committee was mainly male, women largely led the daily activity of the strike, and having a leader that represented them in gender and age was of no small importance in the IWW's drive to emphasize proletarian solidarity without limits.

With the immense female presence of the strike, it is of little surprise that Elizabeth Gurley Flynn played an important role in the IWW and in the strike itself. "In the Good Old Picket Line" posits that after the strike, "Gurley Flynn will be the boss" (line 7). This is a significant line, and it portrays the goals of the strikers and of the IWW. This is sung tongue in cheek since Gurley Flynn, and the IWW, were major proponents of a world without bosses, where workplaces and the economy were run by the workers from the shop floor up instead of by capitalist owners. Stating that the workers want Gurley Flynn as their boss is another way of affirming the workers' goal of obtaining control over their mills.

The stated desire to run the mills for themselves situated the workers in sharp juxtaposition to the AFL and its stated goals. The IWW and the AFL were at odds during this strike, as the goal of the AFL was to have rulings and strategy come down from the top. The IWW ideologically opposed this form of unionism. Gurley Flynn represented a dream of freedom and power for the workers in Lawrence and across the country, and when "Gurley Flynn will be the boss," the workers will be free (7). This theme of industrial democracy rings true to almost every IWW song and is solidified in the infamous opening line of "Solidarity Forever," which reads, "When the Union's inspiration through the worker's blood shall run" (line 1). It is the workers' blood that carries the struggle forward, not their union leadership, the bosses, or their religious leadership.

Clergy of the different religions and sects generally came out against the strike. As traditional forces for reaction, it was unsurprising that the clergy was inimical to the strike, but the revolutionary undertone of the IWW was concerning them almost as much as the IWW's general distrust—if not distaste—toward organized religion.[18] Although originally sympathetic to the plight of his parishioners, Father James O'Reilly, a dominant leader in the local Roman Catholic community, had become increasingly conservative as he gained power and influence. From the pulpit, O'Reilly vehemently urged his parishioners to cross picket lines and noted that the IWW was far more dangerous than poverty (Moran 189–90). In Frank Brechler's "Workers, Shall the Masters Rule Us?," a popular song during the strike, the tension between the strikers and the church's attempt to break solidarity is apparent: "Shall they own this earth and fool us / With that two-faced gospel band" (lines 3–4).[19] The Irish are specifically called out in "In the Good Old Picket Line," as the composer states, "we want to see more Irish in the good old picket line" (line 4). While O'Reilly was relatively successful in keeping Irish workers off the picket line, other clergy had much less clout. Syrian Christians simply ignored their church's advice on breaking the strike, and Italians ignored the pleadings of local *prominenti*, responding with "hisses and jeers" to their clergy's attempts at breaking workers' solidarity (Cameron 134).

When a Franco-American priest advocated a similarly reactionary path for his flock, a crowd of "eight thousand formed on Broadway and paraded to his home," threatening to tear both it and the church down. Ettor sent word from his jail cell to quell the impromptu demolition (Moran 215). Though many militant workers ignored the opinions of their clergy, O'Reilly was relatively successful at forging discipline among his flock. Workers in Lawrence reflected their anger through song. An anonymously penned "Lawrence, Mass., Strike Song" identifies the diversity among the strikers (Kornbluh 180). Sung to the tune of "In the Good Old Summer Time" (179), "In the Good Old Picket Line" is a short and memorable song about the diverse community involved in the strike: the striking workers in Lawrence "are from every place, from nearly every clime" (line 2). Thus the songs reflected not only the reality of the situation, but attempted (through a curious mixture of shame and solidarity) to bring other ethnic groups into the strikers' fold.

With the combined force of the state and religion massed against them, the strikers were perhaps surprised by yet another wall between them and victory, the AFL. The AFL had been active in Lawrence well before the battle erupted in 1912. The leader of the AFL United Textile Workers was John Golden, a firm believer in craft unionism and a staunch opponent of organizing the unskilled and "foreign." Golden told members of his local to report for duty *despite* the strike, as neither he nor the AFL recognized the IWW-led action or the sanctity of their pickets (Moran 199–200). AFL members had retained more skill on the job, were much higher paid, and had more freedom in their work. Despite the attempt by Golden to contain his workers, many soon joined their compatriots on the street, and Golden was widely held in disdain for his attempts at "union scabbing." The songs of the IWW reflect this situation well.

Alongside the nameless strikers who authored "Few of Them are Scabbing It" and "In the Good Old Picket Line," Joe Hill situates "John Golden and the Lawrence Strike" firmly within the Lawrence milieu. Hill positions his song in Lawrence not only in the title but in the first line as well: "In Lawrence, when the starving masses struck for more to eat" (1). According to the song, "John Golden had with Mr. Wood a private interview" (line 17), in which "he told him how to busy up the 'I double double U'" (18). The strikers in Lawrence won their struggle, and the second chorus identifies this victory:

> That's one time Golden did not
> Make it right, all right;
> In spite of all his schemes
> The strikers won the fight.
> When all the workers stand
> United hand in hand,
> The world with all its wealth
> Shall be at their command. (25–32)

These last few lines close the song and ring true to the ultimate goal of not only the IWW but of the workers themselves. These songs stood to create solidarity and unite the workers. The link between song and solidarity is aptly summarized in a dual-purposed line from Brechler's "Workers, Shall the Masters Rule Us?": "Workers, we must stick together; / We must join in one great *band*" (17–18; emphasis added).

We have seen how song occupies a specific place within the particular proletarian struggle in Lawrence. Although at times slippery in manifestation, it is a force of direct praxis, the specific interaction of theory and action, which can divide capitalist hegemony and economic power in the face of workers' cultural production and militant self-activity. According to David A. Carter, "Among the more volatile labor organizations during the early decades of the twentieth century, none aroused more passions, stirred more controversy, nor sang more loudly than the Industrial Workers of the World" (365). Indeed, literature and, in this case, song can be "the strongest and most far-reaching interpreter of our deep-felt dissatisfaction" (Goldman 241). Many of these songs were not just sung by the workers, but the workers who sung them also wrote them, performed them, and felt their influence. "Lawrence was a singing strike," noted Vorse (12); Lawrence was also a singing strike that was victorious. On March 12, the mill owners conceded the core demands of the strikers. Victory represented the power of the "common interest of the working class in bringing all nationalities together" (Dubofsky 147). For the strikers at Lawrence, it seems that in some ways "The Internationale" rang true: the "toilers from shops and fields united, the union we of all who work" were able to unite for victory (lines 37–38). In this victory, the militant, radical, and revolutionary song was an integral aspect of education, solidarity, and action within the public sphere. As an immediate manifestation of proletarian power distinctly within both the public sphere and the class struggle itself, song was a significant element of proletarian revolt, power, and activity for and by the working class.

Notes

1. The singing tradition of the IWW became text merely three years after it was founded in song with the publication of the Spokane Branch's book of songs.

2. Two songs analyzed within this chapter were written by anonymous groups of workers, giving insight into the often-tricky realm of what workers—who left very little in the way of written documentation—were thinking during periods of industrial struggle.

3. It was not only because of the Salvation Army bands that a great number of IWW songs were anticlerical in nature. The IWW was institutionally opposed to religion as it promised "pie in the sky when you die" instead of proletarian betterment. As a revolutionary organization, the IWW had many songs antithetical towards religion, and this was reflected in song (*IWW Songs* 7, 10, 21, 36, 38, 48).

4. The IWW as a dialectically "musical" revolutionary organization of the proletariat was indeed reflected in multiple double entendres. IWW songs such as

"The Preacher and the Slave" and "Count Your Workers, Count Them" were manifestly self-referential in relation to "this fighting band" and "the grand Industrial band" (*IWW Songs* 36, 48). Moreover, in relation to the Lawrence strike, "Workers, Shall the Masters Rule Us?" argued:

> Workers, we must stick together;
> We must join in one great band,
> That's the way to fight the masters,
> So that they'll not rule this land. (lines 17–20)

5. The term "industrial unionism" can be difficult to understand for those not versed in the nomenclature of unionism and the Left. Generally speaking, there are two main ways to organize unions: craft unions and industrial unions—the former organizes by craft, the latter by industry. The discrepancy between the two can be best illustrated using a construction site as an example. Under craft unions, the electricians, carpenters, plumbers, pipefitters, bricklayers, laborers, and ironworkers would all have their own unions. Under industrial unions, they would all be in the same union. Industrial unions tended to increase workers' power.

6. This revolutionary syndicalist outlook is what situates the IWW within the "broad anarchist tradition" of the international revolutionary left (Schmidt and van der Walt 16–17, 159–70). There is an astounding amount of literature on the founding, ideology, and practice of the IWW. For basic overviews, see Melvyn Dubofsky's *We Shall Be All*, Patrick Radshaw's *The Wobblies*, and the aforementioned work by Schmidt and van der Walt.

7. Originally, "The Internationale" was intended to be sung to the tune of "The Marseillaise." Independent music was added in 1888 (Walls 5).

8. All song compositions and verse orders are as listed in *Rebel Voices*, and the line layout published there is the outline for the line number citations. Therefore, only the first instance of the chorus is used in numbering lines.

9. "The Marseillaise" was composed in French and has undergone many additions in many languages.

10. The city had one of the highest rates of infant mortality in the United States. Workers lived in dark, crowded tenements, with little in the way of sanitation. The mills had only the most rudimentary ventilation, and one third of the children working in the mills died before reaching the age of twenty-five (Moran 188).

11. The premium system was a scheme wherein if a worker achieved a certain amount of productivity, they would "earn" extra money. The problem was that the goal was set incredibly high and the period of productivity was four weeks. One missed day of work, a simple breakdown, or a torn piece would result in no "premium," no matter how close the worker was to achieving it.

12. Distinctly apropos, Elizabeth Gurley Flynn argued two years later:

13. "What is a labor victory? I maintain that it is a twofold thing. Workers must gain economic advantage, but they must also gain revolutionary spirit, in order to achieve a complete victory. For workers to gain a few cents more a day, a few

minutes less a day, and go back to work with the same psychology, the same attitude toward society is to achieve a temporary gain and not a lasting victory." (qtd. in Kornbluh 215)

14. In Lawrence, the mill owners banned the strikers from renting halls for their activities, and police and militia often broke up public meetings. The strikers therefore used the meeting halls of different groups who were either sympathetic to the workers' cause or had forced their leadership to be. The center of the strike was at the Franco-Belgian Hall, although many more halls and meeting places were pressed into service.

15. Ironically, the avarice of the landlords accidentally created an interethnic solidarity to bolster class solidarity. As Ardis Cameron noted, "Whereas the mill management systematically sought to use ethnic loyalty to separate workers, crowded living conditions and domestic routine provided a means to overcome ethnic antagonisms and link disparate communities" (91).

16. The militia was a polyglot affair but also made up of students from Harvard, whose president Abbot Lowell (of Lowell textile fame) excused the men from exams for the occasion (Watson 110). One of the militiamen infamously noted that Harvard students "rather enjoyed coming down here to have a fling at those people" (qtd. in Moran 197). The militia was quartered in the empty mills, laying bare whose interests they represented.

17. This was a particularly prescient thought, considering what would happen to families of strikers in Ludlow, Colorado, in April 1914. The Ludlow Massacre occurred when around twenty people died when a coal miners' camp was attacked and burned by the National Guard and accompanying mining officials.

18. While only twenty-one years old during the Lawrence battle, Flynn was already a seasoned militant, having delivered her first public speech, "What Socialism Will Do for Women," at only sixteen (Baxandall 2).

19. For more on the IWW and religion, see Joe Hill's song "The Preacher and the Slave," which pertains to "long-haired preachers" leading the proletariat astray and leaving nothing but "pie in the sky when you die" (Kornbluh 132–33).

20. Although this song is attributed to Frank Brechler, Joe Hill may have used this name as a pseudonym (Kornbluh 179).

Works Cited

Arendt, Hannah. *The Human Condition.* Chicago: U of Chicago P, 1998. Print.
___. *On Violence*. Orlando: Harcourt, 1970. Print.
Baker, Ray Stannard. "The Revolutionary Strike: A New Form of Industrial Struggle as Exemplified at Lawrence, Massachusetts." *American Magazine* May 1912: 18–30. Print.
Baxandall, Rosalyn Fraad. *Words on Fire: The Life and Writing of Elizabeth Gurley Flynn.* New Brunswick: Rutgers UP, 1987. Print.

Brenner, Aaron, Benjamin Day, and Immanuel Ness, eds. *The Encyclopedia of Strikes in American History.* Armonk: Sharpe, 2009. Print.

Cameron, Ardis. *Radicals of the Worst Sort: Laboring Women in Lawrence, Massachusetts, 1860–1912.* Chicago: U of Illinois P, 1993. Print.

Carter, David A. "The Industrial Workers of the World and the Rhetoric of Song." *Quarterly Journal of Speech* 66.4 (1980): 365–74. Print.

Dubofsky, Melvyn. *We Shall Be All: A History of the Industrial Workers of the World.* Ed. Joseph A. McCartin. Chicago: U of Illinois P, 2000. Print.

Flynn, Elizabeth Gurley. *I Speak My Own Piece: Autobiography of "The Rebel Girl."* New York: Masses, 1955. Print.

Furey, Hester L. "IWW Songs as Modernist Poetry." *Journal of the Midwest Mod. Lang. Assn.* 34.2 (2001): 51–72. Print.

Giovannitti, Arturo. *Arrows in the Gale and Other Poems.* Niantic: Quale, 2004. Print.

Goldman, Emma. "The Modern Drama: A Powerful Disseminator of Radical Thought." *Anarchism and Other Essays.* New York: Dover, 1969. 241–71. Print.

Gramsci, Antonio. *The Antonio Gramsci Reader: Selected Writing 1916–1935.* Ed. David Forgacs. New York: NYU P, 2000. Print.

Green, Archie, David Roediger, Franklin Rosemont, and Salvatore Salerno, eds. *The Big Red Songbook.* Chicago: Kerr, 2007. Print.

Hayes, Max S. "The World of Labor." *International Socialist Review* 6.12 (1906): 755–58. Print.

Haywood, William D. *Bill Haywood's Book: The Autobiography of William D. Haywood.* New York: International, 1966. Print.

Industrial Workers of the World. *IWW Songs to Fan the Flames of Discontent.* Chicago: Kerr, 1923. Print.

———. "On the Firing Line: Extracts from the Report of the General Executive Board to the Seventh Annual Convention of the Industrial Workers of the World." Spokane: Industrial Worker, 1912. *Workerseducation.org.* J. D. Crutchfield, 7 May 2007. Web. 2 Jan. 2013.

———. *Proceedings of the First Convention of the Industrial Workers of the World.* New York: New York Labor News, 1905. Print.

Kimeldorf, Howard. *Battling for American Labor: Wobblies, Craft Workers, and the Making of the Union Movement.* Berkeley: U of California P, 1999. Print.

Kornbluh, Joyce L., ed. *Rebel Voices: An IWW Anthology.* Chicago: Kerr, 1998. Print.

Moran, William. *The Belles of New England: The Women of the Textile Mills and the Families Whose Wealth They Wove.* New York: St. Martin's, 2002. Print.

Nolan, Dean, and Fred Thompson. *Joe Hill: IWW Songwriter.* Chicago: Chicago General Membership Branch, IWW, 1979. Print.

Pernicone, Nunzio. *Carlo Tresca: Portrait of a Rebel.* Oakland: AK, 2010. Print.

Schmidt, Michael, and Lucien van der Walt. *Black Flame: The Revolutionary Class Politics of Anarchism and Syndicalism.* Oakland: AK, 2009. Print.

Thompson, Fred W., and Jon Bekken. *The Industrial Workers of the World: Its First 100 Years.* Cincinnati: IWW, 2006. Print.

United States. Bureau of Labor. *Report on Strike of Textile Workers in Lawrence, Mass. in 1912.* Washington: GPO, 1912. Print.

Vorse, Mary Heaton. *A Footnote to Folly: Reminiscences of Mary Heaton Vorse.* New York: Farrar, 1935. Print.

Walls, David. "Billy Bragg's Revival of Aging Anthems: Radical Nostalgia or Activist Inspiration?" Class Matters: Working Class Culture and Counter-Culture. Working Class Studies Assn. St. Paul. 15 June 2007. PDF file.

Watson, Bruce. *Bread and Roses: Mills, Migrants, and the Struggle for the American Dream.* New York: Penguin, 2005. Print.

Dystopia as Protest: Zamyatin's *We* and Orwell's *Nineteen Eighty-Four*

Rachel Stauffer

I. Introduction

Yevgeny Zamyatin's *We* (Russian title: *Мы*, meaning "My"), a dystopian novel written in the early 1920s, is said to have been influenced by H. G. Wells and to have influenced George Orwell's *Nineteen Eighty-Four*, although *We* is less familiar to Western readers than *Nineteen Eighty-Four*. In Soviet Russia, *We* was censored until the late 1980s when General Secretary Mikhail Gorbachev's glasnost policy of openness lifted the ban on the book; the publication of *Nineteen Eighty-Four* and *Brave New World* soon followed (Tall 183). The publication of *We*, *Nineteen Eighty-Four*, and *Brave New World* in Russia therefore coincided directly with the dissolution of the Soviet Union after seventy years of Communist rule. This suggests that some dystopias, by virtue of their content, are texts of social protest. I will explore this first through close examination of Zamyatin's *We* and then through a comparison of *We* with the protest elements of Orwell's *Nineteen Eighty-Four*.

A dystopia firmly rejects the ideal society envisioned by a utopia. The first appearance of the word "utopia" occurs in Thomas More's work *Utopia* in 1516:

> The word *utopia*, first coined by More for his book [*Utopia*], also has a comfortable, modern feeling. It is now a very common term in English, most often carrying the meaning of a vain fantasy, a hopelessly unrealistic reform program, or an entirely impracticable set of social institutions (Sacks 4).

In the text of *Utopia*, More establishes the word by combining the Greek *u*, meaning "not," with *topos*, meaning "place," literally meaning "no place" (More 86). As Sacks points out, in common contemporary parlance, "utopia" has come to mean a place that does not exist because such an unattainable ideal is impossible. The later development of the word "dystopia" unites the Greek *dys*, meaning "bad," with the same root *topos*, giving it the literally meaning "bad place." It is opposed to "utopia," however, as a bad place that has resulted from the attempt to create utopia. Some scholars utilize the term "anti-utopia" in reference to Zamyatin and Orwell because the term "dystopia" does not fully convey an opposition to utopia in the same way that "anti-utopia" succeeds in this regard. Here I will use the term "dystopia" in both its literal and its opposing meanings as a place in which organizing principles of utopia have not exactly yielded utopian ideals or have successfully extinguished organic human desires (such as maternal instincts, love, the search for deeper meaning).

In the foreword to *American Protest Literature*, John Stauffer defines "protest literature" as "the uses of language to transform the self and change society," also asserting:

> The difference between literature and protest literature is that while the former empowers and transforms individuals, the latter strives to give voice to a collective consciousness, uniting isolated or inchoate discontent. Protest literature taps into an ideological vein of dissent and announces to its people that they are not alone in their frustrations. Protest literature is part of its milieu, inextricably linked to its time and place. But it also stands at a remove from prevailing social values, offering a critique of society from the outside. (xii)

Zamyatin's novel is easily contextualized temporally to the establishment of lofty Marxist ideals under Lenin and the Communist Party in post-1917 Russia. He presents a world in which love and imagination are forbidden, urging his reader to reject a world in which individual voices are inaudible over the mass. Orwell's *Nineteen Eighty-Four* offers a similar atmosphere in the context of post–World War II Europe, coincidentally, although probably not intentionally, reminiscent of the Stalin era in Soviet Russia. For both authors, the events of their time— that is, the experiences of revolution and war—seem to have contributed to the writing of these novels, whether consciously or subconsciously. More broadly, within the texts of both *We* and *Nineteen Eighty-Four*, there is clear opposition between human nature and the laws of science. In a dystopia, the former is viewed as a weakness while the latter serves as the foundation of the laws of the land. Human instincts and desires drive both main characters to rebel against state reason and science. As a result, the injustice within the texts creates a sense of the necessity of fundamental human experiences in the reader that, as Stauffer believes, "taps into an ideological vein of dissent and announces to its people that they are not alone in their frustrations," therefore establishing these two dystopias as works of protest literature.

II. Yevgeny Ivanovich Zamyatin (1884–1937)

Because Zamyatin is not a well-known author in the West, there is utility in presenting some basic biographical information about his life, in order to contextualize the discussion of *We* here. Yevgeny Ivanovich Zamyatin was born in the Russian countryside and moved to the city of St. Petersburg as a young adult to study naval engineering. His move to the city coincided with the growing discontent in Russia that led to the 1905 Revolution. In late nineteenth-century Russia, the Industrial Revolution and the end of serfdom in 1861 both contributed to increasing frustration among the working classes. Given the newness of industry in Russia, working conditions were often poor. Over time, the working class, without unions or any sort of provisions to protect them and their well-being (particularly if injured on the job, which, under these working conditions, was common), sought government help. The added industrial burden of the unpopular Russo-Japanese War (1904–5) did not help matters. Protests and strikes were common, though they did not typically yield results. In January 1905, on a day later designated as Bloody Sunday, peaceful protesters outside of the Winter Palace in St.

Petersburg were shot by the czar's guards, who would go on to kill and wound thousands.[1] As an active participant in revolutionary activities that led to the failed revolution, Zamyatin was arrested and exiled. One biographer describes Zamyatin's interest in revolution as "a craving for excitement, allied with a natural rebelliousness" and describes the outcome of his participation in revolutionary activity:

> 1905, the year of the first attempt at revolution in Russia, was full of inci-
> dent for Zamyatin . . . his revolutionary activity continued unabated and in
> December a police raid on the revolutionary headquarters of the Vyborgsk
> Quarter led Zamyatin, along with thirty others, to be arrested, searched,
> and beaten up. For several months he was kept in solitary confinement in
> the Shpalerny Prison, during which time he studied shorthand and English
> and 'inevitably,' as he says, wrote poems. . . . In the Spring of 1906 he was
> freed and sent home . . . and soon slipped back illegally into the capital,
> from where he several times went to Helsinki to revolutionary gatherings.
> (Richards 8–9)

A natural rebel, Zamyatin's defiance of his exile only caused the authorities to re-sentence him to two more years of exile once he was discovered to have, in fact, illicitly returned to St. Petersburg. When his exile sentencing ended and Zamyatin was permitted to return to St. Petersburg in 1913, he undertook more activity in the literary community and published stories and Russian translations of English authors, including H. G. Wells, who is thought to be an important influence in the writing of *We*. Zamyatin was viewed as a leader in literary circles, often mentoring young authors as a member of the Serapion Brotherhood, a group devoted to communion among authors and dedication to craft rather than to ideological content. Edward Brown describes Zamyatin as decidedly apolitical in his philosophy, claiming that he "insisted that literature be free of social or political tendency" and "genuinely indifferent to actual political events and the philosophies that motivated them" (26). Brown simultaneously recognizes this alleged perspective was possibly requisite in the highly politicized and revolutionary climate of early twentieth-century Russia in order to avoid clashes with the government. Regarding *We*, there is a general consensus that it contains a philosophical component that is decidedly absent in Zamyatin's earlier works, possibly because of the heavy impact of the 1917 Revolution, which successfully overthrew the monarchy. David Richards states, "The Russian Revolution of 1917 had a decisive influence on Zamyatin's literary career. Most of his best work, produced in the twenties, reflects more or less directly the Revolution, its effects, its shortcomings and its significance for the future" (11). Since Zamyatin was a rebel and protester himself, it is not surprising that *We* might be considered a work of protest literature.

In the postrevolutionary period, Zamyatin was known as a *poputchik*, or "fellow traveler," the term used to refer to artists and intellectuals who believed in the objectives of the revolution but who did not always agree that Marxist or communist principles were the most effective way to foster new and better conditions. Under Lenin and Trotsky's leadership, the fellow travelers were considered friends of the state, but under Stalin's first Five-Year Plan (1928–33), which dictated that artistic production must align with the goals of the party, Zamyatin's reputation was destroyed. In this repressive climate for artists and intellectuals, many authors were denounced as enemies of the state if or when their texts did not promote the ideals of socialism, did not emphasize the goals of industrialization, or did not joyfully sing the praises of the Communist Party. "Zamyatin's forthright opinions had long made him unpopular with the proletarian critics who now gained wide authority and in 1929 he found himself branded as a traitor and subjected to a prolonged campaign of vilification in the Soviet press," Richards notes (12). As a result, Zamyatin appealed directly to Stalin in 1931 for permission to leave the Soviet Union, which was granted to him and his wife. They moved to France, where he died in 1937. Before his death, Zamyatin is reported to have said, "I am an excommunicant, you know. I had to leave Soviet Russia as a dangerous counterrevolutionary" (qtd.

in Richards 14). Zamyatin's personality—namely, his rebellious nature and questioning of the intentions of communism—significantly contribute as evidence for categorizing *We* as a text of protest.

III. Summary Analysis of *We* as Protest Literature

Zamyatin's novel *We* describes life in a postapocalyptic, collective society in which humans have numbers instead of names, love and imagination are criminalized, and daily life in the nation of One State is meticulously scheduled and highly restrictive. Citizens, known as ciphers, live unquestioningly devoted to the leader, the nation, and the history and philosophy provided by the state. The main character of the novel, D-503, is the author and narrator of the text who also provides the reader with a first-person view of his nation, One State; his leader, the Benefactor; and his creation of the *Integral*, a ship designed to travel to distant galaxies in order to disseminate the One State ideology to the interplanetary masses. D-503 is an engineer with an affinity for mathematics, which personally unites him with the One State mantra of reason and science as the only philosophies under which any society is to survive. Zamyatin's own background as a naval engineer played a role in the development of D-503's character and occupation. D-503 frequently uses math, numbers, and even algebraic equations to rationalize the laws and doctrines of One State. D-503's consistent reference to numbers, logic, and equations always serves its purpose in legitimizing the principles of One State but not in rationalizing an unexpected human emotion: love.

D-503 describes the history of One State and life there early in the novel:

> It may be that you don't know terms like the Table of Hours, the Personal Hour, the Maternal Norm, the Green Wall, the Benefactor. . . . The Table of Hours—it transforms each of us into the real-life, six wheeled, steel heroes of a great epic. Each morning with six-wheeled precision, at the exact same hour, at the exact same minute, we, the millions, rise as one. At the

exact same hour, we uni-millionly start work and uni-millionly stop work. And, merged into a single, million-handed body, at the exact same Table-appointed second, we bring spoons to our lips, we go out for our walk and go to the auditorium, to the Taylor Exercise Hall, go off to sleep . . . Twice a day—from 16:00 to 17:00 and from 21:00 to 22:00—the united powerful organism scatters to its separate cages. These are written into the Table of Hours: the Personal Hours. (Zamyatin, *We* 11–13)

In this passage we see a world in which every activity is rigidly scheduled and idle time is limited. The Green Wall represents an impermeable boundary to the outside world that no cipher is to cross. The walls of One State are made of glass so that every action is visible, and the citizens are dressed and coiffed identically as D-503 describes: "The auditorium. An enormous, sun-saturated hemisphere of glass expanses. Circular rows of noble, spherical, smoothly sheared heads" (16). In another scene later in the novel, D-503 describes a similar gathering: "Cube Plaza. Sixty-six powerful concentric circles: the stands. And sixty-six rows: quiet, bright faces and eyes reflecting the radiance of the skies—or, maybe, the radiance of the One State . . . Profound, strict, gothic silence" (41). The leader of One State, the Benefactor, is described as having "superhuman might" (44), and the execution (by a sort of electric guillotine operated by the Benefactor himself) of disobedient ciphers is common. The failure to maintain expected norms is punishable by death.

Even sexual relationships are governed by One State in order to stifle love and the irrational behavior that accompanies it:

So it's natural that having subjugated Hunger (algebraically = to the sum of material goods), the One State began an offensive against the other master of the world—against Love. Finally, even this natural force was also conquered, i.e., organized and mathematicized . . . and the rest are technicalities. You are thoroughly examined in the laboratories of the Bureau of Sex, the exact sexual hormone content of your blood is determined, and then they generate a corresponding Table of Sex Days for you. Then you make a statement that on your given day you would like to make use of this (or that) cipher, and you receive the appropriate ticket book (pink). And that's it (Zamyatin, 21).

Procreation is also mandated by the state, in order to prevent ciphers from "obliviously giving birth to children" (14). Children belong to and are raised by the state, further enmeshing the ciphers with the only parental figure the state wants them to know, the Benefactor. One character, D-503's regular sexual partner, O-90, is unable to part entirely with her own maternal instincts, despite not being a Maternal Norm. O-90's disappointment about this issue offers a brief but honest point of view that suggests that life in One State is, in fact, not perfect for everyone, and some people still feel twinges of human nature (or later, as we will discover, a soul), no matter how much science and reason may seem to prevail in One State.

The main character who leads D-503 to protest behavior is I-330. D-503 becomes acquainted with I-330 while admiring his surroundings, overcome by the majesty of One State at the beginning of the novel:

I saw it all as though for the very first time: the immutably straight streets, the ray-spraying glass of the sidewalks, the divine parallelepipeds of the transparent buildings, and the quadratic harmony of the gray-blue ranks. And then: it was as if I—not whole generations past—had personally, myself, conquered the old God and the old life. As if I personally had created all this. And I was like a tower, not daring to move even an elbow, for fear of scattering walls, cupolas, machines. . . .

And then there was an echo—a laugh—coming from the right. I spun around: the white—unusually white—and sharp teeth of an unfamiliar face were before my eyes.

"Forgive me," she said, "but you were observing your surroundings with such an inspired look—like some mythical god on the seventh day of creation. It looked as though you actually believed that you, yourself, had created everything—even me! I'm very flattered. . . ." (Zamyatin, *We* 7–8)

D-503 is unsettled by I-330's presence, associating her with the variable *x*, saying, "There was a kind of strange and irritating X to her, and I couldn't pin it down, couldn't give it any numerical expression" (8). As Andrew Barratt observes, D-503's "predicament, as all critics have noted, stems directly from the unexpected intrusion into his previously well-ordered life of the mysterious and alluring I-330. Under her influence, his position as loyal and trusted servant of One State becomes increasingly irksome and untenable, a circumstance which profoundly affects every facet of his life" (660). I-330 is a member of an underground organization within One State, the ME-PHI, whose primary objective is to liberate the people of One State by destroying the Green Wall and freeing the ciphers. Early in the novel, the organization's existence is reported in the daily newspaper, although D-503 is unaware that I-330 is involved: "According to reliable witnesses, new evidence has been found of an organization, which continues to elude us to this day, whose aim is the liberation of the State from its beneficial yoke" (Zamyatin, *We* 33). D-503 is shocked and confused by this news, never thinking that he or any of his acquaintances are connected to the organization, even though he is already infatuated with I-330, one of the MEPHI's most enthusiastic members.

I-330 repeatedly influences D-503 to break the laws of One State. The first occurrence is when they visit the Ancient House, a museum displaying artifacts of twentieth-century life. I-330 is unconcerned with obeying the Table of Hours, claiming that she can get a friend to forge a doctor's note attesting to her absence at a required, scheduled event. D-503, stunned by her apathy, states that, like any loyal cipher, he must report her to the Bureau of Guardians for attempting to falsify her whereabouts. Our first indication that D-503 is beginning to question the authority of One State is his subsequent failure to report I-330 to the bureau after all. The next time they meet, we see how powerless D-503 is in I-330's presence:

> "So you didn't go to the Bureau of Guardians?"
>
> "I was . . . I couldn't. I was sick."
>
> "Yes. Well, I thought so. Something was always going to prevent you—it didn't matter what." Sharp teeth, a smile.
>
> "And so, now you are in my hands. You do remember: 'Any cipher who does not declare themselves to the Bureau in the course of forty-eight hours is considered . . .'"
>
> My heart struck so hard that the twigs bent. Like a little boy—foolish, like a foolish little boy, I had been caught, and foolishly, I stayed silent. (Zamyatin, *We* 47)

D-503 is simultaneously intrigued and revolted by I-330, and her power over him somehow makes him repeatedly neglect his obedience to One State, making him complicit in her own protest against One State. This particular meeting continues in this same way, with I-330 continuing to break more rules, including drinking alcohol and smoking cigarettes, about which D-503 cites verbatim the text of One State's law against these substances. I-330 counters this by saying simply, "You are so sweet—oh, I am sure of that—and you wouldn't think of going to the Bureau and telling them that I drink liqueur and smoke. You will be sick—or you will be busy—or whatever. Furthermore: I am sure that you are going to drink this charming poison with me now" (49–50). Predictably, D-503 takes a drink, once again defying the rules of One State in exchange for I-330's attention and approval.

The first incident of organized protest of One State involving I-330 and the MEPHI occurs on an election holiday when to the surprise of D-503, thousands of ciphers vote against the Benefactor, I-330 included, when normally all votes are in favor of the Benefactor:

"Who says 'No'?"

This was always the most magnificent moment of the holiday: everyone continues to sit, immobile, joyfully bowing their heads to the beneficial yoke of the Cipher of ciphers. But now, to my horror, I heard another rustling: a very light sound . . . I raised my eyes and . . . In the hundredth part of a second, the hairspring of a clock, I saw: thousands of hands wave up—'No'—and fall again. I saw I-330's pale face, marked with a cross and her raised hand. (Zamyatin, *We* 125–26)

Immediately after this incident, D-503's foundation is shaken as he considers those who voted against the Benefactor, saying, "I am ashamed, pained, and scared for them. But who are 'they'? And who am I: 'they' or 'we'? How will I know?" (128). This important moment leads to a climax when D-503 is introduced to the MEPHI as the builder of the *Integral* and realizes that I-330 plans to hijack the *Integral* in order to escape One State:

"Brothers! You all know that there, in the city behind the Wall, they are building the Integral. And you know that the day has arrived when we will destroy this Wall—every wall—so that the green wind can blow from pole to pole—the whole Earth over. But the Integral is taking these walls up there, to the thousands of new Earths, to those that will whisper to you tonight with their fires through the black night leaves. . . . The Integral should be ours. . . . On the day when it first casts off into the sky—we will be on it. Because the Builder of the Integral is here with us. He forsook the Wall and he came here with me, to be among us. All hail the Builder!" (137)

At this moment of introduction, D-503 is fully transformed into a participant in protest when he says, ever mathematically, "I stopped being a component, as I had been, and I became the number one" (138). Moments later he fully complies in the MEPHI protest of One State, explaining that "everyone must go crazy—as soon as possible" (142).

When I-330 questions D-503's newfound protest of One State, reminding him of his lifelong devotion, D-503 becomes defensive. By this time in the novel, D-503 has become as resolute in his protest of One State as he was in his prior loyalty to it, even though he cannot quite define what this means.

I-330's plan to take over the *Integral* requires D-503's consent. I-330 explains D-503's role to him and the order of events that must take place in order for her plan to be realized. Despite his love for I-330 and his newfound support for the cause of the MEPHI, D-503 is concerned about the plan, exclaiming, "This is pointless! This is ridiculous! Isn't it clear to you yet: you are starting what is called—a revolution!" (Zamyatin, *We* 153). The word "revolution" in One State is *verboten* and taught to the ciphers as an impossibility. I-330 appeals again to D-503 with mathematic persuasion: "My sweet, you are a mathematician . . . So then, tell me: what is the final number . . . the last, the highest, the biggest" (153). To this D-503 responds that numbers are infinite, and I-330 responds by saying, "Revolutions are infinite" (153), appeasing D-503's rational side and soliciting his consent to take over the *Integral* upon its first test flight.

The next day, the One State newspaper announces that a procedure has been developed that destroys imagination and that all ciphers are to report to the auditoriums to have the Great Operation. The test flight of the *Integral* is coincidentally postponed. I-330 encourages D-503 to have the operation instead, saying to him that he should cure himself of her (Zamyatin, *We* 162). D-503 puts off the operation, saying, "It was clear to me: everyone was saved, but there was to be no saving me, I don't want saving" (163). Every move that D-503 makes enables the departure of the *Integral*. He and I-330 strategically avoid the Great Operation (another act of protest) and set the stage to launch the *Integral* for its departure from One State, but are unsuccessful. D-503's subversion is driven by love, while I-330's is driven by her cause: "I-330's rebellion against utopia's repression is overtly political: she belongs to the secret underground movement . . . dedicated to overthrowing the Well-Doer, to tearing down the Wall. . . . D-503's rebellion, however, is purely instinctual, that of a man blindly following his heart . . . willing now to do anything to keep her love" (Beauchamp 292). Despite D-503's conditioned and intellectual submission to One State, his proscribed rationality cannot be maintained as a result of his fundamentally human feelings for I-330.

D-503 then receives a call from the Benefactor requesting a meeting in which the Benefactor tells D-503 that I-330 is only interested in him because of his status as builder of the *Integral*. Betrayed by the object of his affection, D-503 returns to the only other love he has known— love for One State. The next day, he confesses everything to the Bureau of Guardians. All of D-503's progress toward protest unravels. He is "cured" of his love and imagination by undergoing the Great Operation and returns to his earlier rational state of mind:

> The facts are these. On that evening, my neighbor, having discovered the finiteness of the universe, and I, and everyone who was with us, were taken, since we did not have Operation certificates, and carried off to the nearest auditorium. . . . There, we were bound to tables and subjected to the Great Operation. The next day, I, D-503 appeared to the Benefactor and told him everything that I knew about the enemies of happiness. How could this have seemed so hard to do before? Incomprehensible. The only explanation: my former sickness (a soul). (Zamyatin, *We* 202–23)

Within the text, there are additional subversive elements not mentioned here but conveyed well by another source:

> Within this plot, there are numerous subplots and subtleties. For example, one can follow the spread of the soul 'epidemic' to other characters in contact with the love-smitten D-503: O-90 falls in love with him, becomes jealous of I-330 and illegally conceives a child by him; U secretly reads his diary, falls in love with him and informs on the other revolutionaries, thus affecting the outcome of the story. One can explore the contrast

between illusion and reality—D-503's initial understanding of the state and the revolutionary movement, and his ultimate realization that he has been used by both. (Kern 13)

The underlying subplots mentioned above are additional elements of protest that contribute to the overall message of social protest conveyed in the novel. As the resistance of the MEPHI in the novel escalates with the destruction of parts of the Green Wall and I-330's coercion of D-503 as the Builder, these other elements similarly communicate the message of protest.

The final words of the novel, however, leave this message unclear. Although it appears that D-503 is no longer protesting One State, his final words act as an invitation to the reader to appeal to his or her reason having now read D-503's diary:

> There is still chaos, howling, corpses, wild beasts, and—unfortunately—a significant number of ciphers betraying reason in the western quarters. But, across the city, on the fortieth avenue, they have managed to construct a temporary wall of high-voltage waves. And I hope we will win. More than that: I know we will win. Because reason should win. (Zamyatin, *We* 203)

This brings up the important issue of the title—*We*. Zamyatin's use of the first-person plural pronoun functions not only in its purpose of talking about the ciphers as a collective, but it also snares the reader as a participant. "And I hope *we* will win. More than that: I know *we* will win." Even though we are meant to believe that D-503 has no recollection of his resistance to One State, writing it off as a sickness, the reader only recalls this opposition. In that context, these two sentences can be interpreted as the reader wishes. Which "we" does the reader select: the "we" of One State's so-called reason or the "we" of the ME-PHI protesters? As Gary Kern states, "*We* . . . would hardly cause a mass revolution, but it might start a little revolution in the mind of each reader" (20). It is difficult to say which "we" D-503 means for us to join, but in the context of postrevolutionary Russia, Zamyatin's intent appears to be clear: *We* must not let One State–like principles thrive.

IV. Comparing Dystopic Protest in *We* and *Nineteen Eighty-Four*

There are many comparisons to be made between *We* and Orwell's *Nineteen Eighty-Four*. Here I will focus on the parallel elements in each that serve as evidence that dystopia is a form of protest literature. The myriad linkages between the two texts has been widely acknowledged in scholarship, often also incorporating Aldous Huxley's 1932 novel, *Brave New World*. Speaking of the similarities between the three, Brown states,

> Some of these are surface and obvious: for instance, Zamyatin's benevolent dictator appears in Huxley's work as the World Controller and in Orwell's as Big Brother; the 'mephi' outside the wall in *We* have their counterpart in Huxley's 'savage reservation' and in Orwell's 'proles.' What is more important and perhaps not so obvious is that all three books share an implicit assumption: that the more complex and highly organized a society becomes, the less free are its individual members. All three works assume the direction of modern European society is toward larger and more complex organization, and that the regimented world of Ford, Taylor, or the proletarian extremists will result at last in the disappearance of the individual human being in favor of the mass. (39)

It is precisely against this "favor of the mass" over the individual that Winston Smith, Julia, D-503, and I-330 protest in *Nineteen Eighty-Four* and *We*. Because of love (an individual affliction), Winston and D-503 become more opposed to blind compliance.

In *Nineteen Eighty-Four*, Winston, unlike D-503, questions the world around him even before becoming driven to subversion by his love for Julia. This is in part owing to his occupation in the Records

Department, which requires him to reconstruct the past on a daily basis in order to align it with the continuous redefinition of the present by the Party (e.g., war with Eastasia one day, war with Eurasia the next, and the rectification of past publications to reflect that the enemy today has always been the enemy). Early in *Nineteen Eighty-Four*, before Winston meets Julia, he has already questioned the world around him:

> Had it always been like this? Had food always tasted like this? He looked round the canteen. A low-ceilinged, crowded room, its walls grimy from the contact of innumerable bodies; battered metal tables and chairs, placed so close together that you sat with elbows touching; bent spoons, dented trays, coarse white mugs; all surfaces greasy, grime in every crack; and a sourish, composite smell of bad gin and bad coffee and metallic stew and dirty clothes. Always in your stomach and in your skin there was a sort of protest, a feeling that you had been cheated of something that you had a right to. . . . Why should one feel it to be intolerable unless one had some kind of ancestral memory that things had once been different? (Orwell 62–63)

Here Winston uses the word "protest"[2] referring to his own sense that there is more to life than that proscribed by the Party. This feeling is one that D-503 encounters through his love for I-330, which brings his soul to life and leads to his willing defiance of One State. Unlike D-503, Winston already suspects that the truth conveyed by the Party and Big Brother is not the Truth:

> How could you tell how much of it was lies? It *might* be true that the average human being was better off now than he had been before the Revolution. The only evidence to the contrary was the mute protest in your own bones, the instinctive feeling that the conditions you lived in were intolerable and that at some other time they must have been different. It struck him that the truly characteristic thing about modern life was not its cruelty and insecurity, but simply its bareness, its dinginess, its listlessness. (76–77)

The word "protest" again appears here and refers to another physical sensation that was described previously: in the first case, it is a feeling in the stomach, and in the second, it is a feeling in the bones. This awareness of missing out on a better life is not something that Winston only imagines in his head, but that he also senses with his entire body. In both novels, physicality plays a central role. Both D-503 and Winston submit to physical lust, a human desire that the state presumably controls. In *Nineteen Eighty-Four*, this manifests in the surface-level physicality of poor living conditions and the beatings and torture that Winston endures. But Winston's observation of feeling something wrong deep inside points to the places that the state cannot control, encouraging the reader to similarly examine from within.

Winston's description of his physically manifested questioning of the Party is similar to D-503's struggle between two desires—his emergent desire for I-330 and his conditioned desire to be loyal to One State. The more enmeshed he becomes with I-330, the more conflicted he is within to accept life as it is in One State. As one scholar has observed, "The central conflict in *We* is the internal struggle of the once-certain D-503. He is constantly torn between his 'old self' of machine-like logic and his 'new self' of primitive passion and human emotion" (Dennis 212). Winston, in contrast, is already alienated by the world around him and somehow internally suspects that a better, or at least different, life may be possible. Unlike D-503, Winston questions even rational (that is, mathematical) Party propositions: "For, after all, how do we know that two and two make four?" (Orwell 84). All the same, despite his questioning and his seeming revulsion for his situation, he is overcome by a sense of helplessness to act: "His heart sank as he thought of the enormous power arrayed against him, the ease with which any Party intellectual would overthrow him in debate, the subtle arguments which he would not be able to understand, much less answer. And yet he was in the right! They were wrong and he was right" (84). This is the beginning of Winston's protest in his own diary, to which he purposefully devotes himself, just like D-503 in *We*.

Julia is the first person Winston meets who openly (at least in private) disagrees with the Party, and she is drawn to him because he feels the same, as she confesses: "I'm good at spotting people who don't belong. As soon as I saw you I knew you were against *them*" (Orwell 128; italics in orig.). The more they talk, the more hopeful Winston becomes: "Anything that hinted at corruption always filled him with a wild hope" (131). As their relationship progresses, Winston and Julia become gradually more subversive: "Sometimes, too, they talked of engaging in active rebellion against the Party, but with no notion of how to take the first step" (159). All of this leads, of course, to their overt protest of the Party when they approach O'Brien:

> We believe that there is some kind of conspiracy, some kind of secret organization working against the Party, and that you are involved in it. We want to join it and work for it. We are enemies of the Party. We disbelieve in the principles of Ingsoc. We are thought-criminals. We are also adulterers. I tell you this because we want to put ourselves at your mercy. If you want us to incriminate ourselves in any other way we are ready. (177)

O'Brien subjects Winston and Julia to a series of questions—asking them how far they are willing to go to protest the Party. They give themselves fully to the mission of the Brotherhood—the secret organization of which O'Brien claims to be part. Winston and Julia are driven by love, but they are more like I-330 than like D-503: they also believe there is something morally, ethically, and terribly wrong with the Party line. Before they are sent to the Ministry of Love, Winston envisions "a world of sanity" (Orwell 229). This is the last hope he will have until the end of the novel when it is determined that "he had won the victory over himself. He loved Big Brother" (311). Just as D-503 ends his diary with his previous loyalty to One State renewed, Winston similarly ends his fight against the Party. But just as Zamyatin has fueled his reader with passionate disagreement for One State, so too has Orwell instilled a disappointment in his reader that Winston and Julia are no longer together and that they are no longer protesting the Party. The ending leaves the reader feeling dissatisfied and uneasy—evoking a feeling of unrest deep within. This aligns perfectly with the definition of protest literature as a medium that "taps into an ideological vein of dissent and announces to its people that they are not alone in their frustrations."

Both Orwell and Zamyatin's intentions were based in some type of existing frustration, it seems. In the case of Zamyatin, the censorship of *We* in Russia at the time of its publication until the 1980s indicates that those in control took issue with the potential for subversion presented by the text. Its later publication in the 1980s alongside *Nineteen Eighty-Four* may very well have led to the protest and revolution that the censors of the 1920s clearly feared. Dystopia, therefore, seems to convey a certain ideological ideal that is counter to freedom and to human nature—both Zamyatin and Orwell successfully enmesh the reader to rebel against such indoctrination.

Notes

1. For additional information on this or other relevant twentieth-century historical information, see Riasanovsky.

2. Interestingly, the word "protest" never appears in *We*. Words with similar meaning appear occasionally: *vozrazit* (to object) and *soprotivljat'sja* (to resist, to oppose). The word *revoljutsija* (revolution) appears three times in the dialogue between D-503 and I-330 cited earlier. In *Nineteen Eighty-Four*, the word "protest" appears four times in nominal or verbal usage. Synonyms such as those found in *We* are similarly more abundant in *Nineteen Eighty-Four* than in Zamyatin's novel. The reasons for this, beyond narrative and theme, may be more indicative of the restrictions on literature in Russia in the 1920s than of authorial intent on Zamyatin's part. Similarly, anti-Western sentiment in the post–World War I and postrevolutionary period may have contributed to a leveling in the usage or borrowing of words of Western origin, a category to which "protest" (Russian: протест) belongs.

Works Cited

Barratt, Andrew. "The X-Factor in Zamyatin's *We*." *Modern Language Review* 80.3 (1985): 659–72. Print.

Beauchamp, Gorman. "Of Man's Last Disobedience: Zamiatin's *We* and Orwell's *1984*." *Comparative Literature Studies* 10.4 (1973): 285–301. Print.

Brown, Edward J. Brave New World, 1984, and We: *An Essay on Anti-Utopia*. Ann Arbor: Ardis, 1976. Print.

Dennis, Bretton J., and Rafeeq O. McGiveron. "Zamyatin's *WE*." *Explicator* 58.4 (2000): 211–13. Print.

Kern, Gary. "Introduction: The Ultimate Anti-Utopia." *Zamyatin's* We: *A Collection of Critical Essays*. Ed. Kern. Ann Arbor: Ardis, 1988. 9–21. Print.

More, Thomas. *Utopia*. 1516. New York: Palgrave, 1999. Print.

Orwell, George. *Nineteen Eighty-Four*. London: Secker, 1987. Print.

Riasanovsky, Nicholas V. *A History of Russia*. 6th ed. New York: Oxford UP, 1999. Print.

Richards, David J. *Zamyatin: A Soviet Heretic*. New York: Hillary, 1962. Print.

Russell, Robert. *Zamyatin's* We. London: Bristol Classical, 2000. Print.

Sacks, David Harris. Introduction. *Utopia*. By Sir Thomas More. New York: Palgrave, 1999. Print.

Shane, Alex. "Zamyatin, Y. I." *Handbook of Russian Literature*. Ed. Victor Terras. New Haven: Yale UP, 1985. 528–29. Print.

Stauffer, John. Foreword. *American Protest Literature*. Ed. Zoe Trodd. Cambridge: Belknap, 2006. xi–xviii. Print.

Tall, Emily. "How *Ulysses* Was Finally Published in the Soviet Union." *Slavic Review* 49.2. (1990): 183–99. Print.

Zamyatin, Yevgeny I. *We*. Trans. Natasha Randall. New York: Modern Lib., 2006. Print.

___. *My* [*We*]. New York: Chekhov, 1952. Print.

scholars see Cummings's recount of his incarceration as ultimately a search for meaning, much like that of Bunyan's hero, Christian. W. Todd Martin argues that through his time spent in prison and through the people he encountered there, "like Christian, he [Cummings] now has the key to understanding the ideals that make up such a Romantic vision of the world and the individual" (130). Martin suggests that Cummings's central goal is to "create a world of Peace and Goodwill" through an understanding of difference (130). Whereas Cummings clearly leaves the confines of La Ferté-Macé with a new understanding of the world and its inhabitants, he does not offer a clear path to a new, more peaceful world. Rather, the often-sardonic tenor of the narrative suggests that Cummings's foremost goals are to celebrate the forgotten underclasses while criticizing the elites as heartless, foolish, and stupid.

In fact, the cutting, often-mocking tone of the novel undercuts any notion of parallelism between Cummings and Bunyan. Paul Headrick argues, in fact, that Cummings's allusions to *Pilgrim's Progress* are ironic. He asserts that Cummings is not parodying the values advocated in Bunyan's work; rather, Cummings attacks "the legacy of Puritanism, those principles that survive covenant theology and the diminishing of Puritanism's importance: anxiety over spiritual status and the expression of this anxiety in conformity, the view of the world as fallen, and the predisposition to allegory itself" (49). He goes on to observe that for Cummings, the journey leads to self-reliance; Cummings grows from a dependence upon B (his abbreviation for his friend and co-inmate William Slater Brown) for survival in the Enormous Room to gaining the ability to stand on his own. Though Headrick's argument is generally sound, limiting the focus to Bunyan and Puritanism misses the obvious: this is a novel about the war.

Though a novel about the war, *The Enormous Room* is about the social politics surrounding the war, rather than the fighting. As such, the novel most clearly reflects the changing face of American society during this era. World War I not only saw a new form of warfare emerge, but also a new form of progressive peace movement, which was more radical, more political, more individualistic, and less concerned with religious doctrine than its predecessors. This new generation of pacifism rejected the ethnocentrism and xenophobia inherent in war propaganda. The young E. E. Cummings, along with many of his colleagues at Harvard, supported this new, liberal pacifism. It is with that in mind that it is important to note that while *The Enormous Room* is set in France (the historical location of Cummings's imprisonment), and the explicit criticism is leveled against the French government, his critiques are implicitly directed at the government of the United States. Cummings, through the various portraits of his fellow inmates, along with himself and B, illustrates how paranoia fuels first the fear of the Other and, subsequently, the fear of one's own populace.

One such governmental reaction was a concerted attempt to stamp out any speech that deviated from the official line. Alan Cywar notes, "Following Congressional approval of Woodrow Wilson's request for a state of war, official manipulation of opinion by the government of the United States brought about a decline by most Americans into an intellectual condition of unquestioning patriotism" (583). Frances H. Early, in her excellent book *A World without War: How U.S. Feminists and Pacifists Resisted World War I*, examines the ways, both subtle and overt, in which the United States government policed dissent as a means of thought control. She says, "It was not long before people discovered that public criticism of [President Woodrow] Wilson, of war decision, or of conscription could lead to police or citizen arrest and a stiff prison sentence" (3). Concluding that any opposition to official governmental policy could undermine the war effort, the US government implemented laws, such as the Espionage Act (1917) and the Sedition Act (1918), to coerce a spirit of nationalism, punishing those who either actively expressed disagreement or who simply did not agree loudly enough.

The former fear is plainly seen in Cummings's and B's initial arrest, which opens the narrative. He says:

To borrow a characteristic cadence from Our Great President:the lively satisfaction which we might be suspected of having derived from the accomplishment of a task so important in the saving of civilization from the clutches of Prussian tyranny was in some degree inhibited, unhappily, by a complete absence of cordial relations between the man whom fate had placed over us and ourselves. Or, to use the vulgar American idiom, B and I and Mr. A [Cummings's unit chief] didn't get on well. (3)[2]

In this portion of the opening paragraph, Cummings establishes the fundamental hypocrisy inherent in the rhetoric surrounding the war—to save free nations from an invading, oppressive force—with the pettiness of the rules surrounding the interactions between the drivers and their boss. His sardonic reference to Wilson as "Our Great President" similarly undercuts Wilson's credibility, highlighting Cummings's disrespect for him and foreshadowing the numerous abuses of power—a decided lack of greatness—that underscore his experiences at La Ferté-Macé.[3]

Cummings continues, noting that the dispute between he, B, and Mr. A. stem from Cummings's and B's habit of spending time with French soldiers, rather than exclusively interacting with their fellow Americans:

We were in fundamental disagreement as to the attitude which we, Americans, should uphold toward the poilus [French soldiers] in whose behalf we had volunteered assistance, Mr. A. maintaining "you boys want to keep away from those dirty Frenchmen" and "we're here to show those bastards how they do things in America", to which we answered by seizing every opportunity for fraternization. (3)

Cummings later reveals that the primary reason for their arrest was that letters written by B had been read by a French censor and contained material deemed to be suitably subversive. He further explains that "Mr. A. and Mr. A.'s translator, both of whom had thankfully testified to the bad character of B and (wishing very naturally to get rid of the both of us at once)had further averred that we were always together and that consequently I might properly be regarded as a suspicious character" (13). Though Cummings is clearly insubordinate, Mr. A.'s somewhat untruthful testimony against him, along with Cummings's resultant imprisonment, emphasizes the hyperbolic governmental response to even the smallest perceived nonconformity, as well as his own antiauthoritarianism.

This account largely comports with the historical account of his imprisonment. Cummings biographer Richard S. Kennedy recalls that Cummings and Brown "heard details about the best-kept secret on the Western front, the mutiny in the French army after General Nivelle's disastrous campaign on the Aisne" (145). He goes on to note that Brown's letters home, relaying this information, and the general pessimism of the French troops "made him appear dangerous to the jumpy French intelligence authorities" (Kennedy 147). Brown was arrested as the author and Cummings as his accomplice. Christopher Sawyer-Lauçanno, in his 2004 biography *E. E. Cummings*, adds that their unit chief, Harry Anderson, "had other issues with his two volunteers, as well, not the least of which was their general dishevelment, which he took as further sign of their insipid insubordination" (115). As both Kennedy and Sawyer-Lauçanno attest, their rocky relationship with Anderson, who was hoping to rid himself of the two rebellious drivers, led directly to their imprisonment. In Cummings's own telling of his ordeal, his narration fairly drips with irony, plainly conveying both his utter disrespect for those who have authority over him and the ridiculousness of the situation in which he has found himself.

Cummings shines a light on the insidious consequences of such wartime paranoia in the above passages. Mr. A.'s jingoism and authority over Cummings and B, who openly disdain him, coupled with a government overly sensitive to subversion, ultimately result in the imprisonment of two men who appear to be no real threat to the war effort. This is a theme repeated throughout the novel, as he paints portraits of his various fellow inmates at La Ferté-Macé, most of whom are described commonly as harmless nonconformists, foreigners, or generally an undesirable Other.

Significantly, none of the inmates of La Ferté-Macé are French. On Cummings's first day at La Ferté, B, while describing their fellow inmates to him, remarks, "Only two or three of them can speak a word of French" (46). This attention to the language barrier shared by so many prisoners is indicative of the inherent xenophobia rampant amongst the French government and general population. In other words, being foreign is grounds for suspicion. David Goldberg, in *Discontented America*, observes that many of the most virulent opponents of United States' entrance into the League of Nations "made demagogic appeals to Americanism and railed against foreign influence" (23). This rabble rousing, Frances Early notes, was essentially futile in its stated goal. She observes that though no actual spies were convicted, hundreds of otherwise innocent pacifists and radicals were kept under strict governmental surveillance for their perceived disloyalty. Cummings and his fellow captives come to represent not only the foreign influence that fuels so much paranoia, but the generally harmless nature of those who often get swept up and punished as a result.

Adding to this notion of a faceless terror, throughout the novel Cummings rarely refers to anyone by their real name, preferring to use a descriptive nickname: the Zulu, the Young Russian, Bill the Hollander, Mexique, and Jean le Nègre. He goes to great lengths to show that the real reason these people are incarcerated is that they do not fit the mold of an authentic Frenchman. Mexique, who traveled to France as a tourist, missed his ship back home, and when he asked a gendarme for help, he was promptly detained:

He [Mexique] had been kindly treated and told that he would be taken to a ship de suite [right away]—had boarded a train in the company of two or three kind gendarmes, ridden a prodigious distance, got off the train finally with high hopes, walked a little distance, come in sight of the grey perspiring wall of La Ferté. (132)

Mexique, like so many others in La Ferté, does not appear to be acting suspiciously other than that he is clearly a foreigner and thus automatically under suspicion.

Cummings describes other inmates who, like Mexique, seem similarly harmless. The Schoolmaster is an old man who spends his days quietly writing at a tiny desk (85). Cummings ironically remarks, "probably The Schoolmaster was a notorious seditionist" (86). The little Machine-Fixer is described as having come "to us with his troubles much as a very minute and helpless child comes to a very large and omnipotent one" (99). Cummings adds that the real dilemma was that "the Machine-Fixer had a soul" (100). And Surplice, one of the Delectable Mountains, whose risk of being a spy is belied by a clear childlike understanding and general lack of awareness of the world around him:

> His filthy rather proudly noble face radiates the pleasure he receives upon being informed that people are killing people for nobody knows what reason, that boats go under water and fire six-foot long bullets at ships, that America is not really just outside this window close to which we are talking, that America is in fact over sea. The sea: is that water? . . . Ah: a great quantity of water . . . (189)

In each of these cases, along with the several others peppered throughout the novel, Cummings showcases the human cost of a fearful government that indiscriminately sweeps up anyone who does not fit the behavioral norm. True danger to the state does not seem to be a criterion for arrest. In effect, Cummings shows the humanity of the innocents who have been sacrificed in order to maintain authoritarian order.

Having taken stock of his fellow inmates, Cummings plainly spells out the insidious arbitrariness of the implementation of antisedition laws, when enforced through a haze of paranoia. He asks:

Who was eligible to La Ferté? Anyone whom the police could find in the lovely country of France (a) who was not guilty of treason (b) who could not prove that he was not guilty of treason. By treason I refer to little annoying habits of independent thought or action which en temps de guerre are put in a hole and covered over, with the somewhat naïve idea that from their cadavers violets will grow whereof the perfume will delight all good men and true and make such worthy citizens forget their sorrows. (83–84)

Cummings's description of the criteria for arrest and incarceration is eerily similar to the targets of harassment, intimidation, and arrest in the United States during this period. Early notes that "anti-radicalism, Germanophobia, and a generalized nativist repugnance for all things foreign fused in the popular mind with the notion of the enemy within" (79). Underlying Cummings's various portraits is a condemnation of the prejudices, hatreds, and phobias that are allowed to fester in these types of conditions. Yet he simultaneously undercuts the basis for those same fears. Cummings's fellow inmates are purely innocuous, and only a state so consumed in fear of the Other could find reason for suspicion and just cause to imprison them.

The rampant political paranoia found in *The Enormous Room* can be traced to the United States' paranoia about revolt at the hands of socialists and other progressives at home. Maureen Flanagan notes that "after the war, the success of Bolshevism abroad meant that every kind of political dissent inspired fears of revolution at home. In this hysterical environment, extreme measures became common" (240). Cummings's focus on the trivialities of his and his fellow inmates' arrests can be viewed as a critique of American war policy both during and after World War I—specifically, the Espionage Act. Enacted in June 1917, it "outlawed any obstruction of military operations during wartime and forbade the use of the mails to disseminate any material advocating treason, insurrection, or forcible resistance to any law of the United States" (Flanagan 234). While being interrogated by a French minister, Cummings states that the reason he and B had been arrested was because "the French censor had intercepted some of B's letters, and had notified Mr. A." (13). As noted previously, it was these letters that gave Mr. A. the excuse to trump up charges against Cummings and B, of whom he wanted to rid himself.

In these letters, Cummings and B request to remain with the French when the Red Cross is taken over by the American military, and this is interpreted as Cummings and B "not only trying to avoid serving in the American Army but . . . contemplating treason as well" (14). While the exact contents of the letter sent by Cummings and B does not relate directly to the specific provisions of the Espionage Act, Flanagan notes that the postmaster applied the legislation broadly, unilaterally banning what he deemed to be objectionable, subversive material. She says, "Individuals were convicted even for discussing whether conscription was constitutional" (Flanagan 234). The innocuous nature of their offense enables Cummings to highlight how the abuse of such broad, ambiguous, repressive legislation results in the wrongful incarceration of those whom it is intended to protect. It is significant to note that upon arriving at La Ferté-Macé, he is told by B that "'all these fine people were arrested as espions'" (46) and that he and Cummings are suspected spies as well. In effect, during times of war, citizens who do not meet strict standards of patriotism are guilty until proven innocent.

The Espionage Act was followed shortly by the Sedition Act, which, according to Flanagan, "made it easier, as the attorney general had requested, to prosecute any 'disloyal utterances'" (235). The law also "declar[ed] it unlawful for anyone to 'willfully utter, print, write, or publish any disloyal, profane, scurrilous, or abusive language'" about any United States government entity, policy, document, military "'or any language intended to bring the form of government of the United States . . . into contempt, scorn, contumely, or disrepute'" (Flanagan 235). It is under these broad and ambiguous guidelines that Cummings is imprisoned. He is asked whether he hates the Germans and, rather than appeasing his interrogators by answering "yes," he answers, "Non. J'aime beaucoup les français [No. I like the French very much]"

(14). Here, Cummings underscores the twisted logic of the act. His refusal to respond in the prescribed way is viewed by his interrogators as disloyalty because, in their mind, loving France and hating Germany are inseparable concepts; therefore, not hating Germans translates to contempt of the French.

This idea of absolute patriotism mirrors the postwar campaigns of so-called 100 percent Americans, who, according to historian John Higham, "'set out to stampede immigrants into citizenship, into adoption of the English language, and into unquestioning reverence for existing American institutions'" (qtd. in Flanagan 233). Flanagan adds, "When war was declared, too many average Americans heard 'Americanism' equated with patriotism and supporting the war" (232). This idea of blind support for the United States grew stronger as the war raged on and eventually morphed into a complete mistrust of any foreign nations. As a result, the Senate rejected the Treaty of Versailles on the basis that, according to Jolyon Girard, "Article X authorized the League to act to enforce its decisions, perhaps with military force" (90), and many senators believed that the League of Nations would then be authorized to send American troops into war without Senate approval. In effect, the fear of foreign influence during and after the war rose to a fever pitch. Cummings and B, two Americans in France, become swept up in the overly patriotic fervor sweeping through many nations during and after the war, and because they did not blindly accept all conventional governmental beliefs, they were incarcerated as a preventive measure, rather than because of any tangible harm done to the nation. Their arrest becomes a perfect analog for American xenophobia.

The exchange between Cummings and his interlocutor highlights the ways in which overzealous underlings manipulate an already oppressive system and showcases the semantic traps that people commonly found themselves in as a result of the overall paranoia of the time. During Cummings's interview, the outright hatred of Germans is the sign that he was suitably allied to the French cause; liking the

French is not enough. Frances Early notes that in America, "soon after the war declaration, the federal government launched a well-orchestrated propaganda campaign to win the unquestioning loyalty of Americans. . . . The nation quickly became saturated with notions of 100 percent Americanism and unthinking patriotism" (19). During his journey to La Ferté-Macé, Cummings notices that his Americanness—in essence, his foreignness—causes many sidelong glances and general disparagement by the locals. He remarks of one such look that is "meant to wipe me off the earth's face" (33). Cummings later muses, "Evidently I was getting to be more of a criminal every minute;I should probably be shot tomorrow" (33). Through his overly casual tone, Cummings draws specific attention to the ease at which authoritarian measures can spiral out of control, especially when they are tacitly sanctioned by the government with little critical oversight. Akin to the 100 percent Americanism described above, the suspicions of French citizens toward Cummings are purely the result of his non-Frenchness.

It is important to note that prior to the United States' involvement in World War I, most pacifist movements eschewed radical political action, preferring philosophical and religious discussion in order to promote a more peaceful, isolationist foreign policy. Charles Chatfield notes, "There had been pacifists in the strict sense before World War I, but for the most part they had been sectarians motivated by obedience to religious injunctions against killing and against complying with the military" (1920). In addition to religious pacifists, numerous primarily isolationist organizations—such as the World Peace Foundation, which boasted Cummings's father as a founding member—believed that through discussion and study, a more perfect society could be created; yet, these groups were against radical challenges to established authorities. Despite their opposition to war, many of these groups firmly believed in American exceptionalism, arguing, "If the nation ever should go to war . . . its democratic politics and humanitarian tradition would guarantee its cause to be just and necessary" (Chatfield 1921).

Many of these pacifists believed that World War I met just such a criteria of a "just war."

Significantly, Cummings's refusal to avow hatred of all Germans, and his preference to admit an appreciation for the French, is reflective of this new generation of American pacifists. During the run up to World War I, many pacifists rejected the view that Germany (and all of its citizens by proxy) was inherently a great evil, and with that, they rejected the idea of a just war, as well as the ethnocentrism and xenophobia of earlier American pacifist groups. Cummings's response likewise undercuts the notion, fundamental to the idea of the just war, of American exceptionalism.

In fact, contrary to the idea of the just war, Sawyer-Lauçanno remarks that Cummings was "certain that the war was fundamentally stupid, and a great waster of the lives of countless human beings" (115). Cummings highlights that stupidity throughout *The Enormous Room*, both through the dimwittedness of those in authority and through the more sympathetic portraits he paints of his fellow inmates. Mexique echoes Cummings's own view of the war, saying, "I t'ink lotta bullshit" (132).

More telling is the story of Jean le Nègre, one of the Delectable Mountains, who is arrested for gleefully impersonating an English captain and strutting around Paris, claiming all the respect and spoils that his rank entitles him:

> Everywhere he met with success. He was frantically pursued by women of all stations from les putains [whores] to les princesses. The police salaamed to him. His arm was wearied with the returning of innumerable salutes. So far did his medals carry him that, although on one occasion a gendarme dared to arrest him for beating in the head of a fellow English officer(who being a mere lieutenant, should not have objected to Captain Jean's stealing the affections of his lady), the sergent de gendarmerie . . . refused to even hear the evidence, and dismissed the case with profuse apologies to the heroic Captain. (201).

Jean's adventures as a faux captain prove to be a severe critique of how authoritarianism comes to thrive when a democracy abandons its principles. Jean's uniform gives him the right to do whatever he wants to whomever he wants, just so long as that person is of lower rank. A public beating meets no reprisal because the arresting officer is his subordinate. Cummings shows, through a humorous encounter, that Paris has become, effectively, a police state. With this episode, Cummings warns of what can happen—even in a democracy—when too much deference is given to the state under the guise of national security.

The Sedition Act, and similar legislation, signaled that the US government was willing to undermine the civil rights of its citizens in order to maintain the façade of the people's unconditional loyalty. Chatfield argues that "pacifists accepted such liberal values of progressivism as . . . the democratic process, and the ultimate worth of the individual" (1926)—each of which the aforementioned legislation was intended to suppress. The majority of the portraits Cummings paints are of simple, often poor people from various countries who have in some way aroused the suspicions of the French government and have found themselves at La Ferté. As such, he continually highlights the inherent irony in the state-sponsored restraint of free expression during a war ostensibly meant to save democracy from tyranny and authoritarianism.

Edward Cain, in his essay "Conscientious Objection in France Britain and the United States," notes that the United States and France "cannot afford to be as relaxed in [their] patriotism as a constitutional monarchy . . . it is much more difficult to draw a line between regime and state" (298). Meaning that without a clear figurehead to rally around, republics like the United States and France count on widespread patriotic feeling among the populace. Cummings shows how this fear of dissent and any unpatriotic grumbling leads to the unnecessary incarceration and abuse of individuals. The vast majority of inmates are themselves confused as to why they have been taken into custody, but Cummings often speculates as to what possible infraction could land these unassuming men in prison. He wonders of the Schoolmaster, "Did he, by any chance, tell the children that there are such monstrous things as peace and good will . . . a corrupter of youth no doubt" (86; ellipses in orig.). Mocking the thin-skinned nature of governments and the ridiculous symbols of national pride during wartime, Cummings speculates, "I bet Emile the Bum insulted two potatoes" (87). And Cummings reasons that a shy, developmentally disabled man with little language at all is "really a super-intelligent crook who had robbed the cabinet of the greatest cabinet-minister of the greatest cabinet-minister's cabinet papers . . . and all the apparent idiocy of the little man with the Orange Cap was a skillfully executed bluff" (88). For Cummings, it seems impossible that any of these men could in any way harm the French nation, yet he shows how often a government declares that maintaining a single political voice takes precedence over the rights of the individual.

For as much sympathy as he gives his fellow inmates, Cummings is equally venomous toward the authorities presiding over his incarceration, waging the war, and marketing the war as a great and noble cause. Cummings's sarcastic voice throughout *The Enormous Room* is on wide display as he frequently makes ironic references to the slogans and propaganda used to convince people to join the war effort as well as those who diligently and unthinkingly carry out governmental orders. Whereas the First World War was billed as the "war to end all wars," Goldberg notes that critics of the Treaty of Versailles argued that it "planted the seeds for another war" (21). Cummings echoes that sentiment, sardonically comparing an injured soldier's recovery duty as a guard at La Ferté to a vacation of sorts: "as soon as they had recovered their health under these salubrious influences they were shipped back to do their bit for world-safety, democracy, freedom, etc., in the trenches" (59). Here, he underscores both the callousness of the government toward its rank-and-file soldiers, sending them back out into the fray after narrowly escaping death, and the relative foolishness of those soldiers who happily enjoy their time as prison guards, imagining that ordering detainees around in a dank and musty detention center is a fun break. In some ways it is, given that they will soon be back in the trenches.

Cummings lampoons the most zealous of the prison guards who does not want the inmates talking loudly at night, saying, "Never have I seen a greater exhibition of bravery that was afforded by The Black Holster, revolver in hand, holding at bay the snoring and weaponless inhabitants of The Enormous Room. Vive les plantons [Long live the orderlies]" (145). Throughout the novel, the Black Holster stands out as the sort of pompous buffoon whose inflated view of his own grandiosity consistently undercuts any authority he might have. The parallels to the France of *The Enormous Room* and the America of the same period are unmistakable here. Cummings ridicules the very institutions and people whom the Sedition Act and Espionage Act were meant to protect, and by doing so, he shows the insanity and inhumanity of those institutions while, at the same time, showing the humanity of those whom those institutions oppress.

While Cummings consistently voices his loathing of the French government, he reserves his harshest criticism for the lower-ranking individuals who dole out the daily abuses in its name: the guards; Monsieur le Directeur, whom he calls Apollyon and describes as "a very definite fiend"; and the commission, referred to as the Three Wise Men (107). La Ferté-Macé is a detention center, not a prison. Every three months, a commission comes to La Ferté and decides the fate of each prisoner; if found guilty, the prisoner is "sent off to a regular prison camp pour la durée de la guerre [the duration of the war];if not guilty, he or she was(in theory)set free" (Cummings 60). The commission represents all the evils of authoritarianism, in which a person is completely at the mercy of another who is working in the interest of the oppressor, not the oppressed, and one wrong word can be the difference between indefinite imprisonment throughout an endless war and potential freedom.

Cummings's most poignant example is the story of the Wanderer, another Delectable Mountain. A soft-spoken, kind man, "guilty of who knows what gentleness, strength and beauty" (166), learns a few weeks after being taken to La Ferté that his wife and child have come to the prison to live because they could not survive without him. The commission finds the Wanderer to be a security threat, and he is sent to different, long-term prison, again dividing his family. Cummings admonishes both the government and its agents, saying, "Let us . . . admit that it takes a good and great government perfectly to negate mercy" (167). Time and time again, prisoners who have been taken off the streets for uncertain crimes are being sent to prison out of both the inhumanity of the governmental machine and that government's fear of all whispers of dissent. When it is finally his turn to face the commission, Cummings sums up his judgment of them and the system that gives them authority: "The thing is this, to look 'em in the eyes and keep cool whatever happens, not for the fraction of a moment forgetting that they are made of merde [shit]" (217).

The Three Wise Men and the minister who first interrogates Cummings also are representative of the governmental paranoia, which is more intent on proving what it already believes to be true than to conduct hearings to discover the truth. Cummings's official hearings are little more than kangaroo courts. It is likewise clear that B is the real target of inquiry and that the interviews of Cummings are purely to find someone to corroborate what they already believe of B. The minister who first interrogates Cummings asks him many questions about B's loyalty to France and only asks Cummings about himself as he relates to B. The minister tells him, "I am sorry for you, but due to your friend you will be detained a little while" (15). The minister's interrogation strategy is almost mirrored by the Three Wise Men. Cummings recalls that the commission "told me, through its sweetish-soap-leader, that my friend was a criminal—this immediately upon my entering—and I told it with a great deal of well-chosen politeness that I disagreed'" (219). In the end, Cummings is allowed to leave La Ferté but is to stay in France as he remains a suspect, but B is convicted and sentenced to prison for the duration of the war. Cummings confounds his questioners by not responding in the expected ways: defending his friend at personal peril. The fact that Cummings comes under suspicion not as a result of evidence against him, but because he questioned the allegations against B underscores the insidious nature of these hearings when fueled by massive distrust of the majority of people. The arbitrary nature of justice is thus emphasized by the Three Wise Men's decision to hold B but release Cummings, since each had been equally indicted by Mr. A.

Whether it is Cummings admitting to liking the French rather than hating Germans or asserting that he rejects their assertions of B's criminality, though it could keep him in prison, Cummings demonstrates both an antiauthoritarian bent and a dedication to his cause that recalls the strongest of the conscientious objectors of the era. Cummings's small rebellion against the French interrogator is remarkable in both its smallness (a seemingly innocent semantic difference) and its enormous consequences (a year in prison). In this, Cummings connects his own story to other objectors and pacifists of the era. Frances Early cites many figures throughout the period who found themselves under intense governmental scrutiny for either espousing unpopular opinions or merely voicing disagreement with official government policy. She identifies the well-known anarchist Emma Goldman as well as people who refused to sign loyalty oaths or belonged to progressive causes as individuals targeted by administrative and government officials for termination or imprisonment. Cummings, in a sense, uses the inmates at La Ferté-Macé to illustrate the wide range of people swept up in the hysteria of war.

While his detestation for his captors is clear throughout the work, Cummings shows that the guards, the oppressors of the inmates in their charge, also fall victim to wartime paranoia. Cain notes, "The [French] Revolution had made it clear that, in any contest, equality is preferred to liberty. Nowhere is this more evident than in the equal demands for fidelity made by patriotism. One may criticize the state, but certainly everyone is expected to rally to its defense in the case of outside attack" (279). Observing that many of the guards at La Ferté are injured soldiers recovering from the front, Cummings learned early on that a sure way to find one's self in solitary confinement, was to "apply to a planton, particularly a permanent planton . . . the term embusqué [shirker of active service]" (59). The implication of cowardice is met with a feeling of humiliation, anger, and fear.

Often, the frustration of these guards who are not testing their manhood in the trenches is taken out on the prisoners, frequently manifesting in the rigid control of prisoners' movements, food, and basic interactions. In the aforementioned late-night conversation incident, Cummings notes that the Black Holster, pistol drawn and irate, "looked for approbation to his trembling assistants. Then he swore twenty or thirty times for luck, turned, and thundered out on the heels of his fleeing confrères" (145). The absurdity of the situation is so palpable that it is obvious even to the Black Holster. It is this very ridiculousness that leads him to overreact. For the Black Holster, the noise itself is irritating in that it prevents him from sleeping but more so in that it signifies a lack of control on the part of the guards. The inmates, in essence, are running the asylum.

While he offers no condolences, Cummings seems to understand the undue pressures placed on his captors by the regime they serve. The Black Holster reacts so violently because he is afraid that he will be punished if others are not allowed to sleep, and in the end, no one is punished for the infraction of the rules. This is significant in that it shows that no one is immune to authoritarian oppression, and it is this understanding that drives the antiauthoritarian sentiment of many liberal pacifists of World War I and that explains why Cummings so readily comes to the defense of B rather than allowing him to be judged a traitor.

It is worth noting that these same types of challenges to one's manliness were often lobbed at male contentious objectors. Early points out that during World War I, "an extreme masculine ideal of the intrepid combat-ready patriot . . . held sway in the minds of many young men" (92). Despite laws and regulations that objectors should face no repercussions, historian John Whiteclay Chambers II reports that "military authorities starved the objectors on bread and water, hanged them by their wrists, forced them to exercise and then drenched them in icy showers, and beat them with belts and broom handles" (qtd. in Early 97). It is therefore little wonder that the *plantons* of La Ferté-Macé would take such umbrage at being called a malingerer.

Interestingly, despite the dour circumstances, the emotion that most clearly pervades *The Enormous Room* is joy. He remarks, on his passage to La Ferté-Macé, "An uncontrollable joy gutted me after three months of humiliation, of being bossed and herded and bullied and insulted. I was myself and my own master" (17). This is echoed by B, on Cummings's first morning: "Cummings, I tell you this is the finest place on earth!" (46). While there is a fair bit of irony in these statements, their happiness to be rid of Mr. A. is clear. Moreover, Cummings, in spite of his incarceration, is more at home with the people populating La Ferté-Macé than he ever was with his fellow Americans. His loving portraits suggest a likeness in spirit, if not ethnicity and origin. Ultimately, Cummings finds that he shares much more in common with men from varying nationalities and classes than he does with the other Americans he has encountered in France. This underscores much of the rising peace movements of the World War I era. Theirs was a unity of common cause, or causes, rather than a tribal connection. People from all walks of life were welcomed into the fold based upon common ideals and shared struggles. The inmates inhabiting La Ferté-Macé were all there for different reasons but shared a humanity and an independent spirit that made them a threat to the social order.

From the very first pages, it is clear that E. E. Cummings's *The Enormous Room* is a war novel unlike any other. His is not a study of the life of the soldier, but a paean to the nonconformists and objectors who were similarly swept up in the tides of war. According to Sawyer-

Lauçanno, "Cummings's decision to volunteer for the ambulance service had little to do with patriotism, nor did it mark a change in his anti-war feelings. Like most young men at the time, he was simply facing a difficult choice" (104)—the choice being to volunteer for the ambulance corps or to be drafted into the trenches. Cummings chose the road less traveled but no less difficult. His account of his imprisonment therefore shines a unique light on the governments that use war and propaganda to forcibly instill patriotism in its people and the insidious ways in which those democracies undermine their own values in a quest for uniformity of opinion in the name of national security. With equal parts irony, anger, and humanity, Cummings celebrates those who would resist a government that no longer lives up to their values.

Notes

1. Cummings alternately describes *The Enormous Room* as both a novel and a memoir. For the sake of simplicity and continuity, I will refer to the work as a novel.
2. Cummings's original text omits spacing between certain in-sentence punctuation and the following words, such as commas, colons, and semicolons. Therefore, throughout this essay, when directly quoting from *The Enormous Room*, the quoted material will reflect Cummings's original spacing.
3. Cummings repeats this device throughout the text, most notably when referring to the Three Wise Men, the commission ruling whether a prisoner is a legitimate threat or can be set free. Like President Woodrow Wilson, the Three Wise Men are unmistakably unwise.

Works Cited

Brosman, Catherine Savage. "The Functions of War Literature." *South Central Review* 9.1 (1992): 85–98. Print.

Cain, Edward R. "Conscientious Objection in France, Britain, and the United States." *Comparative Politics* 2.2 (1970): 275–307. Print.

Chatfield, Charles. "World War I and the Liberal Pacifist in the United States." *American Historical Review* 75.7 (1970): 1920–37. Print.

Cummings, E. E. *The Enormous Room*. 1922. New York: Liveright, 1978. Print.

Cywar, Alan. "John Dewey in World War I: Patriotism and International Progressivism." *American Quarterly* 21.3 (1969): 578–94. Print.

Early, Frances H. *A World without War: How U.S. Feminists and Pacifists Resisted World War I*. Syracuse: Syracuse UP, 1997. Print.

Flanagan, Maureen A. *America Reformed: Progressives and Progressivisms 1890s–1920s*. Oxford: Oxford UP, 2007. Print.

Fussell, Paul. *The Great War and Modern Memory*. 1975. Oxford: Oxford UP, 2000. Print.

Girard, Jolyon P. *America and the World*. Westport: Greenwood, 2001. Print.

Goldberg, David J. *Discontented America: The United States in the 1920s*. Baltimore: Johns Hopkins UP, 1999. Print.

Headrick, Paul. "*The Enormous Room* and the Uses of Parody." *Spring* 2 (1993): 48–56. Print.

Kennedy, Richard S. *Dreams in the Mirror: A Biography of E. E. Cummings*. New York: Liveright, 1980. Print.

Martin, W. Todd. "'The Mysteries of Noyon': Emblem and Meaning in *The Enormous Room*." *Spring* 9 (2000): 125–31. Print.

Sawyer-Lauçanno, Christopher. *E. E. Cummings: A Biography*. Naperville: Sourcebooks, 2004. Print.

Holiness and Heresy: Viramontes, *la Virgen,* and the Mother-Daughter Bond_____

Christi Cook

Young-adult (YA) literature is a marginalized, oft-contested, and sometimes suspect genre existing on the borderlands of the canon of adult literature (Younger). YA literature is difficult to define, according to noteworthy critic of the field Perry Nodelman in *The Hidden Adult.* It bears some similarities to adult literature and other likenesses of children's literature, but Nodelman maintains that YA literature, just like children's literature, is a genre whose intrinsic qualities are significant enough to delineate it clearly from other genres. If a definition of children's literature is possible, though, Nodelman asserts that the most pragmatic definition is that which is listed on the children's list of a publisher. "Children's literature" generally refers to literature appropriate for children up to age twelve or thirteen, although Nodelman uses this term to refer to literature from birth through adolescence (145), while "young-adult literature" usually describes literature for readers aged fourteen and older. Sometimes the term "juvenile literature" is used to include both children's and YA literature. Ultimately, publishers make the final call as to what will be marketed to child readers and what will be targeted toward adults.

Chicano/a literature is also a marginalized genre due to the conditions of its emergence as literature for a politicized, borderlands Mexican American population. The Chicano movement of the 1960s catalyzed a vast wealth of protest literature by writers who embraced some of the indigenous aspects of Mexican culture as they fought against their marginalization in the United States. Therefore, Chicano/a YA literature is doubly in shadow as compared to traditionally canonical literature. Since protest literature is defined as literature written by or about any disenfranchised group of people with the goal of resisting that disenfranchisement, it is clear that most Chicano/a YA literature should be categorized as protest literature. Because postmodern literary studies have promoted the study of literature that was previously on the fringe, more people are critically examining Chicano/a YA literature.

One such protest writer was Rudolfo Anaya, whose 1972 novel *Bless Me, Ultima* simultaneously emerged from and sparked the Chicano movement of the late 1960s and early 1970s. Another complex Chicana writer whose work has consistently been labeled as YA literature is Helena María Viramontes. In 1995, she released *Under the Feet of Jesus*, which is enriched when viewed through a feminist theoretical lens. Viramontes both draws inspiration from and expands on Anaya's vision of an indigenous Chicana literary tradition by moving beyond Chicano focus on Aztlán and creating a feminist model characterized by its focus on female characters and its formal experimentation. In this chapter, I will give an overview of Chicano history and of Chicano and Chicana political and literary approaches, an explanation of the marginalized role of Chicana literature as well as YA literature in general, and an in-depth exploration of *Bless Me, Ultima* as an important precursor to *Under the Feet of Jesus*. I will explore three prominent feminine archetypes significant to both novels: *la Virgen de Guadalupe*, *la Llorona*, and *la Malinche*. I argue that the authors' reconfiguration of these cultural icons alongside their presentation of earth-based spirituality, along with their inclusion of powerful female characters and exploration of the injustice of poverty, is a method of protesting the dominant culture.

Chicano History and Politics

Mexico was populated and governed by indigenous people such as the Aztecs and the Maya until Hernán Cortés, a Spanish conquistador, conquered the land and the people in the early sixteenth century. Feminist theologians, such as Monica Sjöö, Charlene Spretnak, and Barbara Walker, discuss how, historically, when Catholic Spanish missionaries arrived after the indigenous peoples of Mexico were conquered, they often erected churches on sites that were already sacred to the population for worshipping indigenous gods and goddesses. Church officials encouraged worship of the Virgin Mary, since that made for an easier transition for people with a tradition of mother-goddess worship. However, the Christian doctrine that there is only one God and that the way to Him is through His son, Jesus, limited the church's tolerance of earth- or goddess-focused spirituality (cf. Oleszkiewicz-Peralba). The indigenous people were forced to work as slaves on what had been their land, which was redistributed to Spaniards, and to convert to Christianity. A new caste system developed, with Spaniards born in Spain at the top, followed by *criollos*, Spaniards born in Mexico; then *mestizos*, those with mixed Spanish and Mexican heritage; and *indios*, the indigenous people, at the bottom (Arce). In 1820, Mexico became independent from Spain's rule, thus beginning its postcolonial period. During this time, Mexico had to come to terms with its complex, troubled relationship with its mixed Spanish and indigenous heritage. Even today, racial and class stratifications remain.

At that point, a sizable portion of what had been Mexico became the southwest United States as the result of the United States seizing Mexican land following the Mexican-American War. Mexican American families endeavored to gain financial and political power as their land and rights were taken away from them by Anglos. In the following years, numerous Mexican and Mexican American people were forced to work as migrant farmers and other low-paying, backbreaking jobs in order to support themselves.

Frustration over these conditions and other forms of discrimination culminated in the 1960s with the Chicano movement, a political movement coinciding with the 1960s struggle for civil rights for minorities. The term "Chicano" is a politicized term referring to Mexican Americans. "Mexican American" is a less politicized term referring to people of Mexican ancestry currently living in the United States, many of whom descended from Mexican nationals who were living in Mexico until 1848. This movement included activism focused on schools, land rights, political rights, and labor. The activist César Chávez, to whom Viramontes dedicated *Under the Feet of Jesus*, started the group that became the United Farm Workers in 1962. According to the union's website, they use nonviolent activism to advocate for better treatment and payment of migrant farm workers. Losing their native soil as a result of war differentiates Chicanos, and the literature they produce, from minorities and minority literature that are the result of immigration or slavery.

Though many Chicanas participated in the political movement of the 1960s, they often felt sidelined by male leaders, a phenomenon that was widespread in several civil rights movements.[1] Many Chicanas felt silenced and excluded by the patriarchal nature of the Chicano movement, and they responded to this repression politically and artistically. Due to the long-standing tradition of *machismo*—the idea that men are stronger and better equipped to work in the public sphere while women stay primarily inside the home to cook and clean for their husbands and children—the leaders of the Chicano movement, such as Rodolfo "Corky" Gonzáles, Reies López Tijerina, and César Chávez, were primarily male. Chicanas worked to find their own unique voice as women within the movement. One of these Chicanas, Helena María Viramontes, is a part of what Ellen McCracken described, in her comprehensive 1999 work *New Latina Narrative*, as the flood of feminist Chicana voices into literature in the wake of the Chicano movement (4). Viramontes helped bring the concerns and beliefs of Chicanas into the spotlight, where they could be better understood by Chicanos and a broader mainstream audience.

Chicano/a Literary Approaches

Chicano literary approaches tend to have a masculine, land-based focus, while Chicana literary approaches eschew the land in favor of relationships and self-determination. For many Chicanos, cultural pride was tied up with reclaiming the ancestral land of the Southwest, Aztlán, from its unlawful current proprietor. A literary example of this phenomenon appears in *Under the Feet of Jesus*: Perfecto's desire to return to a specific homeland, which is so strong that it feels like "a tumor lodged under the muscle of [his] heart" that gets "larger with every passing day" (Viramontes 82–83), is reminiscent of the nationalistic stance of the Chicano movement exemplified by Corky Gonzales's epic *Yo Soy Joaquín* (1972) and the poet Alurista's concept of Aztlán, although Viramontes seems to critique Perfecto's land-focused position. Signaling a change in focus from a homeland to borderlands, Gloria Anzaldúa changed the conversation entirely when she published her pivotal 1987 text, *Borderlands*. Anzaldúa proclaims the advent of the New Mestiza, who is capable of simultaneously embodying both masculine and feminine as well as numerous nationalities. The New Mestiza consciousness is one that is comfortable inhabiting borderlands without prizing one nation above the other, and the New Mestiza incorporates various cultures and languages holistically in her life. Anzaldúa redefined the landscape for Chicanas and showed them how to use the ubiquity of border consciousness in their lives both formally and thematically in their works (Kaup 199). She integrates numerous languages and styles in her book, which is innovative in a poststructural fashion (208). Anzaldúa's study makes no effort to disguise the fact that her text, like many texts, is constantly spilling out of its conventional borders.

Following in Anzaldúa's tradition, Viramontes encapsulates a borderlands mentality with her shifting formal approach, her positioning of Estrella on the boundary between childhood and adulthood, and her placement of Estrella's feet in both US and Mexican cultures. The thirteen-year-old migrant farm worker attends school occasionally when she is able to do so, but Anglo teachers rudely observe that she is poorly dressed and that her hygiene is substandard. Similar to Donna Haraway's characterization of cyborgs in "A Cyborg Manifesto" (1985), Estrella is both-and (both Mexican and American, both young and old, both powerful and powerless), but she, as Haraway urges all of us to do, uses the tools she has at her disposal to make the most of her current situation rather than trying to return to an Edenic garden.[2] Estrella, like all Chicano/a people, is a hybrid subject. Cultural hybridity is an important, prevalent theme in Chicano/a YA literature because it addresses how a young Chicano/a should function in a dominant culture that is different from his or her heritage.

In order to unpack Viramontes's *Under the Feet of Jesus*, or any work by a Chicana author, it is helpful to have an understanding of Anzaldúa's *Borderlands*, which is a multigenre creative memoir, and McCracken's *New Latina Narrative*, which is a standard work of literary criticism. These two theorists set a foundation for analyzing Chicana narrative structure according to its distinctive patterns. Chicana YA literature's status as a marginalized, contradictory, hybrid art form is best understood with Anzaldúa's framework in mind. For her, hybridity is a positive, empowering status, and the borderlands model invites formal experimentation and an all-encompassing acceptance of cultural "back-and-forths" that previously were neither tolerated nor even conceived of. Viramontes fits into this tradition with her unique poetic, nonchronological style. Since race and ethnicity are such important themes in Chicano/a YA literature, McCracken is helpful for creating a framework to analyze the appearance of race and ethnicity, along with class, sexual orientation, and gender, on various axes in Chicana literature. She provides pointed analysis of Viramontes's works, along with several others, in order to situate Viramontes's writing among her peers. Both Anzaldúa and McCracken are vital to a thorough understanding of the themes of cultural hybridity, power, gender norms and traditions, religion, and sexuality that emerge in Viramontes's work, as well as in most youth literature written for young-adult Latinas. Though these themes are not entirely unique to Chicana literature, their predominance in the literature and their distinct manifestations, detailed throughout this chapter, make them helpful markers for distinction from non-Chicana literature.

Though McCracken is quick to point out that the Chicana authors who emerged in the 1980s and 1990s are not a monolithic group who can or should be ghettoized, she does note several similarities among them. To begin with, Chicana authors like Sandra Cisneros and Helena

María Viramontes were welcomed into late twentieth-century US mainstream culture because in the postmodern age, difference was more valued than at any previous time. McCracken draws a parallel between this ostensible appreciation of diversity and Edward Said's observations about Orientalism: the minority becomes a valuable commodity because s/he presents a nonthreatening amount of deviation from the white standard (McCracken 5). The New Chicana authors write to mostly English-speaking audiences, but they use "tropicalized" English (7); they often insert Spanish words and phrases into a primarily English text in unusual ways, thereby writing back against the colonizer. The concept of "writing back" against an oppressor is a common one in postcolonial studies, the field of study of the inheritance and difficulties faced by peoples who have been oppressed by a colonizing Western nation. Often, the colonized will use the language of the oppressor, along with his or her own tongue, in inventive ways in order to get across an important political or emotional point. For example, in one scene in *Under the Feet of Jesus*, Alejo and his cousin Gumecindo are picking fruit from an orchard when they start discussing Plato. Gumecindo is unfamiliar with the famous Greek philosopher; he thinks Plato is "'plate' in gringo Spanish" (Viramontes 5). When Alejo explains the misunderstanding, the two lose themselves in hysterical laughter. Viramontes uses a moment of cultural and linguistic disconnect to highlight the slippery nature of biculturalism and bilingualism, even though the interaction takes place mainly in English. Hence, the deviation from the Anglo norm is small and easily accepted by the Anglo reader.

Bilingualism is one type of formal experimentation utilized by New Chicana authors; another is their frequent desire to separate themselves from the master text narrative by experimenting with stream of consciousness and nonchronology, as Viramontes does. Her writing is sometimes difficult to follow, as her stories move back and forth through time without transitions. For example, in *Under the Feet of Jesus*, Perfecto Flores, the much-older boyfriend of thirteen-year-old Estrella's beleaguered mother, Petra, seems to begin deteriorating in mental capacity toward the end of the novel. His mind jumps around more and more to the past, and the reader is immersed in various scenes from Perfecto's first marriage, along with his somewhat incoherent articulations about his desire to return home, which may be attributed to his rising panic about his inability to provide for his and Petra's growing family. Perfecto wants to leave the migrant farms of California and return to his ancestral land to die, and he is contemplating leaving Petra, who is pregnant by him, and her five young children, to whom he has been a stepfather. At the end of the novel, Petra stands in a doorway watching Perfecto out by his car. She senses that he might leave her, and she "embrace[s] Estrella so firmly," that Estrella feels "as if the mother [i]s trying to hide her back in her body" (Viramontes 171). The teenaged Estrella is her mother's real source of strength. This closing image of female strength through the mother-daughter bond is comforting since, while the narrative does not indicate whether Perfecto will leave, the reader is nevertheless assured that Petra and Estrella have one another. Novels written by Chicanas often feature strong mothers and their equally daunting daughters. This is important because female characters tended to be less prevalent in works by Chicano authors, and female readers need to be able to see themselves on the page.

Literary Criticism

Power is a key component of feminist criticism; because of her poverty, race, gender, and young age, Estrella is set up to lead a life of little advantage and power. She is an inspirational character, though, because she functions daily by finding ways to regain her power and to protest her oppression. Two significant scenes typify Estrella's determination to push back against the matrices of power that surround her. In one flashback to her earlier life, Estrella recollects a poor Anglo friend she had in a previous migrant community. Maxine cannot read, so she asks Estrella to read some of her brothers' comic books to her. Estrella loves the comic books, and the two girls often relax by enjoying this pastime together. One day they have a disagreement based on racial and sexual undertones they do not even understand at the time: Maxine asks Estrella why Estrella's father is so old, and Estrella clarifies that he is not her father. Maxine then wonders, "Then why you let your grandpa fuck your ma fo'?" (Viramontes 34), and Estrella asserts that her mother and Perfecto do not do that. The battle of words escalates to an all-out brawl in the middle of the neighborhood after Maxine implies that Estrella "don't . . . know nothin'" if she thinks that her mother and Perfecto are not sexually active (35). Estrella does not back down, refusing to accept Maxine's crude assessment of sexuality, even though her participation in the altercation means that her family has to pull up stakes and move on to the next migrant farm, since the white family would receive the benefit of the doubt and the family of color would receive all blame for any incidents of this kind. When a supervisor informs Estrella's family that they need to move since "he wasn't responsible for harm or bodily affliction caused by the devil-sucking vengeful Devridges" (36), the reader may wonder at the injustice of the "devil-sucking" white family being permitted to stay. The balance of power in this scene is interesting, though: Estrella can read and her Anglo counterpart cannot. Estrella embodies Anzaldúa in this scene as she claims the marginal: she crosses back and forth over boundaries of language, gender, and education in order to get what she needs.

Another scene that showcases Estrella's rebellious spirit is the confrontation between Estrella and the white nurse at a remote clinic where Estrella's family takes her love interest, Alejo, after he is sprayed with pesticides while picking fruit. The family struggles to acquire enough money to put gas in the car and to pay for medical attention for Alejo, who is inching closer to death with each passing day. They finally get about ten dollars together and decide, at Estrella's urging, to seek help before the young man dies. When they first pull up to the ramshackle trailer serving as a clinic, Perfecto immediately begins to assess all the problems with the building in the hope that he can trade his handyman services for Alejo's treatment. The family is forced to wait alone for several minutes in the stuffy waiting room before an indifferent nurse finally appears to attend to them. She briefly examines Alejo, proclaims that he is dehydrated and sick, informs the family that they will need to take him into town to the hospital to be treated, and then charges them ten dollars for the visit. Perfecto offers to fix the toilet instead, but the nurse declines. After she hands over all the money the family has and starts walking back to the car, Estrella becomes incensed at the injustice of the whole situation; now there is no money to buy enough gas to get Alejo to the hospital. She tells her family she will fix everything and promptly turns around, grabs a crowbar, and hits the counter, inadvertently smashing the nurse's family photos. Threatening more drastic action, Estrella demands a refund, and the terrified, disheveled nurse hands the money back so that the family is able to take Alejo to the hospital. At this moment, the protagonist says that she feels like two Estrellas: one who is a "silent phantom . . . while the other held the crowbar and the money" (Viramontes 150). Making the pivotal decision to confront an unjust power structure releases Estrella from her status of silent shadow and teaches her how to have agency in her own life. Estrella is no longer the pawn of an unfair system; she has figured out how to speak up for what is wrong and to use her body, and violence, to effect change. At this point, her cultural hybridity is no longer a stumbling block in her life. Rather, as Anzaldúa suggests Chicanas should, Estrella uses all the tools at her disposal to become a fully developed, complex individual who integrates all of the parts of herself in order to find her source of power.

Characters' struggles to maintain power in their lives are ubiquitous in YA literature since, as Roberta Trites argues in *Disturbing the Universe*, the genre itself is designed to repress adolescent readers while teaching them to negotiate the oppressive institutions around them in a manner that is socially acceptable to adults. The literature is written by adults but aimed at teenagers to instruct them how to behave. The added dynamics of race and class often distinguish the types of power struggles that appear in Chicano/a YA literature. In other words, power and repression are integral forces in both Chicano/a YA and

Anglo-American YA literature, but Chicano/a characters have several added layers of repression to struggle against due to their marginalized position in a hegemonic society. This distinction is evident in Viramontes's work. In *Under the Feet of Jesus*, Viramontes explores the difficult life of the Chicano/a migrant farm worker who lives in poverty, works from young childhood to elderly adulthood in harsh weather conditions doing manual labor, and is not allowed to eat the produce he or she picks. Working around pesticides causes some migrant workers' infants to be born disfigured, while other healthy workers, like Alejo, are sprayed or maimed with farm equipment. Casual racism is part of life, as evidenced in the scene where Maxine asks Estrella, "You talk 'merican?" (Viramontes 29). Some Chicanos are legal residents of the United States, while others are not, so worries about *la Migra* (the immigration agency) abound. This is daily life until, after a few days, weeks, or months, migrant families pack up their meager belongings and move to the next *pisca* (harvest) to start the cycle over again. Estrella sums up the life of the migrant farm worker: "People just use you until you're all used up, then rip you into pieces when they're finished using you" (75). Such is the unfair life of a young Chicana, which is held up under a microscope in this novel in order to inform the reader and perhaps inspire her or him to change the injustice.

La Virgen

One force that provides stability and hope for many Chicano/a families is religion. In order to make it through the difficult days, the mothers in Chicana YA literature, much more often than the fathers and children, turn to their Catholic and/or indigenous faith.[3] Emblematic of the blending of Catholicism and indigenous religions is *la Virgen de Guadalupe*, one of three female archetypes that appear throughout much Chicano/a literature. She is a specifically Mexican and Mexican American goddess figure said to have appeared to a Mexican peasant and performed miracles in 1531, and she has been embraced by

Mexicans as a loving guardian who understands them and their unique needs. Her iconography is significant in that it consists of indigenous symbols along with Mexican and Spanish ones, so that she serves as a figure of love and unity for the diverse peoples of Mexican heritage. The other two important Mexican female archetypes are *la Llorona* and *la Malinche*.[4] *La Llorona* is a bogeyman figure who is said to wander at night, often by water, searching for her lost children. Often, parents warn their children to be careful in the evening lest they be abducted by *la Llorona*, who is likely to take them to ease the pain of missing her own children. *La Malinche* is the historical Malíntzin Tenépal, who is often thought of as a traitor for her role as the indigenous woman who translated for and had a sexual relationship with Hernán Cortés, the Spanish conquistador who invaded and conquered Mexico. Many feminist theorists and artists[5] have worked to modernize and reenvision these figures: *la Virgen* is depicted in more sensual and worldly portrayals, *la Llorona* is embraced for her ability to vocalize her feelings, and *la Malinche* is viewed more sympathetically as the mother of modern-day Mexico who did what she had to do in order to survive.

References to *la Virgen* and religious themes abound in *Under the Feet of Jesus*, but in order to understand them fully, I believe it is important to hearken back to Rudolfo Anaya's *Bless Me, Ultima*, which in 1972 laid the foundation for modern-day Chicano YA literature. *Bless Me, Ultima* has been extremely controversial and often banned since its publication; the American Library Association reports that it was one of the ten most banned or challenged books in 2008 (Morales). In the novel, Antonio, the young protagonist, is a tenderhearted mama's boy who forms a special bond with a visiting friend of the family, a *curandera* (holistic healer) named Ultima. Antonio's influences are diverse: Ultima teaches Antonio about the mysteries of the earth's healing powers, his mother inculcates in him her love for *la Virgen*, the priest preaches about appropriate ways to worship Jesus, and a local boy reveals to him an indigenous god that manifests itself as a golden carp. Antonio is confused about these seemingly contradictory religious ideologies, saying, after he sees the golden carp for the first time, "It made me shiver, not because it was cold but because the roots of everything I had ever believed in seemed shaken. If the golden carp was a god, who was the man on the cross? The Virgin? Was my mother praying to the wrong God?" (Anaya 75). After a family friend is murdered in front of him, Antonio begins going to church after school to pray to God for answers about why tragedies occur. He hears no answer from and feels no connection with God, and so he begins praying in front of the altar of the Virgin instead, "because when I talked to Her I felt as if she listened, like my mother listened" (180). There is a conflation of the Virgin Mary and his mother in Antonio's mind because his mother continually prays to her two-foot-tall statue of *la Virgen de Guadalupe* and invokes the Virgin's name throughout the family's daily life. Antonio feels protected and comforted by both his mother and the Virgin, along with Ultima and Mother Earth. He learns, at the end, that his church-based and earth-based beliefs can coexist and that he can work toward unity rather than separation.

Antonio's connection to and respect for both the earth and religion are mirrored by the characters in *Under the Feet of Jesus*. Half of Antonio's family, the Luna side of his mother's relatives, are farmers with a spiritual connection to the land. Similarly, in *Under the Feet of Jesus*, Perfecto has dreams of his native soil, the land to which he feels his spirit is bound. In Anaya's novel, Ultima uses plants and herbs to heal Antonio and others around her, just as, in Viramontes's, Petra uses an egg and various home remedies to attempt to cure Alejo when he is poisoned by pesticides. The fact that Petra fails to cure Alejo while Ultima succeeds in healing others represents Viramontes's portrayal of the maternal role as more complex and troubled than Anaya's depiction of female characters. The mothers in both novels are connected to Catholicism and to *la Virgen*: Antonio's mother prays daily at her altar with its prominent statue of *la Virgen*, and Petra has a large statue of Jesus and a smaller statue of *la Virgen* on an altar that she erects the moment she moves into a new home. Petra's children's legal papers are "under the feet of Jesus" in case they are ever threatened by immigration officials, and she prays at her altar during times of crisis. Toward the end of the novel, Petra's treasured statue of *Jesucristo* breaks, which is a metaphor for her broken relationship with Perfecto and her broken life in general.

Interestingly, the next powerful scene toward the end of the novel, of the entwined mother and daughter on the porch watching Perfecto stand by the car as he considers deserting the family, lends itself to an interpretation of the Petra-Estrella dyad as two sides of an embodied *la Virgen*. Throughout the novel, Petra is consistently referred to as "the mother," rather than "my mom" or another more personal and possessive term. This general modifier, along with Petra's perpetual status as pregnant and/or tending to small children, correlates to *la Virgen*'s revered status of mother to Jesus and to all of the church's followers. Also, in Perfecto's mind, Petra, who eats several cloves of garlic a day, and *la Virgen* are almost synonymous; he longs for his inner demons to stop torturing him so that he can "enjoy the tenderness of a woman who w[ears] an aura of garlic as brilliant as the aura circling La Virgen" (101). While Petra encapsulates *la Virgen*'s mothering side, Estrella represents her youthful, virginal qualities. Throughout the novel, she is portrayed as sexually innocent. When the ill but lovestruck Alejo cuddles up with her in his sick bed, she makes room for him platonically as she would make room for a younger brother or sister. After she stands next to her mother on the porch, in the final scene of the novel, Estrella runs to the crumbling barn near her house and climbs onto the roof. There, the "termite-softened shakes" crunch "beneath her bare feet like the serpent under the feet of Jesus" while Estrella feels her heart beating as strongly as church bells in order "to summon home all those who strayed" (175, 176). This imagery of Estrella likens her to a religious statue as she embodies the love and strength of *la Virgen* for her people. I interpret this ending as Viramontes's subversion of religious iconography; she protests a static, unreachable goddess figure and roots her *Virgen* in a flawed but lovable young girl in an impoverished modern setting.

Even though *Under the Feet of Jesus* is more clearly a feminist text with its focus on female protagonists, *Bless Me, Ultima* is its heretical precursor, since the 1972 text paved the way for a Chicano/a spiritual literary tradition that integrates goddess- and earth-based spirituality with Catholicism. Given the monotheistic history and focus of Christianity, Rudolfo Anaya's presentation of witchcraft, pantheism, premonitory dreams, the Virgin Mary, magic, and Catholicism as forces that coexist in the world has been troubling or offensive to some readers. Similarly, in *Under the Feet of Jesus*, magic, premonitions, and religion exist alongside one another. For example, when Petra is trying to prevent her husband, Estrella's father, from abandoning the family, she puts "a few drops of menstrual blood in his coffee" (23). This type of magical, spiritual remedy is reminiscent of Ultima's use of voodoo dolls to kill the Trementina sisters, although here also Petra fails while Ultima succeeds. At another point in *Under the Feet of Jesus*, Petra believes Estrella to be a victim of the evil eye, harm inflicted by means of a glance. Similarly, dark magic is present in *Bless Me, Ultima* with the evil actions of Tenorio Trementina and his three *bruja* (sorceress) daughters.

La Llorona

La Virgen de Guadalupe and religious themes, including heresy, are some of the most prominent motifs in both *Bless Me, Ultima* and *Under the Feet of Jesus*. However, just as they appear in much Chicano/a literature, the other two primary feminine archetypes are evident in both novels as well. *La Llorona* is prominently featured in one of Antonio's dreams, in which he hears "the tormented cry of a lonely goddess," which makes "the blood of men run cold" (Anaya 23). In the dream, Antonio's brothers, full of fear, tell Antonio that the lonely goddess is *la Llorona*. Antonio reinterprets the cry as the presence of the river itself, which is a powerful but beneficent force that, outside of his dream, Antonio feels on several occasions. Antonio refuses to live in fear of the river and *la Llorona*, which is consistent with his holistic, integrated approach to life. In *Under the Feet of Jesus*, Gumecindo hears screaming he attributes to *la Llorona* when he and his cousin, Alejo, illegally pick fruit from the fields to sell for a profit. Even though he previously believed *la Llorona* to be a myth, when he hears the noise, Gumecindo becomes uneasy and urges his cousin to get out of the tree so that they can leave. This incident, along with a subsequent fruit-picking expedition in which Gumecindo cannot stop fearfully mentioning *la Llorona* each time Alejo ascends a tree, foreshadows Alejo's later spraying by pesticides. After his cousin falls ill, Gumecindo recalls the premonition of the screams and remarks, "I knew something was coming down . . . I just knew it. I could feel it in my bones." Petra replies, "When you feel it that deep, you should listen" (Viramontes 95). Listening to intuition is often characterized as feminine, as in the common phrase "woman's intuition," so it is interesting to see intuition and a female archetype aligned the way they are in this scene. In Antonio's case, Ultima, the female shaman and *curandera*, helps him listen to and follow his dreams and his intuition. *La Llorona*, the earth, and the river are all thought of traditionally as feminine forces, and Antonio is close to all of them, in addition to the close relationships he maintains with his mother and with Ultima. *Bless Me, Ultima* sets the precedent, which is later followed in *Under the Feet of Jesus*, of recasting in a positive light feminine archetypes and attributes that are often looked down upon in a patriarchal society.

Another important motif from both novels that merits further investigation is death, which bears a strong association with *la Llorona*. For Roberta Trites, one of the primary markers of YA literature is the way its protagonists grapple with their own mortality. Death, she asserts, is the sine qua non, or the essential condition, of YA literature. In children's literature like E. B. White's *Charlotte's Web*, death often takes place offstage, whereas in adult literature, death takes its inevitable, somewhat humdrum place within the framework of the story. For young adults, however, death is onstage and laden with the significance of the adolescent coming to terms with her mortality and accepting the limitations of her body. *Bless Me, Ultima* appears to start this trend in Chicano/a YA literature as well. In it, a series of deaths and near deaths shapes Antonio's worldview. The novel opens with his witnessing the death of an acquaintance, climaxes with the murder of Antonio's family friend Narciso, and concludes with the death of his beloved mentor, Ultima. Each of these deaths serves as a marker for Antonio's further initiation into the world of young adulthood. He loses innocence witnessing the first death, separates psychologically from his family with the second one, and finally emerges into a new, unified understanding of his agency in the world around him with the passing of Ultima. In *Under the Feet of Jesus*, actual deaths, such as the passing of Perfecto's first child and the death of an unidentified person in the barn near Perfecto and Petra's bungalow, are more peripheral than the near-death state in which two main characters spend a significant portion of the novel. Perfecto senses that he is close to the end of his days, and for this reason, he longs to leave Petra and his children in order to die on Mexican soil. His closeness to death alters his memory, and his thoughts and actions jumble together between the past and the present. While preparing to abandon the family, Perfecto receives the last sign that it is time to go: Petra insists that the family take in Alejo because if her children were sick in the fields with no one to care for them, she would want someone to tend to them. Perfecto strenuously objects but eventually ends up transporting Alejo to their house. While bringing him in, the older man can "feel the boy's death under his bare feet" (101). Alejo's illness and Perfecto's impending desertion of the family lead to Estrella's defining coming-of-age moments. Alejo's illness sets the stage for Estrella's recognition of her stronger self and her ability to defend herself and her family against injustice. Perfecto's approaching absence leads her to embrace her braver persona again in order to climb on top of the roof of the barn, where she feels empowered and loving. In *Bless Me, Ultima*, it is actual death that shapes Antonio's character, while proximity to death refines Estrella's sense of self in

Under the Feet of Jesus, but both novels feature death as an integral part of an adolescent's emergence into the adult world.

La Malinche

In much the same way as the third archetype, *la Malinche*, is a contradictory figure, sexuality is a theme that manifests itself in Chicana YA literature in interesting, contradictory ways. *La Malinche* is often viewed as a sexual and treasonous woman who betrayed her people for self-serving, material reasons. Nodelman asserts that sexuality is often in shadow in the children's literature genre; he claims that the "hidden adult" author uses the text to share her or his knowledge of the shadow with the young reader. Trites, on the other hand, contends that since YA literature centers on adolescents, who are developing sexually, the genre maintains a consistent focus on sexuality. Trites and Beth Younger both maintain that, as Adrienne Rich points out in her essay "Compulsory Heterosexuality and Lesbian Existence" (1980), heteronormative, monogamous relationships are didactically portrayed as the best choice for teens, and sex is often viewed as dangerous physically and emotionally, especially for girls. For much Chicana YA literature, Nodelman's thesis of sexuality being in the shadow is more applicable, while Trites and Younger's theories have greater bearing on the Anglo-American YA literature. For example, in *Under the Feet of Jesus*, several scenes involving sexuality come to mind, but they are, by and large, subtle, leaving much content in the shadow, unexplained and unexplored for the YA reader. For example, during a sweet encounter underneath the shade of a truck on a scorching day, Estrella and Alejo hold hands and talk. There are sexual undertones to their dialogue, but they are young and the reader understands that their relationship will be sexually innocent. Another moment occurs when Petra and Perfecto are in bed early one morning; Viramontes subtly describes the mother's admiration of Perfecto's arms as she reaches over him to touch his stomach. He rebuffs her advances, and then her attention is drawn to a somewhat romantic dialogue between Estrella and Alejo, which she promptly interrupts. A younger reader would probably not understand that Petra is attempting to have intercourse with Perfecto; thus, that part of the text is in shadow. In another scene, Petra remembers how her first husband's and her "bodies were once like two fingers criss-crossing for good luck" (Viramontes 19). This sexual memory is subtle enough to be missed by younger readers. Finally, Perfecto recalls the first time he had sex with his first wife. This is the most overtly sexual scene in the novel, but even its somewhat lengthy description is told in a poetic, stream-of-consciousness style that appears to avoid open carnality. Compared to Anglo-American novels like Judy Blume's groundbreaking, sex-positive novel *Forever . . .* (1975) and Paul Ruditis's *Rainbow Party* (2005), which details oral sex parties, there is a clear difference in the level of sexuality put on display. Much like the Chicano literature itself, though, this assertion is replete with contradictions and possibilities for deconstruction.

Sexuality in *Bless Me, Ultima* seems more correlated to *la Malinche* than it does in *Under the Feet of Jesus*. In *Bless Me, Ultima*, Antonio feels betrayed by his emerging sexual knowledge. He recalls a situation in which his father and another man, while breeding livestock, made some obscene remarks that he did not understand at the time. Later, when Antonio hides behind a building and observes one of his brothers, Andrew, refusing to leave a brothel, Andrew's actions unleash a series of events that leads to the murder of a trusted family friend. At this point, Antonio connects Rosie's house (the brothel) with his father's prior jokes. He is able to understand what occurs inside the brothel in a way he was previously unable to grasp. Then the young boy has a nightmare in which the prostitute from Rosie's dances nude and wraps Andrew up with her long hair in order to prevent him from leaving to help the family friend. She pulls Antonio's brother away, and he "follow[s] her into the frightful fires of hell" (165). Antonio hears the voice of God condemn Andrew for sinning with a prostitute, and then he hears the soft, forgiving voice of *la Virgen*. Antonio feels betrayed by his brother's choice to stay with a prostitute rather than help the family. In the young boy's estimation, the prostitute is a *Malinche* figure who causes the downfall of Antonio's family.

Featuring *la Virgen*, *la Llorona*, and *la Malinche* and reconfiguring them in a more positive, accepting, Anzaldúan manner is a decisive "protest literature" element of Chicano/a literature. Unapologetically integrating one's unique cultural heritage into the dominant culture requires a certain amount of rebellion and pride. Additionally, highlighting earth-based spirituality alongside traditional religious customs is a way of "writing back" against the dominant culture. Anaya's and Viramontes's inclusion of strong female characters, particularly in a culture renowned for *machismo*, is another element of protest. Finally, helping readers see the injustice in ways of life like migrant farming that are endemic to the Chicano/a population is a prominent element of protest literature. In *Under the Feet of Jesus*, Helena María Viramontes follows in the heretical footsteps of Rudolfo Anaya in utilizing all of these elements in order to connect with and inspire her readers, Chicano/a and non-Chicano/a alike.

Notes

1. For example, when one thinks of the African American civil rights movement, one probably calls to mind names like Martin Luther King Jr. and Malcolm X. Women like Diane Nash were able and willing to lead aspects of the movement as well, but it was usually men who were the figureheads.
2. The Edenic garden in this case could be Aztlán or an earlier time in her life when she was more carefree.
3. This statement is a conclusion I draw in my dissertation, which is a comparative analysis of Chicana and Anglo YA fiction from 1995 to 2010.
4. For further information on these two archetypes, see Blake.
5. See Blake.

Works Cited

"About Us: Our Vision." *United Farm Workers*. United Farm Workers, 2009. Web. 5 Oct. 2012.

Anaya, Rudolfo. *Bless Me, Ultima*. Berkeley: TQS, 1972. Print.

Anzaldúa, Gloria. *Borderlands / La Frontera: The New Mestiza.* San Francisco: Aunt Lute, 1987. Print.

Arce, William. U of Texas at Arlington, Texas. 16 Sept. 2010. Lecture.

Blake, Debra. *Chicana Sexuality and Gender: Cultural Refiguring in Literature, Oral History, and Art.* Durham: Duke UP, 2008. Print.

Kaup, Monika. *Rewriting North American Borders in Chicano and Chicana Narrative.* New York: Lang, 2001. Print.

McCracken, Ellen. *New Latina Narrative: The Feminine Space of Postmodern Ethnicity.* Tucson: U of Arizona P, 1999. Print.

Morales, Macey. "Attempts to Ban Books in U.S. Continue." *ALA.* ALA, 21 Sept. 2009. Web. 25 July 2012.

Nodelman, Perry. *The Hidden Adult: Defining Children's Literature.* Baltimore: Johns Hopkins UP, 2008. Print.

Oleszkiewicz-Peralba, Małgorzata. *The Black Madonna in Latin America and Europe.* Albuquerque: U of New Mexico P, 2007. Print.

Trites, Roberta. *Disturbing the Universe: Power and Repression in Adolescent Literature.* Iowa City: U of Iowa P, 2000. Print.

Viramontes, Helena María. *Under the Feet of Jesus.* New York: Plume, 1995. Print.

Younger, Beth. *Learning Curves: Body Image and Female Sexuality in Young Adult Literature.* Lanham: Scarecrow, 2009. Print.

RESOURCES

Additional Works on the Literature of Protest_____

Anthologies

The Cry for Justice: An Anthology of the Literature of Social Protest edited by Upton Sinclair, 1915

The Best of Bamboo Ridge: The Hawaii Writers' Quarterly edited by Eric Chock and Darrell H. Y. Lum, 1986

Nice Jewish Girls: A Lesbian Anthology edited by Evelyn Torton Beck, 1989

The Tribe of Dina: A Jewish Women's Anthology edited by Irena Klepfitz and Melanie Kaye Kantrowitz, 1989

Making Waves: Writings by and about Asian American Women edited by Diane Yen-Mei Wong, 1989

Calling Home: Working-Class Women's Writings edited by Janet Zandy, 1990

No Walls of Stone: An Anthology of Literature by Deaf and Hard of Hearing Writers edited by Jill Jepson, 1992

With Wings: An Anthology of Literature by and about Women with Disabilities edited by Marsha Saxton and Florence Howe, 1993

Images from the Holocaust: A Literature Anthology edited by Jean Brown, Elaine C. Stephens, and Janet Rubin, 1996

Reinventing the Enemy's Language: Contemporary Native American Women's Writings of North America edited by Gloria Bird and Joy Harjo, 1998

Literature, Class, and Culture edited by Paul Lauter and Ann Fitzgerald, 2000

An Anthology of Disability Literature edited by Christy Thompson Ibrahim, 2011

Songs of Work and Protest: 100 Favorite Songs of American Workers Complete with Music and Historical Notes edited by Edith Fowke, 2012

The Things They Carried by Tim O'Brien, 1990

Drama

Strife by John Galsworthy, 1909

The Children's Hour by Lillian Hellman, 1934

A Raisin in the Sun by Lorraine Hansberry, 1959

Zoot Suit by Luis Valdez, 1978

I'm Black When I'm Singing, I'm Blue When I Ain't by Sonia Sanchez, 1982

Do the Right Thing by Spike Lee, 1989

Roger and Me by Michael Moore, 1989

Angels in America by Tony Kushner, 1993

Ruined by Lynn Nottage, 2007

Long Fiction

Clotel; or, The President's Daughter by William Wells Brown, 1853

Hard Times by Charles Dickens, 1854

Our "Nig" by Harriet Wilson, 1859

Life in the Iron Mills by Rebecca Harding Davis, 1861

Huckleberry Finn by Mark Twain, 1884

New Grub Street by George Gissing, 1891

Iola Leroy; or, Shadows Uplifted by Frances Ellen Watkins Harper, 1892

Maggie, Girl of the Streets by Stephen Crane, 1893

Sister Carrie by Theodore Dreiser, 1900

The Marrow of Tradition by Charles Chesnutt, 1901

The Jungle by Upton Sinclair, 1906

The Iron Heel by Jack London, 1908

The Well of Loneliness by Radclyffe Hall, 1920

Cane by Jean Toomer, 1923

The Trial by Franz Kafka, 1925

Home to Harlem by Claude McKay, 1928

Brave New World by Aldous Huxley, 1932

Call it Sleep by Henry Roth, 1934

Untouchable by Mulk Raj Anand, 1935

Their Eyes Were Watching God by Zora Neale Hurston, 1937

Grapes of Wrath by John Steinbeck, 1939

The Ox-Bow Incident by Walter Van Tilburg Clark, 1940

Let Us Now Praise Famous Men by James Agee and Walker Evans, 1941

If He Hollers, Let Him Go by Chester Himes, 1945

The Street by Ann Petry, 1946

Invisible Man by Ralph Ellison, 1952

Go Tell It on the Mountain by James Baldwin, 1953

Fahrenheit 451 by Ray Bradbury, 1953

The Narrows by Ann Petry, 1953

Giovanni's Room by James Baldwin, 1956

Things Fall Apart by Chinua Achebe, 1957

No-No Boy by John Okada, 1957

All I Asking for Is My Body by Milton Murayama, 1959

Another Country by James Baldwin, 1960

Gorilla, My Love by Toni Cade Bambara, 1960

To Kill a Mockingbird by Harper Lee, 1960

Catch-22 by Joseph Heller, 1961

A Clockwork Orange by Anthony Burgess, 1962

One Day in the Life of Ivan Denisovich by Aleksandr Solzhenitsyn, 1962

The Edible Woman by Margaret Atwood, 1964

Jubilee by Margaret Walker, 1966

This Child's Gonna Live by Sarah Wright, 1969

The Bluest Eye by Toni Morrison, 1970

The Autobiography of Miss Jane Pittman by Ernest J. Gaines, 1971

His Own Where by June Jordan, 1971

Mumbo Jumbo by Ishmael Reed, 1972

Yonnondio: From the Thirties by Tillie Olsen, 1974

The Monkey Wrench Gang by Edward Abbey, 1975

The Painted Bird by Jerzy Kosiński, 1976

Woman on the Edge of Time by Marge Piercy, 1976

Ceremony by Leslie Marmon Silko, 1977

Sitt Marie Rose by Etel Adnan, 1978

Kindred by Octavia Butler, 1979

Waiting for the Barbarians by J. M. Coetzee, 1980

Obasan by Joy Kogawa, 1981

Storyteller by Leslie Marmon Silko, 1981

The Color Purple by Alice Walker, 1982

Heremakhonon by Maryse Condé, 1982

The House on Mango Street by Sandra Cisneros, 1984

The Handmaid's Tale by Margaret Atwood, 1985

Corregidora by Gayl Jones, 1986

Of Love and Shadows by Isabel Allende, 1987

Beloved by Toni Morrison, 1987

Eva Luna by Isabel Allende, 1988

Saturday Night at the Pahala Theater by Lois-Ann Yamanaka, 1990

Almanac of the Dead by Leslie Marmon Silko, 1991

Dogeaters by Jessica Hagedorn, 1991

Bastard Out of Carolina by Dorothy Allison, 1992

Straight Outta Compton by Ricardo Cortez Cruz, 1992

The Lone Ranger and Tonto Fistfight in Heaven by Sherman Alexie, 1993

So Far from God by Ana Castillo, 1993

Stone Butch Blues by Leslie Feinberg, 1993

Native Speaker by Chang-rae Lee, 1995

The God of Small Things by Arundhati Roy, 1997

Yesterday Will Make You Cry by Chester Himes, 1998

Sister of My Heart by Chitra Banerjee Divakaruni, 1999

People of the Whale by Linda Hogan, 2008

Nonfiction

Walden by Henry David Thoreau, 1854

Incidents in the Life of a Slave Girl by Harriet Jacobs, 1861

A Century of Dishonor by Helen Hunt Jackson, 1881

How the Other Half Lives by Jacob Riis, 1890

Up from Slavery: An Autobiography by Booker T. Washington, 1902

The Souls of Black Folk by W. E. B. Du Bois, 1903

An American Testament by Joseph Freeman, 1936

Black Boy: A Record of Childhood and Youth by Richard Wright, 1945

Night by Elie Wiesel, 1960

The Man from Main Street by Sinclair Lewis, 1962

The Autobiography of Malcolm X by Malcolm X and Alex Haley, 1965

The Armies of the Night by Norman Mailer, 1968

I Know Why the Caged Bird Sings by Maya Angelou, 1969

Gemini by Nikki Giovanni, 1971

Camp Notes and Other Writings by Mitsuye Yamada, 1976

On Lies, Secrets, and Silence by Adrienne Rich, 1979

In the Belly of the Beast by Jack Henry Abbott, 1981

A Season in Paradise by Breyten Breytenbach, 1981

Zami: A New Spelling of My Name by Audre Lorde, 1982

Loving in the War Years by Cherríe Moraga, 1983

Living Up the Street by Gary Soto, 1985

Lakota Woman by Mary Crow Dog and Richard Erdoes, 1990

Poetry

Leaves of Grass by Walt Whitman, 1844

"The Ballad of Reading Gaol" by Oscar Wilde, 1898

Harlem Shadows by Claude McKay, 1922

The Book of the Dead by Muriel Rukeyser, 1938

"Strange Fruit" by Abel Meeropol and Billie Holiday, 1937, 1939

Dustbowl Ballads by Woody Guthrie, 1940

A Street in Bronzeville by Gwendolyn Brooks, 1945

Annie Allen by Gwendolyn Brooks, 1950

Howl by Alan Ginsburg, 1955

Preface to a Twenty Volume Suicide Note by Amiri Baraka/Leroi Jones, 1961

Black Feeling, Black Talk, Black Judgement by Nikki Giovanni, 1970

We a Baddddd People by Sonia Sanchez, 1970

No More Masks! An Anthology of Poems by Women by Florence and Ellen Bass Howe, 1973

For Colored Girls Who Have Considered Suicide When the Rainbow is Enuf by Ntozake Shange, 1975

And Still I Rise by Maya Angelou, 1978
Two-Headed Woman by Lucille Clifton, 1980
Satan Says by Sharon Olds 1980
Homegirls and Hand Grenades by Sonia Sanchez, 1985
Rose by Li-Young Lee, 1986
I Shall Not Be Moved by Maya Angelou, 1990
Poetry like Bread: Poets of the Political Imagination from Curbstone Press by
    Martín Espada, 2000
C-Train and Thirteen Mexicans by Jimmy Santiago Baca, 2002
Love Works by Janice Mirikitani, 2003
How We Became Human: New and Selected Poems 1975–2001 by Joy Harjo, 2004
Apprenticed to Justice by Kimberly Blaeser, 2007
Directed by Desire: The Collected Poems of June Jordan by June Jordan, 2007
Selected Poems/Poemas Selectos by Jimmy Santiago Baca, 2009
*Words of Protest, Words of Freedom: Poetry of the American Civil Rights Movement
    and Era*, edited by Jeffrey Coleman, 2012

Short Fiction
The Wife of His Youth and Other Stories of the Color Line by Charles Chesnutt, 1899
"The Pen: Long Days in a County Penitentiary" by Jack London, 1907
"I Stand Here Ironing" by Tillie Olsen, 1961
Labyrinths, Selected Stories and Other Writings by Jorge Luis Borges, 1964
Family Dancing by David Leavitt, 1983
Seventeen Syllables and Other Stories by Hisaye Yamamoto, 1988
The Shawl by Cynthia Ozick, 1989

Bibliography

Aaron, Daniel. *Writers on the Left*. 1961. New York: Columbia UP, 1992. Print.

Abel, Elizabeth, Barbara Christian, and Helene Moglen, eds. *Female Subjects in Black and White: Race, Psychoanalysis, Feminism*. Berkeley: U of California P, 1997. Print.

Allen, Paula Gunn. *The Sacred Hoop: Recovering the Feminine in American Indian Traditions*. Boston: Beacon, 1986. Print.

Anzaldúa, Gloria. *Borderlands: The New Mestiza/La Frontera*. San Francisco: Spinsters/Aunt Lute, 1987. Print.

———, ed. *Making Face, Making Soul/Haciendo Caras*. San Francisco: Aunt Lute, 1990. Print.

Anzaldúa, Gloria, and Cherríe Moraga, eds. *This Bridge Called My Back: Writings by Radical Women of Color*. New York: Kitchen Table, 1981. Print.

Baker, Houston A., Jr. *Blues, Ideology, and Afro-American Literature: A Vernacular Theory*. Chicago: U of Chicago P, 1984. Print.

Bambara, Toni Cade, ed. *The Black Woman: An Anthology*. 1970. New York: Washington Square, 2005. Print.

Bauman, H-Dirksen L., Jennifer L. Nelson, and Heidi M. Rose, eds. *Signing the Body Poetic: Essays on American Sign Language Literature*. Berkeley: U of California P, 2006. Print.

Bogardus, Ralph, and Fred Hobson. Introduction. *Literature at the Barricades: The American Writer in the 1930's*. Ed. Bogardus and Hobson. Tuscaloosa: U of Alabama P, 1982. Print.

Broe, Mary Lynn, and Angela Ingram, eds. *Women's Writing in Exile*. Chapel Hill: U of North Carolina P, 1989. Print.

Butler, Judith. *Gender Trouble: Feminism and the Subversion of Identity*. New York: Routledge, 1990. Print.

Calderón, Héctor. *Narratives of Greater Mexico: Essays on Chicano Literary History, Genre, and Borders*. Austin: U of Texas P, 1995. Print.

Calderón, Héctor, and José David Saldívar, eds. *Criticism in the Borderlands: Studies in Chicano Literature, Culture, and Ideology*. Durham: Duke UP 1991. Print.

Carby, Hazel V. *Reconstructing Womanhood: The Emergence of the Afro-American Woman Novelist*. New York: Oxford UP, 1987. Print.

Chan, Jeffrey Paul, Frank Chin, Lawson Fusao Inada, and Shawn Wong, eds. *The Big Aiiieeeee! An Anthology of Chinese American and Japanese American Literature*. New York: Meridian, 1991. Print.

Cheng, Anne Anlin. *Melancholy of Race: Psychoanalysis, Assimilation, and Hidden Grief*. New York: Oxford UP, 2001. Print.

Chessman, Andrea, and Polly Joan. *Guide to Women's Publishing*. Paradise, CA: Dustbooks, 1988. Print.

Chow, Rey. *Writing Diaspora: Tactics of Intervention in Contemporary Cultural Studies (Arts and Politics of the Everyday)*. Bloomington: Indiana UP, 1993. Print.

Christian, Barbara. *Black Feminist Criticism: Perspectives on Black Women Writers*. New York: Pergamon, 1985. Print.

___. *Black Women Novelists: The Development of a Tradition*. Westport: Greenwood, 1980. Print.

___. *New Black Feminist Criticism, 1985–2000*. Ed. Gloria Bowles, M. Giulia Fabi, and Arlene R. Keizer. Urbana: U of Illinois P, 2007. Print.

Civello, Paul. *American Literary Naturalism and its Twentieth-Century Transformations*. Athens: U of Georgia P, 1994. Print.

Cowley, Malcolm. *Think Back on Us: A Contemporary Chronicle of the 1930s*. Carbondale: Southern Illinois UP, 1967. Print.

Denning, Michael. *Mechanic Accents: Dime Novels and Working Class Culture in America*. London: Verso, 1998. Print.

Drake, Kimberly. *Subjectivity in American Protest Literature*. New York: Palgrave, 2011. Print.

Driskill, Qwo-Li, Chris Finley, Brian Joseph Gilley, and Scott Lauria Morgensen, eds. *Queer Indigenous Studies: Critical Interventions in Theory, Politics, and Literature*. Tucson: U of Arizona P, 2011. Print.

Ervin, Hazel Arnett, ed. *African American Literary Criticism, 1773 to 2000*. New York: Twayne, 1999. Print.

Felman, Shoshana, and Dori Laub. *Testimony: Crises of Witnessing in Literature, Psychoanalysis, and History*. New York: Routledge, 1991. Print.

Franklin, Cynthia. *Writing Women's Communities: The Politics and Poetics of Contemporary Multi-Genre Anthologies*. Madison: U of Wisconsin P, 1997. Print.

Franklin, H. Bruce. *Prison Literature in America: The Victim as Criminal and Artist*. New York: Oxford UP, 1989. Print.

Gates, Henry Louis, Jr., ed. *Black Literature and Literary Theory*. New York: Methuen, 1984. Print.

___, ed. *"Race," Writing, and Difference*. Chicago: U of Chicago, 1986. Print.

___, ed. *Reading Black, Reading Feminist: A Critical Anthology*. New York: Meridian, 1990. Print.

Gilroy, Paul. *The Black Atlantic: Modernity and Double Consciousness*. Cambridge: Harvard UP, 1992. Print.

Gonzalez, Margaret. *The Literature of Protest*. New York: UP of America, 1998. Print.

Griffin, Farah Jasmine. *"Who Set You Flowin'?" The African American Migration Narrative*. New York: Oxford UP, 1995. Print.

Griffin, Susan. *Woman and Nature: The Roaring inside Her*. 1978. San Francisco: Sierra Club, 2000. Print.

Harlow, Barbara. *Barred: Women, Writing, and Political Detention*. Hanover: UP of New England, 1992. Print.

___. *Resistance Literature*. New York: Methuen, 1987. Print.

Hernton, Calvin. *The Sexual Mountain and Black Women Writers*. New York: Doubleday 1987. Print.

Howard, June. *Form and History in American Literary Naturalism*. Chapel Hill: U of North Carolina P, 1985. Print.

Howe, Irving. *Selected Writings, 1950–1990*. San Diego: Harcourt, 1992. Print.

Hooks, Bell. *Black Looks: Race and Representation*. Boston: South End, 1992. Print.

Hull, Gloria T., Patricia Bell Scott, and Barbara Smith, eds. *All the Women Are White, All the Blacks Are Men, but Some of Us Are Brave*. New York: Feminist P, 1982. Print.

Jones, Gavin. *American Hungers: The Problem of Poverty in U.S. Literature, 1840–1945*. Princeton: Princeton UP, 2008. Print.

Kaplan, Amy. *The Social Construction of American Realism*. Chicago: U of Chicago P, 1988. Print.

Krupat, Arnold. *New Voices in Native American Literary Criticism*. Washington: Smithsonian P, 1993. Print.

Lauret, Maria. *Liberating Literature: Feminist Fiction in America*. New York: Routledge, 1994. Print.

Lauter, Paul. *Canons and Contexts*. New York: Oxford UP, 1991. Print.

Lim, Shirley Geok-Lin, and Amy Ling, eds. *Reading the Literatures of Asian America*. Philadelphia: Temple UP, 1992. Print.

Lorde, Audre. *Sister Outsider: Essays and Speeches*. Trumansburg, NY: Crossing, 1984. Print.

Massey, Dennis. *Doing Time in American Prisons: A Study of Modern Novels*. New York: Greenwood, 1989. Print.

Maxwell, William J. *New Negro, Old Left: African-American Writing and Communism between the Wars*. New York: Columbia UP, 1999. Print.

Miller, D. Quentin. *Prose and Cons: Essays on Prison Literature in the United States*. Jefferson, NC: McFarland, 2005. Print.

Mitchell, Lee Clark. *Determined Fictions: American Literary Naturalism*. New York: Columbia UP, 1989. Print.

Mohanty, Chandra Talpade. *Feminism without Borders: Decolonizing Theory, Practicing Solidarity*. Durham: Duke UP, 2003. Print.

Morgan, Robin. *Sisterhood Is Powerful: An Anthology of Writings from the Women's Liberation Movement*. New York: Random, 1970. Print.

Moses, Cathy. *Dissenting Fictions: Identity and Resistance in the Contemporary American Novel*. New York: Garland, 2000. Print.

Munt, Sally. *New Lesbian Criticism: Literary and Cultural Readings*. New York: Columbia UP, 1992. Print.

Netzley, Patrica D. *Social Protest Literature: An Encyclopedia of Works, Characters, Authors, and Themes*. Santa Barbara: ABC-CLIO, 1999. Print.

Novack, George. "Radical Intellectuals in the 1930's." Comp. Daniel Gaido. *International Socialist Review* 29.2 (1967): 21–34. Print.

Pérez, Emma. *The Decolonial Imaginary: Writing Chicanas into History*. Bloomington: Indiana UP, 1999. Print.

Redding, J. Saunders. *To Make a Poet Black*. Ithaca: Cornell UP, 1988. Print.

Reid, Margaret Ann. *Black Protest Poetry: Polemics from the Harlem Renaissance and the Sixties*. New York: Lang, 2001. Print.

Rich, Adrienne. *Blood, Bread, and Poetry: Selected Prose, 1979–1985*. London: Norton, 1994. Print.

Rideout, Walter B. *The Radical Novel in the United States, 1900–1954*. Cambridge: Harvard UP, 1956. Print.

Roof, Judith, and Robyn Wiegman, eds. *Who Can Speak? Authority and Critical Identity*. Urbana: U of Illinois P, 1995. Print.

Salzman, Jack, and Barry Wallenstein, eds. *Years of Protest: A Collection of American Writings of the 1930s*. New York: Pegasus, 1967. Print.

Sánchez, María Carla. *Reforming the World: Social Activism and the Problem of Fiction in Nineteenth-Century America*. Iowa City: U of Iowa P, 2008. Print.

Sandoval, Chela. *Methodology of the Oppressed*. Minneapolis: U of Minnesota P, 2000. Print.

Shevin, David, Janet Zandy, and Larry R. Smith, eds. *Writing Work: Writers on Working-Class Writing*. Huron, OH: Bottom Dog, 1999. Print.

Singh, Amritjit, and Peter Schmidt, eds. *Postcolonial Theory and the United States: Race, Ethnicity, and Literature*. Jackson: UP of Mississippi, 2000. Print.

Smith, Barbara, ed. *Home Girls: A Black Feminist Anthology*. New York: Kitchen Table–Women of Color, 1983. Print.

Spillers, Hortense. *Black, White, and in Color: Essays on American Literature and Culture*. Chicago: U of Chicago P, 2003. Print.

Spivak, Gayatri. *An Aesthetic Education in the Era of Globalization*. Cambridge: Harvard UP, 2012. Print.

Tate, Claudia. *Black Textuality and Psychoanalytic Literary Criticism*. Oxford: Oxford UP, 1998. Print.

Thomson, Rosemarie Garland. *Extraordinary Bodies: Figuring Physical Disability in American Culture and Literature*. New York: Columbia UP, 1996. Print.

Trask, Haunani-Kay. *From a Native Daughter: Colonialism and Sovereignty in Hawai'i*. Honolulu: U of Hawaii P, 1999. Print.

Treuer, David. *Native American Fiction: A User's Manual*. St. Paul: Graywolf, 2006. Print.

Trinh, T. Minh-Ha. *Woman/Native/Other: Writing Postcoloniality and Feminism*. Bloomington: Indiana UP, 1989. Print.

Walker, Cheryl. *Indian Nation: Native American Literature and Nineteenth-Century Nationalisms*. Durham: Duke UP, 1997. Print.

Washington, Mary Helen. *Invented Lives: Narratives of Black Women, 1860–1960*. New York: Doubleday, 1987. Print.

Williams, Patrick, and Laura Chrisman, eds. *Colonial Discourse and Post-Colonial Theory: A Reader*. New York: Columbia UP, 1994. Print.

Wong, Sau-Ling Cynthia. *Reading Asian American Literature*. Princeton: Princeton UP, 1993. Print.

Zandy, Janet. *Hands: Physical Labor, Class, and Cultural Work*. New Brunswick: Rutgers UP, 2004. Print.

Zola, Émile. "The Experimental Novel." *Literary Criticism: From Pope to Croce*. Ed. Gay Wilson and Harry Hayden Clark. Detroit: Wayne State UP, 1962. 589–99. Print.

About the Editor_____

Kimberly Drake directs the writing program and teaches writing and American literature and culture at Scripps College. She received her bachelor's degree and her PhD in English at the University of California, Berkeley, where she focused on nineteenth- and twentieth-century protest fiction by African American and proletarian authors as well as feminist theory and black feminist theory. She also did graduate work in composition studies and worked as a tutor, workshop leader, composition instructor, and fiction-writing instructor during her graduate school years.

Her recently published book *Subjectivity in the American Protest Novel* (2011) concerns trauma theory, double consciousness, and topological constructions of identity in protest novels by Richard Wright, Ann Petry, Chester Himes, Tillie Olsen, and Sarah Wright. She is editing a collection of women's writing about cooking in prison and conducting research for a monograph on social determinism and alternative portrayals of intellectual authority in the American detective novel (Charlotte Perkins Gilman, Rudolph Fisher, William Faulkner, Richard Wright, Chester Himes, Walter Mosely, and Lucha Corpi). Her scholarship includes publications and presentations on the fiction of Richard Wright, Toni Morrison, and Ann Petry; on prison narrative; on the slave narratives of Frederick Douglass and Harriet Jacobs; on trauma theory and detective novels; and on punk rock music and memoir. She is also writing a creative nonfiction piece about her punk rock travel-writing course, an article on gender-neutral pronouns and gender-queer students at a women's college, and a research article about writing assessment.

Contributors_____

Kimberly Drake directs the writing program and teaches writing and American literature and culture at Scripps College. She received her bachelor's degree and her PhD in English at the University of California, Berkeley, where she focused on nineteenth- and twentieth-century protest fiction by African American and proletarian authors as well as feminist theory and black feminist theory. She also completed graduate work in composition studies. Her recently published book *Subjectivity in the American Protest Novel* (2011) concerns trauma theory, double consciousness, and topological constructions of identity in protest novels by Richard Wright, Ann Petry, Chester Himes, Tillie Olsen, and Sarah Wright.

Lydia Willsky is a visiting instructor at Connecticut College in the Department of Religious Studies and a doctoral candidate at Vanderbilt University. She received her BA from Connecticut College in 2005 and her master of theological studies from Harvard Divinity School in 2007. Her most recent research has included "alternative" scriptures, Transcendentalism and social reform, women in liberal Christian movements, and the missionary movements of the Church of Latter-Day Saints (Mormons) and the Watchtower Society (Jehovah's Witnesses).

Jeremiah Garsha is a graduate student in the Department of History at San Francisco State University. His research interests include comparative genocide and the collisions of African and European history under colonialism. He is currently writing his dissertation on German, French, British, and American anticolonial intellectual thought in fin de siècle literature. Beyond academia, he has also worked as a genocide monitor for Zimbabwe under the aegis of the Auschwitz Institute for Peace and Reconciliation, in partnership with the United Nations' Office of the Special Advisor on the Prevention of Genocide.

Babacar M'Baye is an associate professor of English and Pan-African studies at Kent State University. His research interests are varied and include the relationship between intellectuals of the black diaspora and those of continental Africa; African influences in African American, African Caribbean, African British and African Canadian literatures; black travel writings; black Atlantic theories and methods; and the representations of immigration, race, class, gender, and hybrid identities in black literatures, films, and cultures. His work has appeared in the *Journal of African Literature and Culture*, *African and Black Diaspora: An International Journal*, *New England Journal of History*, and other publications. He is the author of *The Trickster Comes West: Pan-African Influence in Early Black Diasporan Narratives* (2009).

Adeline Carrie Koscher earned her PhD in nineteenth-century women's literature from the University of St. Andrews in Scotland, with a focus on the New Woman novelist. She earned an MEd from the University of Massachusetts and a BA in English from Mount Holyoke College. She writes poetry and fiction centered on women's experience, including publication in *Altered States Anthology*, *ninepatch: A Creative Journal for Women and Gender Studies*, *Review Americana*, and the *Lyon Review*. She teaches literature, composition, and creative writing on Cape Cod.

Tara Forbes is completing a master's degree in English literature at Queen's University in Kingston, Ontario, and has been involved in the labor movement extensively for many years.

Mikhail Bjorge is a shop steward for the Canadian Union of Postal Workers and a PhD candidate in history at Queen's University.

Rachel Stauffer teaches courses on Russian cultural history in the Department of Slavic Languages and Literatures at the University of Virginia, where she also coordinates community engagement and outreach on topics of international interest, focusing on the K–14 community throughout Virginia. Currently her research areas include twentieth-century Russian and Soviet literature and film, the teaching of culture and sociolinguistics in foreign-language instruction, and Russian and American English phonology. She holds an MA and PhD in Slavic languages and literatures from the University of Virginia and a BA in Russian studies and Spanish from Randolph-Macon Woman's College.

Seth Johnson is a doctoral candidate at Kent State University. His dissertation, *Across the Borderlands: The Work of Michael Chabon*, examines Chabon's entire literary career, tracing both his celebration of genre fiction and his explorations of the secular and the sacred. His forthcoming essay titled "'An American Golem': The Necessity of Myth in *The Amazing Adventures of Kavalier and Clay*" is to be published in the *Anthology on the Work of Michael Chabon*. His research focuses on twentieth-century American literature and postmodernism, with particular emphasis on religion in the postmodern. He is also interested in how literature influences and is influenced by American social movements.

Christi Cook is an assistant professor of English at Tarrant County College in Fort Worth, Texas. In addition to teaching composition and literature, she offers courses focused on race, class, and gender studies. She plans to graduate from the University of Texas at Arlington in December 2013 after completing her doctoral dissertation, which is a comparative study of gender and sexuality in recent Chicana and Anglo young-adult literature.

Index

A, Mister (*Enormous Room*). *See* Mr. A
(*Enormous Room*)
adolescents. *See* young-adult literature
Africa
European division of, 48
proposed return to, 39, 125, 139
African American protest literature, 66
African Americans
class divisions among, 14
psychoanalysis and, 96–100
slavery, resistance to, 113–141
Alejo (*Under the Feet of Jesus*), 249
American Anti-Imperial League, 57
American Colonization Society, 125
American exceptionalism, 222
American Federation of Labor (AFL),
171, 183, 184
Anderson, Harry, 216
anger displacement, 229
anticolonial protest, 44–63
anti-imperialist protest, 44–63
antislavery narratives, 27–40, 113–141
antitotalitarian fiction, 196–209
anti–Uncle Tom literature, 35
antiwar protest, 211–231
Antonio (*Bless Me, Ultima*). *See* Márez,
Antonio (*Bless Me, Ultima*)
Anzaldúa, Gloria, 237
Apollyon (*Enormous Room*), 226
art
class divisions and, 14, 72
protest literature as, 7–8
Association Internationale Africaine, 47
authenticity
New Woman depictions and, 149
representation and, 18, 74
working class and, 75
authorial identity, 18, 38
authorial intervention, 6

authoritarianism, lack of oversight in,
221
Awakening, The (Chopin), 157–159,
162–164
Baldwin, James, 88
Benefactor, the (*We*), 197–203
Berlin Conference of 1884–85, 48
Bessie (*Native Son*), 103
bilingualism, 239
biographical interpretation, 79, 92–94
black emigration proposal
Frederick Douglass and, 139
Harriet Beecher Stowe and, 39
Henry Clay and, 126
Thomas Jefferson and, 125, 127
black feminist criticism, 95
Black Holster (*Enormous Room*), 229
black nationalism, 114
black radicalism, 114
Bless Me, Ultima (Anaya), 244, 251
Bloody Sunday, 193
bond laws, 40
Borderlands (Anzaldúa), 238
bourgeoisie. *See* class conflict
Brazier, Richard, 168
Bread and Roses Strike. *See* Lawrence
Textile Strike of 1912
caricature, 146–148
"Cat and the Saxophone, The"
(Hughes), 77
Catholic Church
David Walker's opposition to, 120
indigenous spirituality and, 234,
243–247
Lawrence strikers vs., 183–184
censorship, 191, 195
Chicana writers, 236–240
Chicano/a literature, 233
Chicano movement, 235–236

children
    racial uplift through, 69
    state indoctrination of, 198
Children's Exodus, 181
"civilizing mission," 53, 62
civil rights, infringement on, 224
class conflict
    African Americans and, 72
    Russia, 193
    unions vs. employers, 167–186
Clay, Henry, black emigration and, 126
coded language, 14
color motif, 51
coming-of-age. *See* young-adult literature
communism
    dissent under, 195
    Richard Wright and, 89
conformity, racism and, 69
Congo Free State, 51, 60
Congo River, 49
Conrad, Joseph, 44, 46
Covey, Edward, 133
Crane, Helga (*Quicksand*), 77–79, 82–84
crisis novels, 17
"Cross" (Hughes), 80–82
cultural hybridity
    Langston Hughes's poetry, 75
    strength through, 242
cultural imperialism, 13–14
Cummings, E. E., 211–231
death
    coming-of-age and, 248
    contemplation of, 81
    liberation through, 135, 162
    literary device, 31
    master-slave dialectic and, 134
    memory and, 249
    symbols of, 49
Denmark Vesey conspiracy, 128
Devridge, Maxine (*Under the Feet of Jesus*), 240

D-503 (*We*), 196–207
dissent
    Communist Russia and, 195
    policing of, 214
disunity, dangers of, 119
divorce, women's empowerment
    through, 151
Dixon, Ella Hepworth, 149
double consciousness, 100
Douglass, Frederick, 34, 40, 113, 130–140
Du Bois, W. E. B., eugenics and, 68
dystopia, 192
Edna (*Awakening*). *See* Pontellier, Edna (*Awakening*)
"Eight-Hour Song, The" (song), 177
elections, resistance through, 172, 200
Eliza (*Uncle Tom's Cabin*). *See* Harris, Eliza (*Uncle Tom's Cabin*)
Ellison, Ralph, 87
emasculation, 102
emotional appeal, 16, 32
Enormous Room, The (Cummings), 211–231
escape
    antitotalitarian protest through, 201
    marriage and, 153
    slaves', 135–136
Espionage Act (1917), 219
essentialism, 74–75
Estrella (*Under the Feet of Jesus*), 237, 240–242, 246
Ettor, Joseph, 180
eugenics, W. E. B. Du Bois and, 68
families, separation of, 32, 132
"fellow traveler", 195
feminism, race issues within, 95
feminist critique. *See also* black feminist criticism
    gender roles, 146
    marriage, 150–159

Native Son (Wright), 92–94, 100–105
utopian literature and, 152
feminist writing, 144–150
"Few of Them Are Scabbing It" (song), 178
Flores, Perfecto (*Under the Feet of Jesus*), 239, 249
Flynn, Elizabeth Gurley, 182
freedmen, 115–116
Fresleven (*Heart of Darkness*), 47
Freudian psychoanalytic theory, 95
Fugitive Slave Act (1850), 29
Garrison, William Lloyd, 33, 40, 131
gaze, violence through, 101, 105
gender roles
  feminist resistance to, 146
  racial stereotypes and, 67
  war and, 229
genteel antislavery, 29
George (*Uncle Tom's Cabin*). *See* Harris, George (*Uncle Tom's Cabin*)
Gilman, Charlotte Perkins, 148
Giovannitti, Arturo, 180
Golden, John, 184
Gumecindo (*Under the Feet of Jesus*), 248
Gurley Flynn, Elizabeth. *See* Flynn, Elizabeth Gurley
Haitian Revolution, 117
Harlem Renaissance, 66–85
Harris, Eliza (*Uncle Tom's Cabin*), 30, 32
Harris, George (*Uncle Tom's Cabin*), 30, 39
Hawaiian annexation, Mark Twain and, 54
Haywood, Big Bill, 182
Heart of Darkness (Conrad), 44–54
Herland (Gilman), 152, 154–156
"hidden transcript" concept, 15
Hughes, Langston, 12, 66, 74–77, 80–82

hypocrisy, 215
identity
  collective, 204
  commonality in, 230
  group vs. individual, 69
  marriage and, 153–156, 159
  modernist, 82
  New Negro, 73
imprisonment, unjust, 216, 218
individuality, lack of, 69, 105, 197
indoctrination, 198
Industrial Revolution, Russia and, 193
Industrial Workers of the World (IWW), 167–186
"Internationale, The" (song), 176
interracial cooperation, 71, 73
"In the Good Old Picket Line" (song), 182
irony, use of, 212
isolation, 161, 164
I-330 (*We*), 198, 204
Jean le Nègre (*Enormous Room*), 223
Jefferson, Thomas
  black emigration proposal and, 125, 127
  slavery and, 124
"John Golden and the Lawrence Strike" (song), 185
Julia (*Nineteen Eighty-Four*), 205–208
"just war" concept, 223
Karpman, Benjamin, 97
Key to "Uncle Tom's Cabin" (Stowe), 35
King Leopold's Soliloquy (Twain), 59–63
Klein, Georges Antoine, 52
knowledge
  control of, 206
  dangers of, 162–163
  empowerment through, 131, 160–161

Kurtz, Mister (*Heart of Darkness*), 50, 52–54
Lacanian psychoanalytic theory, 99
Lafargue Clinic, 97
La Ferté-Macé detention center, 211
Larsen, Nella, 66, 77–80, 82–84
Lawrence Textile Strike of 1912, 167–186
Legree, Simon (*Uncle Tom's Cabin*), 30, 31
Leopold II (*King Leopold's Soliloquy*), 62
liberation
    death as, 135, 162
    individual and collective, 133, 153, 160–162
liberation literature, goals of, 9
literary canon, exclusion from, 9, 37
Little Red Songbook, The (IWW), 168
Little Sister (Wright), 91
Llorona, la, 244, 247–250
Lo Pizzo, Anna, 182
L'Ouverture, Toussaint, 118
Lowell, Abbott, 188
loyalty, disruption of, 199, 207–209
Ludlow Massacre, 188
Lyndall (*Story of an African Farm*), 145
Machine Fixer (*Enormous Room*), 218
machismo, Chicana response to, 236
Malinche, la, 244, 250–252
Márez, Antonio (*Bless Me, Ultima*), 244, 247, 251
Marlow, Charlie (*Heart of Darkness*), 45
marriage, critiques of, 150–159
"Marseillaise, The" (song), 175
masculinity, war and, 229
master-slave dialectic, 134–135
MEPHI, 199
Mexican-American War, consequences of, 235
Mexico, history of, 234–235
Mexique (*Enormous Room*), 217

miseducation, 120
misogyny, author's vs. characters', 93–94
Missouri Compromise, 129
mixed-race characters. *See also* tragic mulatto figure
    alienation of, 81
    outsider perspective through, 78
    Uncle Tom's Cabin and, 39
modernist literature, New Negro movement and, 73–74
Mr. A (*Enormous Room*), 215
music. *See* song, radical function of
narration
    coercive, 90
    nonchronological, 239
    sarcastic, 225
    third-person limited, 90
Narrative of the Life of Frederick Douglass (Douglass), 113, 129–140
Native Son (Wright), 87, 90–92
naturalism, 88
"Negro Artist and the Racial Mountain, The" (Hughes), 13, 74–75
New Latina Narrative (McCracken), 238
New Mestiza, 237
New Negro movement, 66
New Woman, 144–164
Nineteen Eighty-Four (Orwell), 205–209
Notes on the State of Virginia (Jefferson), 124
100 percent Americanism, 221
One State, 196
O-90 (*We*), 198
oppression
    institutionalized, reaction to, 83
    knowledge and power systems in, 18
    rationalization of, 196, 207
O'Reilly, Fr. James, 183

pacifism
  pre–World War I movements, 222
  progressive, 214
paranoia, 212, 216–222, 227
patriotism, republics and, 224
Perfecto (*Under the Feet of Jesus*). *See*
  Flores, Perfecto (*Under the Feet of
  Jesus*)
Petra (*Under the Feet of Jesus*), 245
Philippines, American occupation of, 56
photography, consciousness raising
  through, 61
Pilgrim's Progress (Bunyan), Cummings
  parallel, 212–213
Pontellier, Edna (*Awakening*), 157–159,
  162
Pontellier, Léonce (*Awakening*), 158
possession
  self, joy through, 230
  wife by husband, 151, 158
postmodernism, protest literature and,
  17
power
  imbalance of, 240
  violence vs., 172
premium wage system, 187
prison guards, 226, 228
procreation, state mandated, 198
proletariat. *See* class conflict; working
  classes
proslavery literature, 36
protest literature
  definition of, 192
  goals of, 8
  mainstream absorption of, 17
  postmodernism and, 17
  types of, 3
  understanding trauma in, 18
psychoanalytic criticism
  definition of, 96
  Native Son (Wright), 98–105

psychology, protest literature and, 18
"public sphere" concept, 173
Quicksand (Larsen), 69, 77–80, 82–84
racial categories
  American, Frederick Douglass on,
    139
  Mexican, 235
  stratification of, 39
racial hatred, political tool of, 138
racial uplift
  critique of, 78–79
  relationships and, 68
  stereotyping and, 67
Ramey, John, 182
rape
  marital, 153, 156–157
  metaphoric, 101–104
readability, 14
reader identification
  emotional effects of, 16
  forced, 91
  New Woman novels and, 148–149
  strategies for, 3–9
readership
  reviewers as proxy, 4
  women, Harriet Beecher Stowe and,
    38
reality, representations of, 12
rebellion, exhortation to, 122
Reisz, Mademoiselle (*Awakening*),
  163–164
repetition, trauma and, 101
representation
  authenticity in, 18, 74
  counter-representation and, 19
  crisis of, 18, 73
  problematic, 39
repression
  psychoanalytic understanding of, 101
  sexual relationships in *We*, 197
  YA literature and, 242

republics, patriotism and, 224
resistance
    differing reasons for, 202
    love inspiring, 199, 202–203, 208
    physical sensation of, 206–207
    song as, 168–170
revolution, use of term, 202
revolutionary countermood, 1–3
Rom, Léon, 52
Russian Revolution, impacts of, 195, 219
Saint-Domingue uprising. *See* Haitian Revolution
Schoolmaster (*Enormous Room*), 218
science, social control through, 68, 196–197
Sedition Act (1918), 220
self-actualization, struggle for, 145
self-discovery, 160
sentimental fiction, 36–38
sexuality
    awakening of, 158
    coming-of-age literature and, 250–252
    racial stereotypes about, 67
    state repression of, 197
shock value, 15, 17
slavery, impact on slaveholders, 31. *See also* antislavery narratives; black emigration proposal; genteel antislavery
Smith, Winston (*Nineteen Eighty-Four*), 205–208
song, radical function of, 168–170
Spanish-American War, 55
speech, restriction of, 214
Stalinism, 195
stereotypes. *See also* tragic mulatto figure
    black rapist, 68, 103
    dumb servant, 105

jezebel, 67
    racial uplift and, 67
Story of a Modern Woman, The (Dixon), 149
Stowe, Harriet Beecher, 27–40
structural blindness, 104
Surplice (*Enormous Room*), 218
teenagers. *See* young-adult literature
Thames River, 45
"Theme for English B" (Hughes), 82
Thomas, Bigger (*Native Son*), 101–105
Three Wise Men (*Enormous Room*), 226, 227
tokenism, 19
"To the Person Sitting in Darkness" (Twain), 57–59
tragic mulatto figure, 80–83. *See also* stereotypes
trauma, reaction to, 83
trauma theory, 18, 100
truth and lies, 206, 211
Twain, Mark, 44, 54–57
Uncle Tom (*Uncle Tom's Cabin*), 30, 31
Uncle Tom's Cabin (Stowe), 11, 27–40
Under the Feet of Jesus (Viramontes), 245, 250
unionism
    religion vs., 183
    types of, 187
universality, 10
utopian fiction
    dystopian vs., 191
    feminism and, 152
Vayle, James (*Quicksand*), 69
vernacular language, 75–77
violence
    global colonial, 57
    literary depiction of, 15
    power vs., 172
    women victims in *Native Son* (Wright), 91–94

Virgen de Guadalupe, la, 243–247

visibility, race and, 104–105

Walker, David, 113, 115–129

Walker's Appeal, in Four Articles (Walker), 113, 115–129

Wanderer (*Enormous Room*), 227

war, critique of, 211–231

We (Zamyatin), 191, 192–193, 196–209

"Weary Blues, The" (Hughes), 76

Wertham, Fredric, 97

"White Man's Burden, The" (Kipling), 55

whiteness, symbolism of, 50

wife, concept of, 154

Winston (*Nineteen Eighty-Four*). *See* Smith, Winston (*Nineteen Eighty-Four*)

Wobblies. *See* Industrial Workers of the World (IWW)

working class. *See also* class conflict

authenticity in, 75

Russia, revolutions of, 193

unionism and, 167–186

World's Temperance Convention (1846), 137

Wright, Richard, 88–90

writing back, 13, 239

xenophobia, war and, 217

"Yellow Wall-paper, The" (Gilman), 160–162

young-adult literature

death in, 248

definition of, 233

power struggles in, 242–243

sexuality in, 250–252

Zamyatin, Yevgeny Ivanovich, 193–196